Guide and Reference to
the Crocodilians, Turtles, and Lizards
of Eastern and Central North America
(North of Mexico)

D1484218

UNIVERSITY PRESS OF FLORIDA

Florida A&M University, Tallahassee
Florida Atlantic University, Boca Raton
Florida Gulf Coast University, Ft. Myers
Florida International University, Miami
Florida State University, Tallahassee
University of Central Florida, Orlando
University of Florida, Gainesville
University of North Florida, Jacksonville
University of South Florida, Tampa
University of West Florida, Pensacola

# Crocodilians, Turtles, and Lizards

of Eastern and Central North America (North of Mexico)

R. D. Bartlett and Patricia P. Bartlett

University Press of Florida

GAINESVILLE · TALLAHASSEE · TAMPA · BOCA RATON

PENSACOLA · ORLANDO · MIAMI · JACKSONVILLE · FT. MYERS

10  09  08  07  06  05   6  5  4  3  2  1

Library of Congress Cataloging-in-Publication Data
Bartlett, Richard D., 1938–
Guide and reference to the crocodilians, turtles, and lizards of Eastern and Central
North America (North of Mexico)/R.D. Bartlett and Patricia P. Bartlett
p.cm.
Includes bibliographical references (p. ).
ISBN 0-8130-2946-5 (alk. paper)
1. Crocodilians—North America—Identification. 2. Turtles—North America—
Identification. 3. Lizards—North America—Identification.
I. Bartlett, Patricia Pope, 1949– II. Title.
QL666.C9B37 2006
597.98097—dc22      2005058573

The University Press of Florida is the scholarly publishing agency for the State
University System of Florida, comprising Florida A&M University, Florida Atlantic
University, Florida Gulf Coast University, Florida International University, Florida
State University, University of Central Florida, University of Florida, University
of North Florida, University of South Florida, and University of West Florida.

University Press of Florida
15 Northwest 15th Street
Gainesville, FL 32611-2079
http://www.upf.com

# Contents

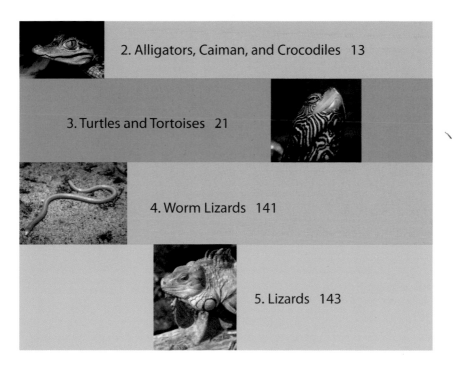

# Species List

## Crocodilians: Alligators, Caiman, and Crocodiles

### Alligators and Caiman, family Alligatoridae

(1) American Alligator, *Alligator mississippiensis*
(2) Spectacled Caiman, *Caiman crocodilus* (introduced)

### Crocodiles, family Crocodylidae

(3) American Crocodile, *Crocodylus acutus*

## Turtles and Tortoises

### Snapping, Musk, and Mud Turtles

Snapping Turtles, family Chelydridae

(4) Common Snapping Turtle, *Chelydra serpentina serpentina*
   (5) Florida Snapping Turtle, *Chelydra serpentina osceola*
(6) Alligator Snapping Turtle, *Macrochelys temminckii*

Mud and Musk Turtles, family Kinosternidae

(7) Striped Mud Turtle, *Kinosternon baurii*
(8) Yellow Mud Turtle, *Kinosternon flavescens flavescens*
(9) Mexican Plateau Mud Turtle, *Kinosternon hirtipes murrayi*
(10) Eastern Mud Turtle, *Kinosternon subrubrum subrubrum*
   (11) Mississippi Mud Turtle, *Kinosternon subrubrum hippocrepis*
   (12) Florida Mud Turtle, *Kinosternon subrubrum steindachneri*
(13) Razor-backed Musk Turtle, *Sternotherus carinatus*
(14) Flattened Musk Turtle, *Sternotherus depressus*
(15) Loggerhead Musk Turtle, *Sternotherus minor minor*

(16) Stripe-necked Musk Turtle, *Sternotherus minor peltifer*
(17) Common Musk Turtle (Stinkpot), *Sternotherus odoratus*

## Basking Turtles

Sliders, Map Turtles, Pond Turtles, Box Turtles, and relatives, family Emydidae

### PAINTED TURTLES

(18) Eastern Painted Turtle, *Chrysemys picta picta*
   (19) Western Painted Turtle, *Chrysemys picta bellii*
   (20) Southern Painted Turtle, *Chrysemys picta dorsalis*
   (21) Midland Painted Turtle, *Chrysemys picta marginata*

### RIVER COOTERS

(22) Eastern River Cooter, *Pseudemys concinna concinna*
   (23) Suwannee Cooter, *Pseudemys concinna suwanniensis*
(24) Western River Cooter, *Pseudemys gorzugi*
(25) Texas River Cooter, *Pseudemys texana*

### COASTAL PLAIN COOTERS

(26) Coastal Plain Cooter, *Pseudemys floridana floridana*
(27) Peninsula Cooter, *Pseudemys floridana peninsularis*

### RED-BELLIED COOTERS

(28) Alabama Red-bellied Cooter, *Pseudemys alabamensis*
(29) Florida Red-bellied Cooter, *Pseudemys nelsoni*
(30) Northern Red-bellied Cooter, *Pseudemys rubriventris*

### SLIDERS

(31) Big Bend Slider, *Trachemys gaigeae*
(32) Yellow-bellied Slider, *Trachemys scripta scripta*
   (33) Red-eared Slider, *Trachemys scripta elegans*
   (34) Cumberland Slider, *Trachemys scripta troosti*

### POND TURTLES

(35) Spotted Turtle, *Clemmys guttata*
(36) Wood Turtle, *Glyptemys insculpta*
(37) Bog Turtle, *Glyptemys muhlenbergi*

## MAP TURTLES

(38) Barbour's Map Turtle, *Graptemys barbouri*

(39) Cagle's Map Turtle, *Graptemys caglei*

(40) Escambia Map Turtle, *Graptemys ernsti*

(41) Yellow-blotched Map Turtle, *Graptemys flavimaculata*

(42) Northern Map Turtle, *Graptemys geographica*

(43) Pascagoula Map Turtle, *Graptemys gibbonsi*

(44) Black-knobbed Map Turtle, *Graptemys nigrinoda nigrinoda*

    (45) Delta Map Turtle, *Graptemys nigrinoda delticola*

(46) Ringed Map Turtle, *Graptemys oculifera*

(47) Ouachita Map Turtle, *Graptemys ouachitensis ouachitensis*

    (48) Sabine Map Turtle, *Graptemys ouachitensis sabinensis*

(49) False Map Turtle, *Graptemys pseudogeographica pseudogeographica*

    (50) Mississippi Map Turtle, *Graptemys pseudogeographica kohnii*

(51) Alabama Map Turtle, *Graptemys pulchra*

(52) Texas Map Turtle, *Graptemys versa*

## DIAMOND-BACKED TERRAPINS

(53) Northern Diamond-backed Terrapin, *Malaclemys terrapin terrapin*

    (54) Carolina Diamond-backed Terrapin, *Malaclemys terrapin centrata*

    (55) Texas Diamond-backed Terrapin, *Malaclemys terrapin littoralis*

    (56) Ornate Diamond-backed Terrapin, *Malaclemys terrapin macrospilota*

    (57) Mississippi Diamond-backed Terrapin, *Malaclemys terrapin pileata*

    (58) Mangrove Diamond-backed Terrapin, *Malaclemys terrapin rhizophorarum*

    (59) Florida East Coast Terrapin, *Malaclemys terrapin tequesta*

## CHICKEN TURTLES AND BLANDING'S TURTLE

(60) Eastern Chicken Turtle, *Deirochelys reticularia reticularia*

    (61) Florida Chicken Turtle, *Deirochelys reticularia chrysea*

    (62) Western Chicken Turtle, *Deirochelys reticularia miaria*

(63) Blanding's Turtle, *Emydoidea blandingii*

## BOX TURTLES

(64) Eastern Box Turtle, *Terrapene carolina carolina*

    (65) Florida Box Turtle, *Terrapene carolina bauri*

    (66) Gulf Coast Box Turtle, *Terrapene carolina major*

    (67) Three-toed Box Turtle, *Terrapene carolina triunguis*

(68) Ornate Box Turtle, *Terrapene ornata ornata*
   (69) Desert Box Turtle, *Terrapene ornata luteola*

SOUTH AMERICAN WOOD TURTLE

(70) Spotted-legged Wood Turtle, *Rhinoclemmys punctularia punctularia* (introduced)

Afro-Neotropical Side-necked Turtles, family Pelomedusidae

RIVER TURTLES

(71) Yellow-spotted River Turtle, *Podocnemis unifilis* (introduced)

## Tortoises

Tortoises, family Testudinidae

(72) Texas Tortoise, *Gopherus berlandieri*
(73) Gopher Tortoise, *Gopherus polyphemus*

## Soft-shelled Turtles

Soft-shelled Turtles, family Trionychidae

(74) Florida Soft-shelled Turtle, *Apalone ferox*
(75) Midland Smooth Soft-shelled Turtle, *Apalone mutica mutica*
   (76) Gulf Coast Smooth Soft-shelled Turtle, *Apalone mutica calvata*
(77) Eastern Spiny Soft-shelled Turtle, *Apalone spinifera spinifera*
   (78) Gulf Coast Spiny Soft-shelled Turtle, *Apalone spinifera aspera*
   (79) Texas Spiny Soft-shelled Turtle, *Apalone spinifera emoryi*
   (80) Guadalupe Spiny Soft-shelled Turtle, *Apalone spinifera guadalupensis*
   (81) Western Spiny Soft-shelled Turtle, *Apalone spinifera hartwegi*
   (82) Pallid Spiny Soft-shelled Turtle, *Apalone spinifera pallida*

## Marine Turtles

Sea Turtles, family Cheloniidae

(83) Loggerhead Sea Turtle, *Caretta caretta*
(84) Green Sea Turtle, *Chelonia mydas*
(85) Atlantic Hawksbill Sea Turtle, *Eretmochelys imbricata imbricata*
(86) Kemp's Ridley Sea Turtle, *Lepidochelys kempii*

Leatherback, family Dermochelyidae

(87) Leather-backed Sea Turtle, *Dermochelys coriacea*

## Amphisbaenids

### Wide-snouted Worm Lizards

Florida Worm Lizard, family Rhineuridae

(88) Florida Worm Lizard, *Rhineura floridana*

## Lizards

### Agamid Lizards

Agamas and Tree Lizards, family Agamidae

(89) African Red-headed Agama, *Agama agama* (introduced)
(90) Indochinese Tree Lizard, *Calotes mystaceus* (introduced)
(91) Butterfly Lizard, *Leiolepis belliana* ssp.

### Anguid Lizards

Glass Lizards and Alligator Lizards, family Anguidae

(92) Texas Alligator Lizard, *Gerrhonotus infernalis*
(93) Western Slender Glass Lizard, *Ophisaurus attenuatus attenuatus*
   (94) Eastern Slender Glass Lizard, *Ophisaurus attenuatus longicaudus*
(95) Island Glass Lizard, *Ophisaurus compressus*
(96) Mimic Glass Lizard, *Ophisaurus mimicus*
(97) Eastern Glass Lizard, *Ophisaurus ventralis*

### Gekkonid Lizards

Eyelidded Geckos, family Eublepharidae

(98) Texas Banded Gecko, *Coleonyx brevis*
(99) Reticulated Gecko, *Coleonyx reticulatus*

## Typical Geckos and Sphaerodactyline Geckos, family Gekkonidae

TYPICAL GECKOS, SUBFAMILY GEKKONINAE

(100) Flat-tailed House Gecko, *Cosymbotus platyurus* (introduced)
(101) Rough-tailed Gecko, *Cyrtopodion scabrum* (introduced)
(102) Tokay Gecko, *Gekko gecko* (introduced)
(103) Common House Gecko, *Hemidactylus frenatus* (introduced)
(104) Indo-Pacific House Gecko, *Hemidactylus garnotii* (introduced)
(105) Amerafrican House Gecko, *Hemidactylus mabouia* (introduced)
(106) Mediterranean House Gecko, *Hemidactylus turcicus* (introduced)
(107) Bibron's Gecko, *Pachydactylus bibroni* (introduced)
(108) Gold-dust Day Gecko, *Phelsuma laticauda laticauda* (introduced)
(109) Giant Day Gecko, *Phelsuma madagascariensis grandis* (introduced)
(110) White-spotted Wall Gecko, *Tarentola annularis* (introduced)
(111) Moorish Wall Gecko, *Tarentola mauritanica* (introduced)

NEOTROPICAL BENT-TOED GECKOS AND DWARF GECKOS, SUBFAMILY SPHAERODACTYLINAE

(112) Dusky Yellow-headed Gecko, *Gonatodes albogularis fuscus* (introduced)
(113) Ocellated Gecko, *Sphaerodactylus argus argus* (introduced)
(114) Cuban Ashy Gecko, *Sphaerodactylus elegans elegans* (introduced)
(115) Florida Reef Gecko, *Sphaerodactylus notatus notatus*

## Iguanid Lizards

Typical Lizards, family Iguanidae

CASQUE-HEADED LIZARDS, SUBFAMILY CORYTOPHANINAE

(116) Northern Brown Basilisk, *Basiliscus vittatus* (introduced)

COLLARED LIZARDS AND LEOPARD LIZARDS, SUBFAMILY CROTAPHYTINAE

(117) Eastern Collared Lizard, *Crotaphytus collaris*
(118) Reticulated Collared Lizard, *Crotaphytus reticulatus*
(119) Long-nosed Leopard Lizard, *Gambelia wislizenii wislizenii*

IGUANAS, SUBFAMILY IGUANINAE

(120) Western Spiny-tailed Iguana, *Ctenosaura pectinata* (introduced)

(121) Black Spiny-tailed Iguana, *Ctenosaura similis* (introduced)

(122) Green Iguana, *Iguana iguana* (introduced)

HORNED LIZARDS, SPINY LIZARDS, AND RELATIVES,
SUBFAMILY PHRYNOSOMATINAE

**Earless Lizards**

(123) Texas Greater Earless Lizard, *Cophosaurus texanus texanus*

   (124) Chihuahuan Greater Earless Lizard, *Cophosaurus texanus scitulus*

(125) Northern Spotted-tailed Earless Lizard, *Holbrookia lacerata lacerata*

   (126) Southern Spotted-tailed Earless Lizard, *Holbrookia lacerata subcaudalis*

(127) Great Plains Earless Lizard, *Holbrookia maculata maculata*

   (128) Speckled Earless Lizard, *Holbrookia maculata approximans*

   (129) Prairie Earless Lizard, *Holbrookia maculata perspicua*

(130) Northern Keeled Earless Lizard, *Holbrookia propinqua propinqua*

**Horned Lizards**

(131) Texas Horned Lizard, *Phrynosoma cornutum*

(132) Mountain Short-horned Lizard, *Phrynosoma hernandesi hernandesi*

   (132a) Eastern Short-horned Lizard, *Phrynosoma hernandesi brevirostre*

(133) Round-tailed Horned Lizard, *Phrynosoma modestum*

**Spiny Lizards, Fence Lizards, and Swifts**

(134) Dunes Sagebrush Lizard, *Sceloporus arenicolous*

(135) Blue Spiny Lizard, *Sceloporus cyanogenys*

(136) Northern Sagebrush Lizard, *Sceloporus graciosus graciosus*

(137) Mesquite Lizard, *Sceloporus grammicus microlepidotus*

(138) Twin-spotted Spiny Lizard, *Sceloporus magister bimaculosus*

(139) Merriam's Canyon Lizard, *Sceloporus merriami merriami*

   (140) Big Bend Canyon Lizard, *Sceloporus merriami annulatus*

   (141) Presidio Canyon Lizard, *Sceloporus merriami longipunctatus*

(142) Texas Spiny Lizard, *Sceloporus olivaceus*

(143) Crevice Spiny Lizard, *Sceloporus poinsettii poinsettii*

(144) Southern Fence Lizard, *Sceloporus undulatus undulatus*

   (145) Southern Prairie Lizard, *Sceloporus undulatus consobrinus*

   (146) Red-lipped Prairie Lizard, *Sceloporus undulatus erythrocheilus*

   (147) Northern Prairie Lizard, *Sceloporus undulatus garmani*

   (148) Northern Fence Lizard, *Sceloporus undulatus hyacinthinus*

   (149) Mescalero Prairie Lizard, *Sceloporus undulatus tedbrowni*

(150) Texas Rose-bellied Lizard, *Sceloporus variabilis marmoratus*
(151) Florida Scrub Lizard, *Sceloporus woodi*
(152) Texas Tree Lizard, *Urosaurus ornatus ornatus*
(153) Big Bend Tree Lizard, *Urosaurus ornatus schmidti*
(154) Eastern Side-blotched Lizard, *Uta stansburiana stejnegeri*

ANOLES, SUBFAMILY POLYCHROTINAE

**Green Anoles**
(155) Northern Green Anole, *Anolis carolinensis carolinensis*
   (156) Pale-throated Green Anole, *Anolis carolinensis seminolus*
(157) Hispaniolan Green Anole, *Anolis chlorocyanus* (introduced)
(158) Cuban Green Anole, *Anolis porcatus* (introduced)
**Giant Anoles**
(159) Western Knight Anole, *Anolis equestris equestris* (introduced)
(160) Jamaican Giant Anole, *Anolis garmani* (introduced)
**Brown Anoles**
(161) Cuban Brown Anole, *Anolis sagrei sagrei* (introduced)
(162) Puerto Rican Crested Anole, *Anolis cristatellus cristatellus* (introduced)
(163) Common Large-headed Anole, *Anolis cybotes cybotes* (introduced)
**Bark Anole**
(164) Bark Anole, *Anolis distichus* (introduced)

CURLY-TAILED LIZARDS, SUBFAMILY TROPIDURINAE

(165) Little Bahama Curly-tailed Lizard, *Leiocephalus carinatus armouri* (introduced)
(166) Green-legged Curly-tailed Lizard, *Leiocephalus personatus scalaris* (introduced)
(167) Red-sided Curly-tailed Lizard, *Leiocephalus schreibersi schreibersi* (introduced)

## Lacertid Lizards

Wall Lizards and Green Lizards, family Lacertidae

(168) Western Green Lizard, *Lacerta bilineata* (introduced)
(169) Common Wall Lizard, *Podarcis muralis* (introduced)
(170) Italian Wall Lizard, *Podarcis sicula* (introduced)

## Scincid Lizards

Skinks, family Scincidae

(171) Northern Coal Skink, *Eumeces anthracinus anthracinus*
  (172) Southern Coal Skink, *Eumeces anthracinus pluvialis*
(173) Florida Keys Mole Skink, *Eumeces egregius egregius*
  (174) Cedar Key Mole Skink, *Eumeces egregius insularis*
  (175) Blue-tailed Mole Skink, *Eumeces egregius lividus*
  (176) Peninsula Mole Skink, *Eumeces egregius onocrepis*
  (177) Northern Mole Skink, *Eumeces egregius similis*
(178) Common Five-lined Skink, *Eumeces fasciatus*
(179) Southeastern Five-lined Skink, *Eumeces inexpectatus*
(180) Broad-headed Skink, *Eumeces laticeps*
(181) Northern Many lined Skink, *Eumeces multivirgatus multivirgatus*
  (182) Variable Skink, *Eumeces multivirgatus epipleurotus*
(183) Great Plains Skink, *Eumeces obsoletus*
(184) Northern Prairie Skink, *Eumeces septentrionalis septentrionalis*
  (185) Southern Prairie Skink, *Eumeces septentrionalis obtusirostris*
(186) Four-lined Skink, *Eumeces tetragrammus tetragrammus*
  (187) Short-lined Skink, *Eumeces tetragrammus brevilineatus*
(188) Brown Mabuya, *Mabuya multifasciata* (introduced)
(189) Florida Sand Skink, *Neoseps reynoldsi*
(190) Ground Skink, *Scincella lateralis*

## Teiid Lizards

Whiptails and Racerunners, family Teiidae

(191) Giant Ameiva, *Ameiva ameiva* (introduced)
(192) Gray-checkered Whiptail, *Aspidoscelis dixoni*
(193) Chihuahuan Spotted Whiptail, *Aspidoscelis exsanguis*
(194) Texas Spotted Whiptail, *Aspidoscelis gularis gularis*
(195) Trans-Pecos Striped Whiptail, *Aspidoscelis inornatus heptagrammus*
(196) Laredo Striped Whiptail, *Aspidoscelis laredoensis*
(197) Western Marbled Whiptail, *Aspidoscelis marmoratus marmoratus*
  (198) Eastern Marbled Whiptail, *Aspidoscelis marmoratus reticuloriens*
(199) Giant Whiptail, *Aspidoscelis motaguae* (introduced)
(200) New Mexican Whiptail, *Aspidoscelis neomexicanus*
(201) Big Bend Spotted Whiptail, *Aspidoscelis septemvittatus septemvittatus*
(202) Six-lined Racerunner, *Aspidoscelis sexlineatus sexlineatus*

(203) Texas Yellow-headed Racerunner, *Aspidoscelis sexlineatus stephensae*
(204) Prairie Racerunner, *Aspidoscelis sexlineatus viridis*
(205) Common Checkered Whiptail, *Aspidoscelis tesselatus* complex
(206) Desert Grassland Whiptail, *Aspidoscelis uniparens*
(207) Rainbow Whiptail, *Cnemidophorus lemniscatus* complex (introduced)

## Varanid Lizards

Monitors, family Varanidae

(208) Nile Monitor, *Varanus niloticus* (introduced)

# Preface

Today, as interest in and knowledge of our reptile fauna increase exponentially, so, too, do the challenges facing the continued existence of many of these interesting creatures. The problems of habitat destruction (including fragmentation), vehicular reptilicide, collection for the pet trade, and pressures from introduced species must all be addressed.

On the plus side, there's a burgeoning interest in these creatures. Interpretive programs are presented regularly in many grade schools. Programs, projects, and studies continue through middle school and into high school, and there is now a proliferation of undergraduate and postgraduate college courses. Ecotours that focus on our reptile fauna are also becoming more common.

The vast landmass east of our point of delineation is home to 416 species and subspecies of reptiles. Of this number, 207 are lizards, turtles, and crocodilians. Most are native, but more than 60 species are introduced and established alien forms. Some of these are probably of minimal consequence to our native herpetofauna, but some, such as the large and predatory Nile monitor and spectacled caiman could be of significant concern.

*The Ecological Impact of Man on the South Florida Herpetofauna*, by Larry David Wilson and Louis Porras and published in 1983, detailed the presence and effects of the twenty-five species of alien herpetofauna then established in the state. Although now dated (there are now more than sixty introduced and established species of herpetofauna, dozens of birds, and a few mammal species in the state) the book remains of tremendous interest. The term "eco-collapse" was used to describe what they felt were ever worsening (and, twenty years later, still unreversed) environmental and ecological conditions in Florida south of Lake Okeechobee. Since it is in Florida (and Texas) that most species of introduced reptiles are established, this book should still be of interest to researchers.

Even within their range, reptiles are not evenly distributed. Some occur only between certain elevations in mountain chains (a few only on a specific mountain), some occur only in acidic bogs, others are dwellers of aridland habitats, and still others may predominate in wetlands or even in suburban settings. A specific reptile may be abundant in one state, yet so rare in another that it is considered endangered. But there are also a few species that are habitat generalists and common. Among these are anole lizards, rat snakes, and garter snakes.

Because of the varying and ever changing state laws, we have not attempted in most cases to advise readers of the legal status of a reptile, but may occasionally make generalities. However, we urge that before seeking a particular species you check both federal and state laws to determine its legal status. In some cases you may need a permit (usually issued only for research purposes) before seeking a specific reptile.

We now invite you to join us as we tour mountains, deserts, woodlands, and backyards, looking along canal edges and beneath rocks, in grass tussocks and under human-generated debris, searching for the lizards, crocodilians, and turtles now found in eastern North America north of Mexico.

## Acknowledgments

The success of a publication such as this is due largely to the efforts and generosity of colleagues and friends. With this in mind, we gratefully acknowledge the comments and concerns of Kevin Enge, Richard Franz, Paul Moler, and R. Wayne VanDevender.

We are grateful to David Auth, who allowed us access to the study collection of the Florida Museum of Natural History, where we were able to see the enigmatic South Florida rainbow snake firsthand.

Collette Adams, Ray E. Ashton, Chris Bednarski, Bill and Marcia Brant, Karin Burns, Dennis Cathcart, Scott Cushnir, Norm Damm, John Decker, C. Kenneth Dodd, Lance Jarzynka, Dennie Miller, Norm Nunley, Justin Garza, Esther Goldhammer, Billy Griswold, Jim Harding, Manuel G. Hernandez, Terry Hibbits, Toby Hibbitts, Troy Hibbitts, Joe Hiduke, Steven Johnson, F. Wayne King, Ken King, Kenney Krysko, John Lewis, Dave Manke, John McGonigal, Carl May, Mike Manfredi, Barry Mansell, Brian Mealey, Flavio Morrissey, David Nelson, Sandy Oldershaw, Regis Opferman, Charlie Painter, Greta Parks, Dan Pearson, Nicole Pinder, Andy Price, Mike Price, Gus Rentfro, Alan Resetar, Dan Scolaro, Don Sias, Brian Smith, Mike Smith, Tom Tyning, Rick Van Dyke, Jerry Walls, Frank Weed, Pete Wilson, Larry Wood, Maria Camarilla Wray, and Kenny Wray either joined us, or allowed us to join them, in the field, provided specimens for us to photograph, or, in some cases, provided the photographs themselves. Dale Johnson did many of the illustrations. Thanks all.

Bill Love, Rob MacInnes, Chris McQuade, and Eric Thiss all allowed us great latitude in photographing many of the reptiles pertinent to this volume.

Walter Meshaka shared with us his accrued knowledge of the introduced reptiles and amphibians of Florida, and induced us into the field that we might photograph many alien species in the wild.

# 1

## Introduction

Reptile ancestors in some obscure and poorly understood form evolved from amphibian stock more than 315 million years ago, during the early Upper Carboniferous Period. What are called the modern reptiles can be traced back some 280 million years to the Permian Era.

Many reptiles have come down through the ages almost unchanged in form. This enduring sameness is exemplified by the two species of New Zealand tuataras, creatures dramatically different from lizards despite their lizardlike appearance. The tuataras are classed as rhynchocephalians, beak-heads, for which readily recognizable ancestors have been found that are thought to date back to the Mesozoic, some 220 million years ago.

Traditionally, snakes, lizards, turtles, crocodilians, and sphenodons have been placed within the class Reptilia. It has recently been suggested that crocodilians and turtles belong each to their own class. We retain the conservative (traditional) approach here, and maintain all within Reptilia.

The class Reptilia contains some 6,600+ species in 900+ genera, 48+ families, and four orders.

In this book, we discuss 208 species and subspecies found in eastern and central North America, comprising three species of crocodilians (order Crocodylia), 53 species of turtles and tortoises (order Chelonia), and 96 species of lizards and amphisbaenians (order Squamata) and assorted subspecies.

Some of these are newcomers. The southern states are particularly hospitable to new species. There are today, in South Florida alone, more than 55 introduced species of reptiles. Miami is the epicenter of introduced reptiles, with very many reptile importers and dealers. In Brownsville, Texas, the new species lists includes two species of iguana, at least one species of gecko, and a tiny burrowing snake. Kansas, Ohio, and New York each have one or two established alien lizard species.

These additions have all happened in only about 50 years, or two-thirds of a human lifespan. We do not yet know what pressures (if any) these creatures will eventually place on native reptiles.

Many biologists, no matter their affiliation, feel that the levels of protection for native reptiles should be increased.

Whether we are researchers or herpetoculturists, or merely have an interest in the creatures with whom we share our world, it is time for us to join forces and promote the conservation of these interesting, beneficial, and highly specialized animals.

We hope our comments in this identification guide will help you to better understand and appreciate the intricate lifestyles of our eastern reptiles.

## How to Use This Book

In this volume we present the lizards, turtles, and crocodilians that may be seen in eastern North America.

Some are easily identifiable. Others can be separated from closely allied species only by DNA analysis. A few may take some detective work for identification: there are skinks and basking turtles that undergo age-related color changes, subspecies (or even different species) of reptiles that interbreed and produce young with a confusing suite of characteristics, and others capable of changing their color from brown to green, then back again. Many reptiles may be very dark when cold or quiet and very light when warm or active.

Subtle characteristics, like the presence or absence of webbing on the hind feet or the number of toes on the hind feet, can be important identification factors. For turtles, the presence or absence of a hinge on the bottom shell (the plastron), and the number of plastron hinges is critical. Is the plastron noticeably reduced in size? Are the creature's pupils vertically elliptical or round? Many of these characteristics are not easily determined unless the reptile is in hand—and there are some reptiles that you just should not have in hand, either for your own safety or for legal reasons.

There are times when a reptile is so aberrant that no normally pertinent factor will help you with identification. Albinism or scalelessness can obliterate patterns and scale characteristics. Then range and gestalt—the whole of the creature's behavior, environment, and morphology—must be identifying factors.

We have numbered all species and subspecies in the table of contents, and these coincide with the numbers assigned in both text and photographs. All species and subspecies are pictured.

## A Comment on Taxonomy

The science of classification, of naming species, is called taxonomy. The basic building block is the scientific name, a descriptive name that is of Latin or Greek derivation. The name can be binomial (two names) or trinomial (three names).

A trinomial indicates that a species has more than one recognized subspecies or race.

Taxonomy is used to indicate links or relationships among animals. As in any other discipline, those who work within the field have diverging beliefs, techniques, and applications.

Two taxonomic approaches, of traditional evolutionary systematics on one hand and the newer cladistics on the other, approach classification from different perspectives. The proponents of either often vociferously decry the suggestions and conclusions of the other.

There is also a current school of thought that allopatrism (noncontiguous populations) equates to speciation, that if identical appearing lizards are separated geographically they are different species. This would make the designation of subspecies by geographical origin, a traditional manner of recognizing different populations, invalid.

Because traditional systematics has "worked well" over the years, and because we feel that a field guide is not the proper forum for arguing taxonomic principles, we continue to take this comfortable and conservative approach in these pages. Almost certainly some names will change in future editions.

Wherever we felt it possible, both the common and scientific names used in this book are those suggested in *Scientific and Standard Common Names of Amphibians and Reptiles of North America North of Mexico, with Comments Regarding Confidence in our Understanding* (SSAR Circular no. 29).

## Captive Care

The collecting of reptiles from the wild for the pet trade is less acceptable today than in bygone years, yet it is entirely legal in many areas. Even if certain jurisdictions do not allow commercial collecting, they often do allow collection of one to several specimens for personal use. Many states have no restrictions on the collecting of introduced alien reptiles.

If trade in wild-collected reptiles is not allowed, the sale of captive-bred native reptiles may be legal. We urge that you support captive propagation whenever possible.

Before seeking reptiles in the wild, or keeping them in captivity, check the legal status of these animals with that state's wildlife agencies as well as with the U.S. Fish and Wildlife Service. Reptiles of protected or regulated status should not be collected, or even molested, without specific permits.

The keeping of reptiles and amphibians in captivity, snakes in particular, has become a popular hobby. Providing the animals and the necessary equipment and supplies to an eager populace is a multimillion-dollar business.

The keeping of reptiles and amphibians in captivity has become a mainstream hobby. Providing the animals and the necessary equipment and supplies is a multimillion-dollar business. Some reptiles are easily kept, requiring only a secure terrarium, food, water, and periodic cleaning to live quietly for many years. Other species (and an occasional individual of normally easily kept kinds) may prove to be very difficult captives.

There was a time when the short-term keeping of reptiles was an accepted practice. A specimen would be found, picked up, and brought home by an enthusiast, kept for a period of time, and then released. It has been learned that this is not really a suitable practice. These animals have difficulty establishing a new territory among other territories, for one thing. Unless they are released in exactly the same spot from which they were collected, many reptiles are not able to reacclimatize and their survival rate is dismal. Secondly, there is always the chance of introducing a potential pathogen from you or from your other reptiles into wild populations.

With this said, we feel that unless you are prepared to undergo a commitment of ten years or more per animal, you should not collect animals from the wild. Finding, observing, and photographing them may be a viable alternative.

What are suitable terrarium/cage conditions for one species of reptile may not be adequate for another. For example, something as simple as providing drinking water to a pet reptile can be problematic because not all reptiles obtain their moisture the same way. Although a dish of drinking water may be suitable for box turtles, anoles and geckos drink hanging water droplets.

Providing the needed ultraviolet rays UVA and UVB for turtles and lizards (crocodilians do not seem so dependent on sunlight) can also be difficult. Basking in natural sunlight allows most reptiles to synthesize vitamin $D_3$ in their skin, and $D_3$ facilitates the normal metabolizing of calcium from food. Without these rays (and particularly without UVB), the natural uptake of calcium slows nearly to a halt. When calcium is not continually available from the diet, it is pulled from the bones. Soon the bones become soft and unable to support the animal's weight.

The best source of ultraviolet rays is natural, unfiltered sunlight. There are some incandescent and fluorescent bulbs now on the market that provide ultraviolet rays. Dietary supplementation with vitamin $D_3$ and calcium may help to retain the needed amount of both, but it is now suspected that very little calcium is actually metabolized properly from dietary additives if UVB light is not present. In fact, if too much calcium is added to the diet it can actually be harmful because it can cause visceral gout.

We urge that, whenever possible, vitamin $D_3$ and calcium requirements be met through access to natural unfiltered sunlight or high-output full-spectrum bulbs and a good diet. Provide additives, but do so sparingly and use mixtures that have at least twice as much calcium as phosphorus.

Many lizards previously thought to be solely insectivorous or carnivorous will readily consume blossoms, leaves, and nectar. We suggest that you provide your lizards (especially anoles, geckos, basilisks, and curly-tails) with a liquid honey-fruit mixture. The following formula is suitable: ⅓ pureed apricot or mango baby food, ⅓ water, and ⅓ honey. Add a little powdered D3–calcium additive, mix well, serve fresh daily. Keep unused portion in the refrigerator but discard all not used weekly.

Provide secure terraria or cages that are as large as possible (some states have laws regulating cage size relative to reptile size).

In general, reptiles need to be kept warm to remain active and to allow natural bodily functions. Thermal gradients should be provided in the terrarium; i.e., warm on one end, cooler on the other. Heat can be provided through the use of overhead bulbs. The suggested basking temperature for woodland, nocturnal desert, and burrowing reptiles is in the mid 90s F; for diurnal, basking desert lizards, and all basking turtles and crocodilians, a hot-spot temperature of about 105°F is suitable. Be sure the cool end of the cage is at least 10°F cooler.

Although there are many types of cages specifically for reptiles now available, we usually use covered aquaria. Choose one spacious enough for the creature(s) you wish to keep. Providing a tight cover is a necessity. Never place a glass terrarium or cage in full-strength sunlight. Glass intensifies and concentrates the heat and the elevated temperatures will quickly kill even the most heat-tolerant reptiles.

#### CROCODILIANS

Three species of crocodilians, one introduced and two native, occur in eastern and central North America. Although babies are easily maintained, larger individuals can be quite aggressive. No matter how long they have been captive, these powerful predators should *never* be considered tame.

Crocodilians are carnivores and will accept fish, worms, and suitably sized mice in captivity. Handle these reptiles with extreme care.

Babies can be maintained in a large aquarium containing several inches of tepid water and a warmed and illuminated smooth haul-out area where the creature can bask and dry. Water cleanliness must be maintained.

Many states prohibit the keeping of crocodilians without a permit; the American crocodile and the American alligator are federally protected.

## LIZARDS AND AMPHISBAENIDS

The lizards of eastern North America may be nocturnal (geckos) or diurnal (all others). They may inhabit moist areas (some skinks and eastern glass lizards) or woodlands (some anoles and fence lizards), but most prefer open areas with well-drained soils. Others are creatures of deserts and other arid lands. They may be arboreal (anoles, fence lizards) or primarily terrestrial (glass lizards, horned lizards, most skinks). Some dwell on rocks (collared lizards, canyon lizards) and a very few readily swim (coal skinks). Mole skinks and worm lizards burrow persistently in yielding sands.

Provide dry quarters with climbing facilities for fence and scrub lizards, curly-tails, brown anoles, and most skinks. Primarily terrestrial lizards such as green and wall lizards, collared lizards, and racerunners or whiptails would probably utilize rocks more efficiently than limbs. The substrate can be sandy loam (recommended), newspaper or paper towels, or flat, dry leaves (such as those of the live oak). Glass lizards will prefer a few inches of barely moistened sand or sandy loam, topped with an inch or two of dry leaves or with a flat board under which they may seclude themselves. Glass lizards desiccate quickly, so be sure fresh water is always present.

When first collected collared lizards and leopard lizards are nervous and may injure themselves by running into the glass sides of their enclosure. Taping paper over the outside of the glass will usually curtail this behavior. These two lizards are also very predatory and will eat smaller cagemates as well as insects.

Arboreal lizards such as the various color-changing anoles, geckos, basilisks, and baby iguanas will do best in a vertically oriented terrarium. Basilisks are nervous lizards prone to dashing into the glass of a terrarium when the cage is approached. A visual barrier such as piece of cloth or newspaper may need to be taped to the front of the cage to prevent frightening these remarkable-appearing lizards.

Green and spiny-tailed iguanas do well as captives provided they are given sufficient space and a primarily vegetable diet. Despite the fact that iguanas of both genera eagerly eat insects and meat, there is now irrefutable evidence that diets high in animal proteins have a negative impact on long-range health. The diet for these lizards should be vitamin- and mineral-rich greens that do not contain oxalic acid (oxalic acid inhibits the use of calcium). It appears that neither green nor spiny-tailed iguanas metabolize orally given calcium well. This is especially so when they are not provided with strong, full-spectrum lighting. If you are availing these lizards of natural sunlight, *do not* put their glass terrarium in the sun, or you will literally cook them.

## TURTLES AND TORTOISES

With sufficient space, cleanliness, temperature, and food, most turtles and tortoises are rather easy to keep and have very long lives. Although most will bite if handled carelessly, they make alert and enjoyable captives.

The flippered marine species and the gopher and Texas tortoises are protected and must not be collected or harassed. Laws have also been enacted to protect the three pond turtles: wood, bog, and spotted turtles. Check your state's laws before removing any of these from the wild.

Most aquatic turtles eventually attain a quite considerable size, a fact that should be considered before you elect to keep any. They are also messy captives that require a regular regimen of cleaning.

Most cooters and sliders attain an adult length of 7–10 inches. Some can reach a length of 16 inches. This large adult size makes these beautiful turtles candidates more for an outside or atrium pool than for an indoor setup. However, many species are cold sensitive and not able to tolerate winter temperatures unless they are in a natural pond that enables them to hibernate through the months of winter. As the cooters and sliders grow, they become more herbivorous. Captive adults will do well on a diet of water plants, lettuces (but not iceberg lettuce), other greens, and a little low-fat dog chow.

Painted turtles are quite similar in lifestyle to the cooters and sliders, but are smaller and somewhat more carnivorous.

The chicken turtle is a rather poorly understood species that spends much time in shallow water but wanders far afield, sometimes for weeks on end. Chicken turtles seem to do best on a diet high in worms, crickets, other invertebrates, and low-fat dog foods. They do not seem particularly fond of fruits or vegetation.

Captive eastern box turtles usually thrive in areas of comparatively high humidity, but may decline where humidity is low. Conversely, the western box turtles prefer a low humidity. Both are terrestrial turtles that often do best in outside garden pens, with full access to Mother Nature. Box turtles are omnivorous, feeding on worms, crickets, and carrion, as well as mushrooms, berries, and some greens. Captives seem to do well on these items plus low-fat dog food with a few berries and bananas added.

Diamond-backed terrapins are a brackish and saltwater species. They may adapt to fresh water, but if injured (bruised or bitten) while in fresh water, a difficult-to-eradicate fungus may invade the injuries. We believe that keeping these turtles in water made brackish by the addition of uniodized table salt is better overall. Diamond-backs feed in the wild on mollusks, crustaceans, worms, and other such fare. Females develop an enlarged head that helps them crush the shells of prey items.

Most of what has been said for diamond-backed terrapins in captivity applies equally to map turtles. However, map turtles are *freshwater* species that do not tolerate salt content well. The females of many map turtle species are significantly larger than the males. Females of some species develop enormously enlarged heads and change from the worm and insect diet of the juveniles to one of shellfish. These turtles need very clean water lest they develop bacterial shell diseases.

Soft-shelled turtles are fully aquatic and as long as high water quality is maintained they will thrive for years in aquaria. The substrate should be a layer of fine sand. Soft-shells readily accept minnows (the long-term use of goldfish is contraindicated), worms, and some prepared foods.

We have found hatchlings of the Florida soft-shelled turtle difficult to acclimate. These little turtles have a tendency to develop fungal problems no matter how clean their water. Perhaps highly acid water and a substrate of sand for shell scrubbing would overcome this problem.

It is a good idea to keep soft-shells singly. By doing so, you eliminate the possibility of them scratching one another and eliminate at least one cause of fungus infection.

Babies of the sliders, cooters, and other freshwater turtles usually thrive in an aquarium with several inches of water and a brightly illuminated and warmed haul-out area. Babies of these turtles feed largely on insects, worms, and small gastropods. In captivity, they will readily accept any good quality prepared turtle diet as well as crickets, small worms, and pieces of fresh fish.

## Cautionary Notes

Do not approach large crocodilians and use care when handling large turtles, iguanas, and monitors.

There are no venomous lizards native to eastern North America, but an encounter with a crocodilian can be fatal, and with a large turtle or lizard, painfully memorable. If approached or handled carelessly iguanas are capable of causing injury to a human. Abrasions or bites by these should be thoroughly cleansed; if the wound is serious, medical attention should be sought.

There is a chance of contamination by *Salmonella* or other pathogens from any reptile, as well as a chance of infection from any reptile bite. Also, for the safety of the reptiles and for your own, we urge that you wash your hands thoroughly both before and after handling any.

## Key to the Families of Crocodilians, Turtles, and Lizards of Eastern and Central North America

### CROCODILIANS

   1a. Snout narrow, notched anteriorly, 4th tooth of lower jaw exposed: family Crocodylidae, crocodiles

   1b. Snout broader, no anterior notch, 4th tooth of lower jaw not exposed: family Alligatoridae, alligators and caiman

### TURTLES

Note: The large family Emydidae, the basking turtles, are variable and diverse. The turtles of this family appear in several couplets below.

   1a. Upper and lower shell covered with large, discernible horny plates . . 2
   1b. Upper and lower shell covered with skin . . . . . . . . . . . . . . . . . . . . . . . 10

   2a. Forelimbs normal, not flippers . . . . . . . . . . . . . . . . . . . . . . . . . . . . . . . .3
   2b. Forelimbs are flippers: family Cheloniidae, marine turtles

   3a. Plastron not hinged . . . . . . . . . . . . . . . . . . . . . . . . . . . . . . . . . . . . . . . .7
   3b. Plastron hinged . . . . . . . . . . . . . . . . . . . . . . . . . . . . . . . . . . . . . . . . . . .4

   4a. Plastron with a single hinge . . . . . . . . . . . . . . . . . . . . . . . . . . . . . . . . .5
   4b. Plastron large with a double hinge: family Kinosternidae, in part, mud turtles

   5a. Feet webbed, upper jaw notched, throat yellow: family Emydidae, in part, Blanding's turtle
   5b. Plastron small and crosslike with a single anterior hinge . . . . . . . . . .6

   6a. Feet webbed, tail short: family Kinosternidae, in part, musk turtles
   6b. Feet not webbed, plastron large: family Emydidae, in part, box turtle

   7a. Carapace (top shell) high domed, often with growth rings, forefeet not webbed, but flattened and spadelike: family Testudinidae, tortoises
   7b. Carapace moderately high domed . . . . . . . . . . . . . . . . . . . . . . . . . . . .8

   8a. Plastron large, carapace smoothly domed: family Emydidae, basking turtles
   8b. Plastron narrow . . . . . . . . . . . . . . . . . . . . . . . . . . . . . . . . . . . . . . . . . .9

    9a. Feet strongly webbed, face often with yellow spots: family Pelomedusidae, river turtles

    9b. Plastron small and crosslike, tail very long: family Chelydridae, snapping turtles

    10a. Forelimbs normal, but fully webbed, snorkel-like snout: family Trionychidae, soft-shelled turtles

    10b. Forelimbs are flippers: family Dermochelyidae, leather-backed sea turtle

### LIZARDS

Note: The agamid, iguanid, lacertid, and teiid lizards are very difficult to differentiate by assessment of external characteristics.

    1a. Scales not shiny . . . . . . . . . . . . . . . . . . . . . . . . . . . . . . . . . . . . . . . . . . . .2

    1b. Scales shiny. . . . . . . . . . . . . . . . . . . . . . . . . . . . . . . . . . . . . . . . . . . . . . .7

    2a. Nonfunctional eyelids and/or vertical pupils . . . . . . . . . . . . . . . . . . . .4

    2b. Dorsal and lateral scales tiny, belly plates large. . . . . . . . . . . . . . . . . . .5

    3a. No dramatically enlarged belly plates; elongated, bifurcate tongue    6

    3b. No dramatically enlarged belly plates; short, simple tongue. . . . . . . . .7

    4a. Most species with vertical pupils and expanded toepads: family Gekkonidae, typical geckos

    4b. Vertical pupils, functional eyelids: family Eublepharidae, eyelidded geckos

    5a. Belly plates in 6 or 8 rows, single enlarged preanal plate: family Lacertidae, wall lizards and green lizard

    5b. Belly plates in 8, 10, or 12 rows, 3 enlarged preanal plates: family Teiidae, ameivas, whiptails, and racerunners

    6a. Adults huge, tail strongly keeled, strong limbs, black with cross bands of yellow spots, long body: family Varanidae

    6b. Appearance very variable, parietal (pineal) eye usually visible, limbs always present, body scales weakly to strongly keeled, subdigital scales keeled, expanded toepads present on anoles: families Agamidae and

Iguanidae, agamas, butterfly lizards, horned lizards, anoles, spiny lizards.

7a. Limbs lacking, conspicuous longitudinal fold along side of body: family Anguidae, glass lizards and alligator lizards
7b. Limbs present, no lateral fold: family Scincidae, skinks

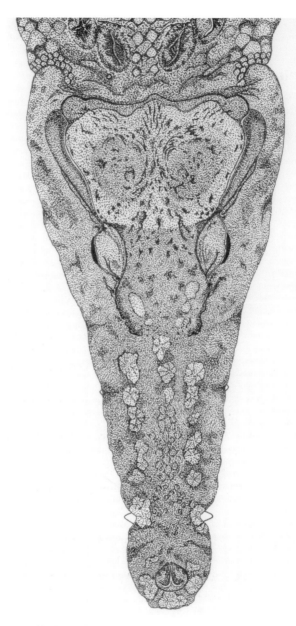

Crocodile head. Illustration by K. P. Wray III.

# 2

## Alligators, Caiman, and Crocodiles, order Crocodylia

### CROCODILIANS

The crocodilians are among the most readily recognized of the reptiles. All, even the smallest, are comparatively immense, semiaquatic creatures with bony backs and broadly flattened snouts that are either variably rounded (alligators and caiman) or variably pointed (crocodiles).

All are highly predatory, and family pets regularly fall prey to alligators. American crocodiles prefer prey such as fish or waterbirds. The males of alligators and caiman are quite cannibalistic, whereas females provide care and protection at least of nests and sometimes of hatchlings. Female American alligators and spectacled caiman gather vegetation into nest mounds; female American crocodiles dig a nest above the vegetation line in a low mound of scraped-together sand and beach debris or merely in the beach sand. The female American crocodile provides less protection of nest and hatchlings than the alligator and caiman.

Female alligators and caiman are noticeably smaller than the adult males. There is less sexual dimorphism in the crocodiles.

Comparatively huge American alligators may survive in relatively small (usually) freshwater waterholes that they may enlarge as needed. American crocodiles are creatures of tidally influenced estuarine areas. All crocodilians bask for extended periods. They are active both by day and after nightfall.

All have a strongly developed homing instinct. Relocated "problem" specimens will return time and again to their home territory.

These reptiles all have voices. During the breeding and nesting season adults are quite vocal and may be more irascible than at other times.

Both the American alligator and the American crocodile are protected; the introduced spectacled caiman is not.

American alligators have caused human fatalities. Extreme care should be used near large specimens.

The alligator and caiman are in the family Alligatoridae. The crocodile is in the family Crocodilidae.

## Family Alligatoridae

Alligators, genus *Alligator* and Caiman, genus *Caiman* (in part)

The genus *Alligator* contains only two species, the American alligator of the southeastern United States and the Chinese alligator of China. In the mid-twentieth century the American alligator was hunted almost to extinction for its skin but once protected, rebounded dramatically. It is estimated that there are now more than one million alligators in Florida alone; populations in other states have also increased greatly.

Although the Chinese alligator does continue to exist, its status is so precarious that it remains listed as an endangered species.

From 20 to 50+ eggs are laid annually. Hatching occurs after 65–75 days of incubation. Females may protect both the eggs and the young. Alligators usually walk with their body held high above the ground, with only their tailtip dragging. They can run fast but tire quickly.

Visitors on vacation in Florida almost invariably want to see an alligator. This is a wish that was not easily granted in the past, because by the mid-twentieth century alligators had been hunted so persistently for their hides that their very existence was precarious. But a recovery plan was implemented and today on waterways and especially in refuges from the Carolinas to Texas finding an American alligator during the months of summer usually involves little more than making a cursory search. From Laguna Atascosa National Wildlife Reserve on the southeastern coast of Texas to Swan Quarter National Wildlife Refuge in northeastern North Carolina and in most areas in between, American alligators abound. It is not impossible to see more than a hundred on a good alligator day in Paynes' Prairie State Preserve in north central Florida, and during the hatching season the number can be double or triple that.

The American alligator's survival—an exemplary tribute to modern conservation techniques!

## 1. American Alligator

*Alligator mississippiensis*

**Abundance/Range:** This huge reptile is now a common sight throughout its range. It may be found from northeastern North Carolina to southern Texas.
**Habitat:** Although this is primarily a species of freshwater ponds, canals, lakes, rivers, large streams, borrow pits, swamps, and marshes or virtually any other

American alligators, adults

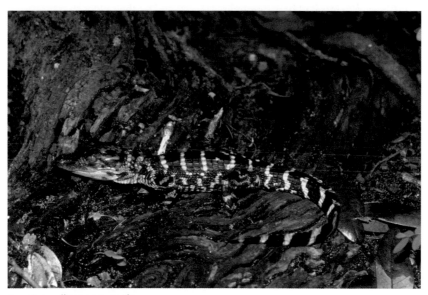

American alligator, juvenile

water-retaining habitat including backyard fishponds and swimming pools, it may be occasionally encountered in estuarine or saltwater habitats.

**Size:** Females often attain 7 feet in length, and occasionally may reach 8 feet; males routinely attain 11 feet. The girth of a healthy, well-fed adult is proportionately immense. The reported record size is 19 feet 2 inches (but this is now suspect)! A male measuring 14 feet ⅝ inch was found recently in central Florida. Hatchlings are about 9½ inches long.

**Identifying features:** This is the darkest of our crocodilians in color. Baby alligators are black with yellow cross bands. With growth, the colors become muted and adults are largely or entirely a dusky olive black. If yellow markings are retained, they will be most prominent on the sides. The snout is bluntly rounded.

**Voice:** Babies produce a high-pitched grunt. Adults voice muffled, spluttering, roars.

**Similar species:** Neither the spectacled caiman nor the American crocodile have yellow cross bands. Both are dark olive green or olive gray with darker banding. Both have narrower snouts. The spectacled caiman has a bony ridge crossing the snout and touching each eyelid. American crocodiles are most apt to be encountered in brackish or saltwater habitats.


Caiman, genus *Caiman*

This is a small group of Latin American alligator look-alikes. One, the spectacled caiman, was once commonly seen in the American pet trade and escapees are now established in southern Florida and possibly in southern Texas.

From 10 to about 40 eggs are laid in summer. Large females usually produce the largest clutches. Incubation is of variable duration but in South Florida seems in the range of 75–95 days. Hatchlings are about 8½ inches long and more contrastingly patterned than the adults.

Spectacled caiman seldom stray far from the water's edge. They are active day and night.

## 2. Spectacled Caiman

*Caiman crocodilus*

**Abundance/Range:** This Neotropical crocodilian is rare and of very localized distribution. In the United States, it is known to breed only in extreme southern Florida. Feral individuals have been seen elsewhere in Florida, in the lower Rio Grande valley of Texas, and sparingly in other states. This cold-sensitive tropical crocodilian is probably unable to survive the winter except in extreme southern Florida and is native from Mexico to northern South America.

**Habitat:** This species occurs in freshwater marshes and heavily vegetated pond, lake, and canal edges.

**Size:** Florida specimens seldom exceed 6 feet in total length. In tropical America this feisty crocodilian may occasionally attain a length of 8 feet.

**Identifying features:** A curved bony ridge extends across the base of the moderately sharp snout, between the eyes, like the nosepiece of spectacles, giving rise to the species' common name. Adult spectacled caiman appear a unicolored dark olive dorsally. Hatchlings are banded with very dark brown on a dark olive ground.

2. Spectacled caiman

**Voice:** Hatchlings communicate in high-pitched grunts. Adult males produce a spluttering roar.

**Similar species:** American alligators are black with yellow banding and a broad snout. American crocodiles have a sharp snout and are usually found in brackish or saltwater habitats.

## Crocodiles, family Crocodylidae

Most of the true crocodiles are more slender snouted than the alligators and caiman. Although some, such as the Nile crocodile of Africa and the saltwater crocodiles of Australia, are confirmed maneaters, in its Florida range the shy and secretive American crocodile eats fish, waterbirds, and small mammals. The population in Florida reportedly now hovers at about 1,000 animals and is slowly increasing.

### Crocodiles, genus *Crocodylus* (in part)

The American crocodile is a shy, quiet, and normally inoffensive creature. It often thermoregulates in the morning while lying half in the water, half out, or by hauling entirely out of the water onto a smooth bank.

From 20 to 50+ eggs are laid in a hole dug in the shore sand. Incubation takes about 3 months. Females assist in the escape of the young from the nest, may carry the young to the water, but offer no further maternal assistance. Hatchlings are about 10 inches in total length.

Seeing a crocodile in the United States can be much more problematic than seeing an alligator. About the only place that you may be reasonably assured of seeing one is at the fish cleaning area at the boat ramp in the village of Flamingo in Everglades National Park, Florida. Two or three crocs have been sunning in that area on sunny days for years. These crocs are of fair size, perhaps 6–8 feet in length and, although fairly well habituated to the presence of humans, remain very much wild animals. Remain a prudent distance away.

## 3. American Crocodile

*Crocodylus acutus*

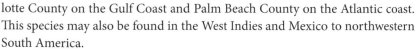

**Abundance/Range:** In Florida, this crocodile is both rare and local. It regularly occurs only in Dade and Monroe counties, but occasional specimens find their way northward to Charlotte County on the Gulf Coast and Palm Beach County on the Atlantic coast. This species may also be found in the West Indies and Mexico to northwestern South America.

**Habitat:** The American crocodile hauls out to thermoregulate on mudflats, exposed rocks, or grassy banks. It favors brackish and saltwater situations.

**Size:** Adults in Florida attain a length of 8–12 feet. Hatchlings are about 10 inches in length.

**Identifying features:** This species has a ground color of muddy brown to dark olive green. The cross bands are darker. The pattern is more prominent on juveniles than on adults. The snout is slender and tapering. Because the upper jaw is notched anteriorly the 4th tooth of the lower jaw is always visible.

**Voice:** Recent hatchlings produce a high-pitched croaking grunt, but specimens of more than a few weeks of age seldom vocalize.

3a. American crocodile, adult

3b. American crocodile, juvenile

**Similar species:** The American alligator is black with yellow cross bands and has a bluntly rounded snout. The spectacled caiman is colored somewhat like the crocodile but occurs in freshwater habitats and has a more bluntly rounded snout.

**Comments:** The American crocodile is now routinely seen on Sanibel, Captiva, and Pine Islands on Florida's Gulf coast as well as in various locations of Collier County. Recent reports indicate that an occasional specimen is making its way northward along Florida's Atlantic coast at least to Palm Beach County.

# 3

## Turtles and Tortoises, order Testudines

### CHELONIANS

Although easily recognized as turtles, these creatures are not so easy to identify as to species.

Despite their obvious similarities, turtles and tortoises are a diverse lot with widely varying needs and lifestyles. Contained in the 13 families are some 75+ genera and about 250 species.

Of these, eight families are represented in the eastern and central United States by a total of 53 species having 84 subspecies:

- Family Cheloniidae, Typical Sea Turtles (4 species)
- Family Chelydridae, Snapping Turtles (2 species)
- Family Dermochelyidae, Leatherback Sea Turtle (1 species)
- Family Emydidae, Basking and Box Turtles (32 species)
- Family Kinosternidae, Musk and Mud Turtles (8 species)
- Family Pelomedusidae, Afro-Neotropical Side-necked Turtles (1 species)
- Family Testudinidae, Tortoises (2 species)
- Family Trionychidae, Soft-shelled Turtles (3 species)

The terms turtle and terrapin are used differently by different cultures. In the United States the term "turtle" is used for both freshwater and marine species. The terms "cooter" (of African derivation) and "slider," heard in the southeastern United States, are used to designate some of the larger basking turtles. In the United States, "terrapin" is reserved for the brackish and saltwater emydines known commonly as diamondbacks. The term "tortoise" is applied only to the exclusively terrestrial species.

The turtle's shell helps protect it from attacks and predation, but it is not impervious. In the southeastern states, even adults of freshwater basking chelonians are crushed and eaten by alligators. Predation by raccoons, opossums, dogs, and cats takes its toll of young turtles, hatchlings, and eggs. Turtles crossing roadways are readily crushed by autos.

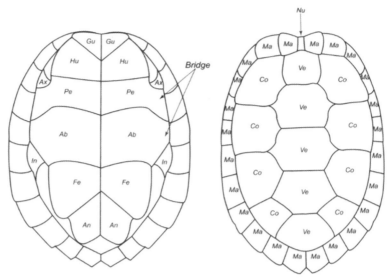

Turtle shells

*PLASTRON*

Gu = gular
Hu = humeral
Pe = Pectoral
Ab = Abdominal
Fe = Femoral
An = Anal
Ax = Axillary
In = Inguinal

*CARAPACE*

Nu = nuchal
Ma = marginal
Co = costal
Ve = vertebral

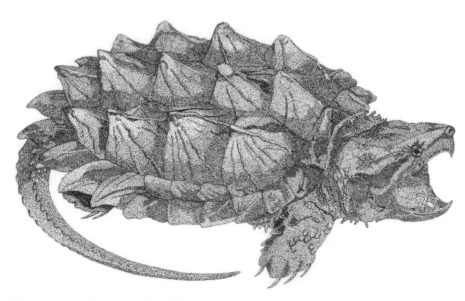

Alligator snapper. Illustration by K. P. Wray III.

## Snapping Turtles, family Chelydridae

This family contains only two species. Both are large; one, the alligator snapping turtle, is the largest freshwater turtle in the United States and one of the largest in the world. Male alligator snappers occasionally exceed 200 pounds, and there is a believable anecdotal report of an alligator snapper weighing more than 300 pounds. This short-necked, strong-jawed turtle will bite readily if molested, especially if on land.

The common snapper is much smaller, but still well worthy of extreme care when approached on land. The long neck of this turtle gives it a great reach when snapping aggressively. In the water, snappers are usually benign.

Both species of snapping turtle have a long tail and a roughened mud-colored carapace that provides excellent camouflage. The plastron of both is comparatively tiny and offers little protection to the soft parts.

Snapping turtles are predominantly carnivorous, eating all manner of animal matter, including other turtles.

---

I (RDB) can remember tirades against the common snapping turtle from days long ago when I was growing up in New England. Every spring skeins of mallard ducklings would trail their mothers across the shallow ponds in a nearby city park. Every year, one by one, the ducklings would disappear, and the cause, according to everyone who was rooting for the success of the ducks, was invariably "those horrible snapping turtles." Every snapper found by the park managers and bird club members paid the ultimate price. But there must have been an amazing population of the big turtles, for no matter how many snappers were killed the ducklings continued to disappear. Strangely, no one ever suggested that raccoons, or herons, or other predators might have been the cause. It was always the snappers.

Somehow, despite this, I grew up liking (and rooting for) the snappers. I marveled at the seeming plodding solemnity of a big female searching out a nesting site. And on rare occasions I watched the hatchling turtles as they emerged from the nest and made their way helter-skelter (in a turtley way) to the nearest water, to undertake the Herculean tasks associated with day to day life.

Today, we realize that snapping turtles are very much a part of the natural realm. We enjoy finding and watching these wonderful, once maligned creatures, wherever our paths happen to cross.

---

### Common Snapping Turtle, genus *Chelydra*

### Alligator Snapping Turtle, genus *Macrochelys*

Each genus contains only a single species. The common snapping turtle is divided into several subspecies that occur southward from southern Canada to Ecuador whereas the alligator snapper is resident of the southeastern and central United States.

Nesting females often first dig a body pit and then the nesting chamber. More than 50 eggs can be laid. Females nest only once annually. Incubation may take from slightly less than two months to more than four months.

These turtles can swim, but usually prefer to walk slowly along the bottom of their pond or river. Common snappers may thermoregulate by floating at the top of deep water or lying in shallows with the carapace partially exposed.

## 4. Common Snapping Turtle

*Chelydra serpentina serpentina*

**Abundance/Range:** This turtle remains one of the most common chelonians in eastern North America. It is found from western Texas and extreme southwestern Saskatchewan eastward to Nova Scotia and extreme northeastern Florida.

**Habitat:** Nearly any quiet or slowly flowing and heavily vegetated body of freshwater is acceptable habitat for this very aquatic turtle. It may be occasionally found in estuarine and salt marsh habitats.

**Size:** A shell length of 19 inches and a weight of more than 50 pounds may be attained. Hatchlings have a shell length of 1–1¼ inches.

**Identifying features:** The carapace may be brown, tan, horn, or olive gray. Darker radiating markings may be present on the costal scutes. The head, neck, limbs, and tail are usually brown, sometimes with olive tones. The mandibles are often lighter than the rest of the head and face. The carapacial scutes are roughened and have a projection near the upper posterior corner of each scute. The posterior marginal scutes are serrate. The plastron is tiny and offers little protection to the turtle. However, once the turtle grows beyond a few inches

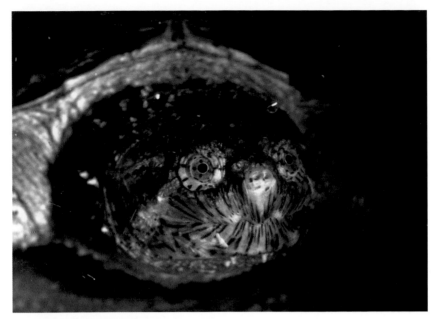

4. Common snapping turtle

in carapace length, its strong jaws (which bear a weak beak) and defensive attitude make up for this lack of armor plating. The very long tail has a prominent dorsal keel and the papillae on the neck are rounded. The carapace of some old examples may be worn almost smooth.

**Similar species:** The alligator snapper has a more massive head with a strongly down-hooked beak, a shorter neck, and it lacks a strongly serrated dorsal tail crest. Musk turtles are small and have a short tail. Mud turtles are small and have a short tail and a proportionately large, hinged, plastron.

### Additional Subspecies

5. The Florida Snapping Turtle, *Chelydra serpentina osceola*, is a little smaller (carapace length to 17 inches and about 25 pounds) than its northern relative. It is found from the southernmost tip of Florida northward to extreme south central Georgia. The chestnut brown hatchlings have a light spot on the outer edge of each marginal scute. Adults are somewhat smoother and olive brown to dark brown in color. The plastron is very small and pliable. The papillae on the neck are conical and pointed.

5a. Florida snapping turtle, adult

5b. Florida snapping
turtle, juvenile

## 6. Alligator Snapping Turtle

*Macrochelys temminckii*

**Abundance/Range:** This turtle is found from eastern Texas to northeastern Florida, and northward to southeastern Kansas and central western Illinois. It is a moderately common turtle that is so persistently aquatic and secretive that its true numbers are often not suspected.

**Habitat:** This is a turtle of big rivers, big creeks, backwaters, and reservoirs.

It can sometimes be seen at night by walking the banks with a flashlight; it is also occasionally caught on hook and line.

**Size:** Males may attain a shell length of 20–24 inches and a weight of more than

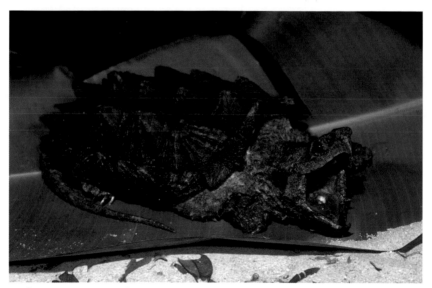

6. Alligator snapping turtle

250 pounds. Adult females usually weigh less than 55 pounds. Hatchlings have a shell length of 1¼–1¾ inches.

**Coloration/pattern:** Both hatchlings and adults are some shade of brown above and below. Some are quite pale, but most are mud colored. Hatchlings have a very rough carapace, but this becomes smoother with growth. The plastron is very small. Although not easily seen, there is an extra row of scutes, the supramarginals, between the costals and the marginal scutes. The jaws are immensely powerful and strongly beaked. The head is large and cannot be withdrawn entirely within the shell. The long tail bears a weakly serrate middorsal keel.

This turtle has a tongue appendage resembling a worm that is white when at rest, red when in use. When the turtle is hunting, the mouth is opened widely and the appendage flicked; when a passing fish swims into the mouth to investigate the "worm," the jaws snap shut.

**Similar species:** Common snappers have very long necks, proportionately smaller heads, and strongly serrate tails.

## Mud and Musk Turtles, family Kinosternidae

Of the ten species of musk and mud turtles found in the United States, all but two occur in the eastern and central states. These small turtles have rather highly domed, often elongate, carapaces. They are basically aquatic in habits but often occur in shallow water situations. Some wander far afield and may be encountered long distances from the nearest water source.

Musk turtles have small plastrons that leave the soft parts unprotected. They have pointed conical noses. Musk turtles have a movable front plastral lobe. Males have considerable expanses of skin showing between the plastral scutes; females have almost none.

Mud turtles have plastrons proportionately larger than those of the musk turtles but which still do not provide complete protection for the turtle. The

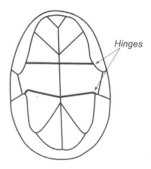
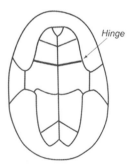

Mud turtle and musk turtle plastrons

plastron has two hinges. The front lobe (consisting of the gular, humeral, and pectoral scutes) and the rear lobe (consisting of the femoral and anal scutes) are movable to a degree. Mud turtles have less sharply pointed noses.

Adult male musk and mud turtles have a heavy, enlarged tail that is usually tipped with a curved spur.

Despite their small size, musk and mud turtles all have strong jaws and will try to bite if restrained or prodded. The musky exudate for which these turtles are so well known is produced in glands at each side of each bridge where the skin meets the shell.

None of these species are brightly colored.

---

Herp people do strange things. We had been walking around the perimeter of a small pond in South Carolina looking at whatever we could see. That in itself isn't awfully strange, but the time was about two o'clock in the morning and it was pouring! It was a warm spring night, the kind of night when reptiles and amphibians are most active, especially immediately after emerging from winter's dormancy. We had already seen several species of frogs, but were now looking for water snakes and other such reptiles. We had pretty much made the whole circle and were standing talking, with flashlight beams lazily sweeping the pond bottom. As we watched, a rounded blob of mud sprouted a head and legs and began to walk slowly from the shallows into deeper water. It warranted jumping in to retrieve the departing creature, an eastern mud turtle, a common chelonian of the eastern seaboard.

For the most part, the above description fits most of the mud and musk turtles, not only of North America but of Central and South America as well. They are predominantly aquatic, smoothly domed or moderately keeled, and prefer to walk rather than swim from point A to point B. And most are pretty common throughout their respective ranges.

The most divergent of these turtles in appearance is also the rarest and has the most restricted range. This is the interesting little flattened musk turtle, a species restricted to clear-water streams and rivers in north central Alabama. It is the only endangered species in the group.

---

## Mud Turtles, genus *Kinosternon* and Musk Turtles, genus *Sternotherus*

The turtles in these two genera are very similar and thought by some authorities to comprise a single genus.

Adult females lay several clutches of 1–7 eggs annually. The nesting site may be in soil or decaying aquatic vegetation at water's edge or in thick floating mats of vegetation. Incubation takes 3–4 months. Hatchlings are about 1 inch long.

These turtles may be active by day but actively forage in shallow water situations after nightfall. They may bury deeply into the mud when the water source dries, or search for another water hole.

### 7. Striped Mud Turtle

*Kinosternon baurii*

**Abundance/Range:** Although this abundant turtle occurs primarily in freshwater habitats, it is occasionally found in brackish water situations. This species ranges southward from southeastern Virginia to peninsular Florida and the Keys.
**Habitat:** This ubiquitous turtle may be found in all manner of water holes and can be particularly abundant in shallow roadside ditches. It may be found in estuaries and other weakly brackish situations. The striped mud turtle often wanders far from water and may sometimes be found beneath boards or other surface debris.

7. Striped mud turtle

**Size:** Adults may be up to 5 inches in length but are often an inch shorter. Hatchlings measure about 1 inch in length.

**Identifying features:** These turtles are one of the most distinctively marked of the genus. Except in a few areas (Florida's Gulf Hammock, the Lower Keys, and Georgia's Okefenokee) at least traces of 3 longitudinal yellowish lines are usually present on the carapace. The plastron is olive yellow to orange with dark pigment outlining each scute. The head is usually dark but has 2 variably prominent stripes on each side of the face. Yellow facial mottling may be so prominent that it all but obscures the stripes, or may be absent. There is a yellowish chin stripe.

**Similar species:** The common mud turtle (especially the Mississippi race) may have facial stripes but usually lacks carapacial stripes. Use range as an identification tool.

**Comments:** Many of the striped mud turtles from the lower Florida Keys have a particularly translucent carapace. They also seem to have a proportionately shorter snout. The Lower Key populations are considered to be endangered and are protected.

## 8. Yellow Mud Turtle

*Kinosternon flavescens flavescens*

**Abundance/Range:** This is a common turtle that occurs throughout the western two-thirds of Texas, eastern New Mexico, southeastern Arizona, and adjacent Mexico. From Texas, its range extends northward to Nebraska and, in disjunct populations, to northeastern Missouri and central Illinois.

**Habitat:** This mud turtle inhabits all manner of freshwater situations. It may occasionally be found far from water beneath surface debris or trekking steadfastly across seemingly inhospitable terrain.

**Size:** Although the yellow mud turtle occasionally attains (or barely exceeds) 6 inches in length, 4–5 inches is the more typical length. Males are slightly larger than females. Hatchlings measure a bit more than 1 inch in length.

**Identifying features:** The high-domed carapace is flattened centrally. The overall carapacial color is olive brown to olive tan (very dark near Presidio, Texas).

8. Yellow mud turtle

The marginal scutes may be lighter in color than the rest of the carapace and often have darker smudges. Marginal scutes 9 and 10 (counting from the front of the shell, but excluding the centermost anterior scute [the nuchal scute]) are significantly higher than marginal number 8. The head is somewhat flattened and proportionately larger in males than in females. The top of the head, neck, and limbs are usually of the same color as the carapace. The chin, cheeks, and underside of the neck and forelimbs are usually yellowish. The jaws may be flecked with dark pigment. There are 2 well-developed barbels (downward projecting papillae) on the chin. The plastron is yellowish, olive yellow, or brownish, edged with darker pigment.

**Similar species:** The common musk turtle has a reduced plastron and usually has facial stripes. The Mexican Plateau mud turtle has only marginal number 10 higher than the others and has a peaked carapace.

## 9. Mexican Plateau Mud Turtle

*Kinosternon hirtipes murrayi*

**Abundance:** Although common in some parts of its rather extensive Mexican range, in the United States this turtle is found only in a few ponds and stock watering tanks in the vicinity of Presidio, Texas.

**Habitat:** In Mexico, this is a species of riverine situations and their associated ponds, resacas, and oxbows.

9. Mexican Plateau mud turtle

In Texas the habitat of this turtle seems restricted to spring-fed cattle tanks and associated permanent ponds in the mesquite grasslands of the Rio Alamitos drainage area.

**Size:** This is marginally the largest kinosternid turtle of the United States. It attains an adult size of 5½–7 inches. Hatchlings measure about 1¼ inches.

**Identifying features:** This seldom seen and poorly understood mud turtle has a high-domed, peaked, weakly tricarinate carapace, with the vertebral keel being the strongest. The carapace, head, neck, and limbs of this turtle are a warm to dark olive brown. Scute seams may be darker. The head and face bear a reticulated pattern and vary from olive black to a rather light olive gray. The plastron is tan, yellow orange, or brown and may bear irregular and poorly defined areas of dark pigment. The two plastral hinges are well developed. Three pairs of chin barbels are present. The jaws of many specimens are lighter than the cheeks and the mandibles may be streaked with dark pigment.    Hatchlings have a rough carapace and an orange-red plastron.

**Similar species:** Yellow mud turtles from western Texas may be very similar in color to the Mexican Plateau mud turtle. However, the carapace of the yellow mud turtle is flattened on top, and marginal scutes 9 *and* 10 are higher than the rest.

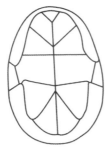 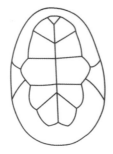

*Kinosternon subrubrum subrubrum*        *Kinosternon subrubrum steindachneri*

Mud turtle plastrons

## 10. Eastern Mud Turtle

*Kinosternon subrubrum subrubrum*

eastern
Mississippi
Florida

**Abundance/Range:** This common but seldom seen turtle ranges southward from Long Island, New York, and northern New Jersey to north central Florida.

**Habitat:** This little turtle utilizes all manner of freshwater habitats. Expect to find it in ponds, lakes, ditches, river edges, and estuarine situations. It also occasionally wanders far from water or may be found burrowed into leaf litter at the base of a tree or against a fallen log.

**Size:** This is one of the smaller mud turtles. It is adult at 4½ inches or less. Hatchlings measure about 1 inch in length.

**Identifying features:** The carapace and head of this turtle are a warm to dark olive brown. The posterior edge of each carapacial scute, including the marginals, may be weakly outlined by dark pigment. There may be olive-yellow spots or reticulations on the cheeks and jaws. The plastron is orangish and relatively large. Hatchlings have a roughened carapace and pinkish plastron.

**Similar species:** The striped mud turtle is much darker and usually has carapacial stripes.

**Comments:** Intergrades between the various races of the eastern mud turtle are commonly found.

10. Eastern mud turtle

**Subspecies**

11. The Mississippi Mud Turtle, *Kinosternon subrubrum hippocrepis*, is found from eastern Texas to southwestern Alabama and northward to northeastern Oklahoma and northeastern Missouri. Its size is identical to that of the eastern mud turtle. The elongate carapace is rather highly domed and not flattened centrally. The general coloration of the carapace and head is warm to dark olive brown to nearly black. There are occasionally 3 weakly developed light stripes

11. Mississippi mud turtle

12. Florida mud turtle

on the carapace. There are irregular yellow facial stripes. The jaws of many specimens are lighter than the head and may be flecked with black. Aged males may develop a moderately enlarged head. The plastron is orangish and bears 2 well-developed hinges.

12. The Florida Mud Turtle, *Kinosternon subrubrum steindachneri*, is the southeasternmost representative of this group. It occurs throughout the southern three-quarters of the peninsula and on Key Largo. It tops out at 4½ inches in length. The carapace and head of this turtle are a warm to dark olive brown. There may be yellowish spots on the cheeks. The jaws may be lighter than the head. With old age, many males develop an enormously enlarged head. The plastron is orangish. The rear lobe of the plastron of this subspecies is quite small and, when closed, leaves much skin exposed.

## 13. Razor-backed Musk Turtle

*Sternotherus carinatus*

**Abundance:** This is a common chelonian from eastern Texas to eastern Mississippi and northward to southeastern Oklahoma and throughout much of the southern half of Arkansas.

**Habitat:** This musk turtle is associated with slow-flowing areas of rivers, streams, and associated swamps and marshes.

**Size:** An adult size of 5 inches (rarely to 6 inches) is attained. Hatchlings measure about 1 inch in length.

**Identifying features:** This is a very highly domed but elongate musk turtle. The carapace color may vary from dark brown to a brownish orange and has downward radiating dark lines. Carapacial scutes are slightly imbricate. The head and limbs are grayish to pinkish brown and liberally peppered with black dots. The small plastron is yellowish, may show some vague dark smudging, and lacks a gular scute. With advancing age, males may darken in color.

The mandibles are vertically striped. Hatchlings have a light tan carapace and brighter yellow plastron, and are less strongly domed than the adults

**Similar species:** Mud turtles have larger plastrons. The common musk turtle usually has yellow facial stripes and a gular scute. The very similar loggerhead musk turtle has 3 keels on the carapace, is not as strongly domed, and overlaps the range of the razor-backed musk turtle only in eastern Mississippi.

13. Razor-backed musk turtle

### 14. Flattened Musk Turtle

*Sternotherus depressus*

**Abundance/Range:** This is an uncommon, federally endangered species of north central Alabama.

**Habitat:** The very aquatic flattened musk turtle is found in clear-water streams of the Black Warrior River drainage. Its flattened shape allows the turtle to hide in crevices that would prohibit the entry of turtles with a more domed carapace.

**Size:** The adult size is 3¾–4⅝ inches. Hatchlings are just about 1 inch in length.

**Identifying features:** This is a small, flattened musk turtle with a big head and strong jaws. The upper jaw may be either weakly notched or weakly beaked. The head is dark olive, variably marked with darker specks or lines. The head may appear either dark or light. Similarly, the carapace may appear dark with vague lighter markings (younger turtles), or may be predominantly light with indistinct dark smudging that are especially prominent at the scute seams (older turtles). The small plastron is pinkish. The neck may or may not be lightly striped. The limbs are usually dark olive with darker flecks, but the skin at the attachment of the carapace may be light olive yellow.

14. Flattened musk turtle

**Similar species:** There are no other mud or musk turtles with such a notably depressed carapace.

## 15. Loggerhead Musk Turtle

*Sternotherus minor minor*

**Abundance/Range:** This common musk is a denizen of the clear springs and spring-fed rivers found in the northern half of the Florida peninsula, in the eastern half of Florida's panhandle, and throughout most of Georgia. Where the ranges abut, it intergrades freely with the striped-necked musk turtle.

loggerhead
striped-neck

**Habitat:** With rare exceptions, the loggerhead musk turtle is associated with flowing, freshwater habitats and their associated overflows and drainages. Very occasional specimens have been found in clear ponds and lakes. These turtles often ascend the submerged roots of cypress and other river-edge trees to the water's surface.

**Size:** An adult size of 5 inches is attained by this species. Hatchlings are about 1 inch long.

**Identifying features:** The high, 3-keeled carapace is of some shade of brown. Darker streaks and lines radiate downward and are most prominent on the

15a. Loggerhead musk turtle, adult

15b. Loggerhead musk turtle, juvenile

costal scutes. The dark-spotted head is grayish. The plastron is quite small and yellowish in color. These turtles, and especially the males, darken with advancing age. Old males have an enormous head, and may have light mandibles. Hatchlings have a light tan carapace and a bright pink plastron.

**Similar species:** Mud turtles have proportionately larger plastrons. The razor-backed musk turtle is very similar but has only a single carapacial keel.

### Subspecies

16. The Striped-necked Musk Turtle, *Sternotherus minor peltifer*, ranges throughout most of Alabama, eastern Mississippi, and immediately adjacent

16. Striped-necked musk turtle

Louisiana. It is also found in eastern Tennessee, western North Carolina, and extreme western Virginia.

The carapace is somewhat flatter than that of the loggerhead musk turtle and the 2 dorsolateral keels are less prominent. The overall color may be darker and the head and neck spots coalesce into stripes. This race occurs in creeks, streams, lakes, and reservoirs, and can be particularly common in impoundments.

## 17. Common Musk Turtle (Stinkpot)

*Sternotherus odoratus*

**Abundance/Range:** An abundant turtle, this species occurs throughout most of the eastern United States and is also found in southern Ontario.

**Habitat:** The common musk turtle may be found in most ponds, slow rivers, lakes, backwaters, and oxbows.

**Size:** Adults attain a length of 3–4½ inches. Hatchlings measure about 1 inch in length.

17. Common musk turtle

**Identification features:** Babies have a rough, keeled, black carapace. The shell of old adults is smooth domed and somewhat elongate. The carapace may be olive black (rarely olive), black stippled, or solid black. The small plastron is horn colored. The skin of the head and limbs is dark, and there are 2 variably prominent yellow lines on the side of the head.

**Similar species:** The striped mud turtle not only has a yellow-striped face but also usually has a striped carapace. Mississippi mud turtles have yellow on the sides of the face and lack carapacial striping. Both of these have a large, two-hinged plastron.

## Basking Turtles

### Sliders, Map Turtles, Pond Turtles, Box Turtles, and relatives, family Emydidae

This is the largest family of turtles in North America. There are several species of basking turtles in eastern and central North America. One or more species may be encountered from the Florida Keys to southern Canada and from western Texas to the Dakotas. Basking turtles are poorly represented in the American West.

There are several rather specialized species of basking turtles. Among these are the highly domed, primarily terrestrial box turtles and the somewhat less terrestrial wood turtle. Blanding's and chicken turtles may also spend considerable time on land. Diamond-backed terrapins are adapted for life in brackish and salt waters. Although a few other species are occasionally seen in tidally influenced estuarine habitats, most are firmly associated with freshwater. Of these latter, some prefer quiet ponds, lakes, and lagoons, whereas others are riverine specialists and a few are bog dwellers.

Many of these turtles are brightly colored, especially as babies, and some remain adorned with brilliant reds, yellows, and greens, throughout their long lives of 25–100+ years!

Many basking turtles have immense geographic ranges and are conspicuous. Others have restricted ranges and are quite rare. A few types have become so uncommon that they are now designated as threatened or endangered on a state or federal level.

Interestingly, rather than being genetically determined, the sex of many turtle species is determined by incubation temperature. Females are produced at higher incubation temperatures and males at lower ones. Thus, nests that are positioned poorly and subjected to an inordinate amount of either sunlight or shade may produce small turtles, popularly called "turtlets," all of one sex.

Floating silently in a canoe down the Apalachicola River on Florida's panhandle offers a naturalist a chance to see many reptiles and amphibians. Water snakes drape themselves on overhanging branches. Loggerhead musk turtles prowl the shallows, ascending cypress knees to reach the surface where they can draw a deep breath. Hulking alligator snappers, a species that can reach 150 pounds or more, are in the deeper parts of the river. And if you look hard enough where the river sweeps over its bed of limestone, you are apt to see one of the prettiest turtles on our continent—the Barbour's map turtle.

The Barbour's map turtle is only one of many beautifully colored basking turtles of the eastern and central states and provinces. As you walk through verdant woodlands you might come across a box turtle or a wood turtle looking for berries or worms. If, with binoculars, you scan some of the dark blobs on the distant shore of a northeastern pond yet rimmed in ice, those blobs may resolve themselves into basking painted turtles, a dark colored turtle that avails itself of the warming rays of the early spring sun. Or that yellow beacon moving slowly through the still-cold shallows of a Michigan marsh can be seen to be the throat of a Blanding's turtle.

The best known of our basking turtles is the red-eared slider, a species sold by the millions each year in the pet trades of the world. It is also one of the hardiest turtles and has now colonized suitable waters in Australia, France, South America, our Southeast, and our Pacific Northwest—all areas where it is neither native nor wanted.

Many basking turtles are very common, but a few are uncommon to rare. Common or rare, large or small, aquatic or terrestrial, all are pretty and interesting components of our natural heritage, creatures deserving of protection and understanding, not disregard and exploitation.

## PAINTED TURTLES, COOTERS, AND SLIDERS

These are three closely allied genera of turtles that were all, at one time or another, considered congeneric (in the same genus). They are currently broken into three genera: *Chrysemys*, the painted turtles; *Pseudemys*, the cooters; and *Trachemys*, the sliders.

The painted turtles are named for the brilliance of their shells and the sliders for their habit of sliding quickly from their basking sites (a habit shared with most other members of this turtle family) into the safety of the water when disturbed. The name "cooter" has been derived from "kuta," a word meaning turtle in several African dialects.

The turtles of these genera are primarily pond dwellers and river dwellers. One, the federally endangered Alabama red-bellied cooter, is a denizen of freshwater habitats but may occasionally enter the brackish waters of Mobile Bay, Alabama. These turtles are active throughout much of the year. Painted turtles often emerge from hibernation while ice still rims the ponds and may remain active until the ice again covers the ponds in late autumn. All bask persistently, sometimes completely filling the surfaces of choice sunning spots. They may occasionally pile several deep in an attempt to partake most fully of the sun's warming and purifying rays.

Sexually mature males of many species develop greatly lengthened foreclaws that are used to caress the head and neck of the female during courtship.

Depending on the species, and on the health and size of the female, a clutch may contain 4–30 eggs. Most females lay 2–4 clutches annually. Some, among them the river cooters, flank their main nest with one or two satellite nests that are thought to act as decoys for predators. Normally the hatchlings, measuring 1–1¼ inches, emerge following an incubation period of 2–2½ months. Those from the clutches laid last may overwinter in the nest. Then mortality may be quite high.

The taxonomy of the painted turtle and the river cooters is unstable at the moment.

### Painted Turtles, genus *Chrysemys*

The single species in this genus contains four subspecies. The carapace is smoothly domed, not keeled. Marginal scutes are not serrate.

## 18. Eastern Painted Turtle, *Chrysemys picta picta*

18. Eastern painted turtle

**Abundance/Range:** This turtle is common to abundant from Nova Scotia southward to northern Georgia. Although it is a turtle of the Atlantic Coastal Plain in the more northerly regions, from southern North Carolina to northern Georgia it becomes an inhabitant of the more inland Piedmont habitats. It intergrades with the midland painted turtle in western New England and adjacent New York, eastern Pennsylvania, and western Maryland, and again in northeastern Alabama.

**Habitat:** The eastern painted turtle may be seen in ponds, marshes, lakes, and slowly flowing rivers and their oxbows.

**Size:** This turtle is adult at a carapace length of 4–5 inches but may occasionally attain a full 7 inches. Hatchlings are about an inch in length, are less brightly colored than the adults, and often have a thin, greenish vertebral stripe.

**Identifying features:** This turtle has a smooth olive black to black carapace. The scute seams are normally much lighter than the scutes they outline. The carapacial scutes are almost aligned across the back. The marginal scutes are smooth edged and prominently marked with red lines. The plastron is yellow and lacks any dark central markings. The head, neck, and limbs are dark. Yellow lines adorn the head. These shade to red on the neck. A bright yellow postocular spot is an excellent field mark. Limb markings are usually reddish. Both sexes are colored similarly.

**Similar species:** Other basking turtles in this family in eastern North America are larger and have a spotted or streaked carapace, a dark plastral marking, and serrate posterior marginals, or lack the discrete yellow postorbital marking.

## Additional Subspecies

19. The Western Painted Turtle, *Chrysemys picta bellii*, is the largest of the four subspecies. It has a smooth greenish carapace patterned with dark-edged lighter green lines. The marginals are nonserrate and each has yellowish lines flanking a vertical red central bar. The plastron may be yellowish but is often red with an extensive dark plastral figure. The head, neck, and limbs are dark. Yellow

19. Western painted turtle

lines pattern the head, but there is no postorbital spot. The neck stripes are red. Limb striping is yellow or reddish. Hatchlings usually have a bright red plastral ground color. Adults are 6–8 inches in length, but occasional examples may attain 9 inches. This is a turtle of the Plains states and the adjacent Canadian provinces, but it ranges westward to Washington, California, Arizona, and New Mexico. It intergrades with the midland painted turtle along the eastern periphery of its range.

20. The Southern Painted Turtle, *Chrysemys picta dorsalis*, is the smallest race. Typical adults measure 5–6 inches in length. This pretty turtle has a dark brown to blackish carapace and a prominent yellow, orange, or red vertebral stripe. The carapacial scutes are often outlined in orange or tan. Marginals are dark and poorly marked on top, but prominently brown and yellow below. The plastron is usually an unrelieved yellow to pale orange. The black head is striped with yellow; the dark neck and limbs are striped with red. The bright vertebral stripe is diagnostic. The southern painted turtle often inhabits quiet, warm, duckweed-choked ponds, lakes, and bayous; when it emerges from the water, a patina of clinging plant life obliterates all diagnostic markings. This is a turtle of western Kentucky, western Tennessee, and adjacent Missouri, as well as most of Arkansas, Louisiana, Mississippi, and western Alabama.

21. The Midland Painted Turtle, *Chrysemys picta marginata*, ranges northward from central Tennessee to the Great Lakes states, adjacent Ontario and Manitoba, Canada, and western New England. This race is most like the eastern painted turtle in appearance but has a dark central figure on the plastron. When

20. Southern painted turtle

21. Midland painted turtle (photo by James Harding)

the turtle is viewed from the side, the anterior and posterior seams of the vertebral and costal scutes are staggered rather than in a straight line. This pretty and common turtle attains a length of about 6 inches.

### Cooters, genus *Pseudemys*

Depending on the species (there are eight), these big turtles may be seen in rivers, spring runs, ponds, lakes, ditches, marshes, and canals. They are, for the most part, of southeastern distribution. Females may be somewhat larger than the males. Males of some species develop very long foreclaws that are employed in a complex courtship ritual while the turtles are swimming.

Both adults and hatchlings can be very brightly colored. The heads and necks of most are strongly striped with narrow yellow lines.

Location of the highest point on the carapace (anterior to midpoint or at midpoint) may be as important in reaching a positive identification as are shell and head pattern.

Compare the colors and patterns on the second costal scute. Patterns are best seen and colors look brightest when turtles are wet. The posterior marginals may be serrate.

Taxonomy of many of these big turtles, especially the river cooters and coastal plain cooters, is in disarray at the moment.

## 22. Eastern River Cooter

*Pseudemys concinna concinna*

**Abundance/Range:** This pretty and wary turtle is common throughout its range. Although there are many disjunct populations in the north, this turtle ranges south and west from northern Virginia to Florida's western panhandle, eastern Texas, and southeastern Kansas.

**Habitat:** As indicated by its common name, this turtle is usually associated with flowing waters. Primary habitats include springs, spring runs, rivers, and large creeks. However, it may also be found in large lakes and occasionally in estuarine situations.

22. Eastern river cooter

**Size:** At 12–15 inches in length (females), this is one of the larger basking turtles of the Southeast. Males are usually somewhat smaller than females. Hatchlings measure about 1½ inches long.

**Identifying features:** Patterns and colors are variable. Hatchlings are green smudged with black spots and bars. Throughout most of the range adults have a busily patterned carapace of olive brown, dark brown, and nearly black with lighter carapacial markings. Carapace markings may be sparse to virtually missing on turtles from the westernmost areas of the range. Even when profusely marked, the carapacial markings may be difficult to discern and are best seen when the turtle is wet. In eastern populations, the second costal scute usually contains a backward-oriented, stylized C along the posterior margin. The C may continue on the third scute when it then forms an O. Consider *only* the part of the marking in the second scute. Western populations may lack the C, having instead a series of curved, vertically oriented light bars. The plastron is yellow(ish), smudged along the scute seams with dark pigment. The dark areas fade with growth. Ocelli occur on the underside of each marginal. Each ocellus involves the rear of one marginal scute and the anterior of the next. The shell is deepest at about midpoint.

The head and legs are very dark with well-defined orangish to yellow markings. There are several interorbital stripes; the center stripe is usually the broadest. Although the stripes converge on the snout, the anterior tips of the outermost ones usually do not actually touch the tip of the central stripe. Males have elongated foreclaws.

**Similar species:** Chicken turtles have a single broad stripe on each forelimb, a narrow head, a very long neck, and an unmarked plastron. Coastal Plain cooters have an unmarked plastron and no C on the second costal scute. The yellow-bellied slider has a prominent yellow cheek patch. The red-eared slider has a red postorbital bar. The Florida red-bellied cooter has an arrow point on the snout and usually a single broad (usually orange) vertical bar in each costal scute.

**Comments:** The taxonomy of this species and the Coastal Plain cooter is muddled. Until recently this turtle species was divided into several subspecies that were variable and difficult to differentiate. There is a current tendency to not recognize the Mobile cooter, the Missouri cooter, or the hieroglyphic cooter and to consider the Suwannee cooter a full species. Some authorities now consider the Coastal Plain cooter a recognizable subspecies of the river cooter. Since this remains controversial, we will retain the Coastal Plain cooter as a full and separate species. We also retain the Suwannee cooter as a recognizable race of the river cooter rather than as a full species.

### Additional Subspecies

23. The Suwannee Cooter, *Pseudemys concinna suwanniensis*, is found in the springs and spring runs from Florida's Big Bend region (Wakulla County) southward to Hillsborough County.

The Suwannee cooter is very similar to the eastern river cooter but larger when adult. This subspecies occasionally reaches a length of slightly more than 17 inches. The striping tends to be pale, with white, pale yellow, or greenish yellow as the norm. The upper surface of the rear feet lack striping. The ground

23. Suwannee cooter

color is very dark. The shell is deepest anterior to the midpoint. Positive identification can be problematic. Rely on the range.

## 24. Western River Cooter (Rio Grande River Cooter)

*Pseudemys gorzugi*

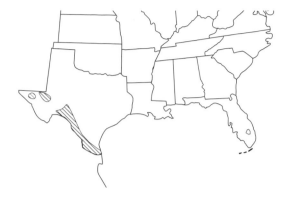

**Abundance/Range:** Although it now seems to be absent in areas where it was once plentiful, this pretty cooter remains common along some suitable stretches of rivers in the Rio Grande and Pecos River drainages of Texas and New Mexico. There are two populations separated by a hiatus of 100 or more miles.

**Habitat:** The western river cooter seems most common in nonpolluted stretches of permanently flowing rivers, but is also found in some of the permanent lakes and ponds associated with those river systems. It is often seen basking atop bent cattails and other such vegetation on the water's surface or on protruding snags.

**Size:** This is a heavy-shelled turtle that is smaller when adult than other races of the river cooter complex. It is thought that neither sex attains a length of more

24. Rio Grande cooter

than 10 inches. Females average about an inch longer than the males. Hatchlings measure about 1½ inches long.

**Identifying features:** Hatchlings have a green carapace busily patterned with dark ocelli. The plastron is yellow with extensive dark markings following the scute seams. The green head and legs are brightly marked with yellow.

Adults are duller but retain a variable but always intricate carapacial pattern. The carapace has a ground color of medium olive to olive brown and a pattern of curved yellow(ish) and dark olive lines surrounding yellow-centered black blotches. The rear margin of the carapace is noticeably serrate. The second costal is patterned with several (usually four) irregular concentric rings. One of these *may* take the form of the rearward-directed C so typical of the river cooters in general. Submarginal markings are in the form of ocelli. The plastron is yellow(ish) and bears a dark, variably distinct, seam-following figure of variable size. Head, neck, and limbs are dark green. The head and neck have numerous, thin, bright yellow stripes, yellow cheek spots, and a wide yellow oval to elongate postorbital blotch on each side. The limbs and tail are lined with yellow and/or orange (or rose). The upper jaw bears neither a central notch nor flanking cusps. Aged specimens become suffused with pattern-obscuring black pigment (melanin). The shell is deepest at about midpoint. Adult males have long foreclaws.

**Similar species:** Use range to differentiate this species from the eastern river cooter. Both the western painted turtle and the red-eared slider have nonserrate posterior marginals. Both the red-eared slider and the Big Bend slider also have one or two red blotches behind the eyes.

## 25. Texas River Cooter

*Pseudemys texana*

**Abundance/Range:** Until recently, this pretty river cooter was considered a subspecies of *P. concinna*. This is a common species in suitable aquatic habitats in central and southeastern Texas.

**Habitat:** The Texas river cooter occurs in vegetated areas of slow-moving rivers as well as in ponds, lakes, oxbows, cattle tanks, and other such permanent bodies of water.

**Size:** In this moderately domed basking turtle, females may attain 12 inches in length and the males about 9 inches. Hatchlings measure about 1½ inches long.

25a. Texas river cooter, adult

25b. Texas river cooter, hatchling (center turtle)

**Identifying features:** The green hatchlings and juveniles of the Texas river cooter have a busy pattern of stripes and whorls. The yellow to yellow-orange plastron contains an extensive dark figure that is most prominent anteriorly and along the scute seams. The green head and legs are brightly marked with yellow.

With growth the carapacial ground color dulls to brown or olive black and the pattern becomes at least partially obscured. There are several intricate whorls on the second costal, but the definitive, rearward-facing C so typical of most river cooters may be absent. The rear margin of the carapace is moderately serrate. The marginals may be tinted on the outermost edges with orange. A vertical yellow bar is present in the center of each marginal. Poorly defined ocelli, formed by half-circle meeting half-circle, are present on the upper front and rear of each marginal. Submarginal markings are in the form of well-defined ocelli. This turtle species often becomes darker with advancing age. The plastron is yellow(ish) and may or may not bear remnants of the dark central figure. The shell is deepest at midpoint. Head, neck, and limbs are dark green to black with numerous thin, bright yellow stripes and cheek spots. A vertical yellow bar is usually present near the articulation of the jaw. Other face and neck stripes are diagonal. The limbs and tail are lined with yellow and/or orange (or rose). A medial notch is present in the upper jaw and is flanked on each side by a downward-projecting cusp. Males have long foreclaws.

**Similar species:** The light whorls on the carapace of the eastern river cooter tend to be heavy and comparatively few. Those of the Texas river cooter are thin and profuse. Both lack a well-defined medial jaw notch and cusps. The red-eared slider has smooth posterior marginals and the namesake red ear marking. Map turtles have a prominent vertebral keel.

## 26. Coastal Plain Cooter

*Pseudemys floridana floridana*

**Abundance/Range:** This common turtle may be encountered from eastern Alabama and northern peninsular Florida, northward in coastal plain habitats to extreme southeastern Virginia. It was formerly called the Florida cooter.

**Habitat:** The Coastal Plain cooter dwells in bodies of still or slowly running water.

26. Coastal Plain cooter

**Size:** Females are the larger sex. Although the largest females may barely exceed 15 inches in carapace length, most are several inches smaller. The usual size range for both sizes is 8–12 inches. Hatchlings are about 1¼ inches in length.

**Identifying features:** This turtle has an olive green to olive brown carapace. It *lacks* a light hairpin marking on the head and has neither notch nor cusps on the upper jaw. The second costal scute often bears a light, broad, irregular, vertically oriented bar. This may be forked or take the form of a Z at its extremities. The carapace is deepest at midpoint. The submarginals bear either solid oval spots or ocelli. The yellow to pale orange plastron is unmarked. Hatchlings are much brighter in color than the adults. Mature males have elongated claws.

**Similar species:** Chicken turtles have a narrow head, long neck, and single broad stripe on the forelimbs. Eastern river cooters have a light letter C on the second costal. The yellow-bellied slider has a large yellow cheek patch. The red-eared slider has a broad reddish postorbital stripe. The Florida red-bellied cooter has a yellow arrow extending to the snout from between the eyes. The peninsula cooter usually has stylized hairpin-shaped markings on each side of the head.

**Comments:** Florida cooters are known to hybridize with river cooters, producing specimens that are difficult to identify. Sometimes the best an observer can do is say that a questionable specimen most closely resembles one or the other species.

27. Peninsula cooter

## Additional Subspecies

27. The Peninsula Cooter, *Pseudemys floridana peninsularis*, is restricted in distribution to peninsular Florida. It is an abundant species from Monroe County at the southernmost tip of the state to Levy, Alachua, and Duval counties in the north. Wherever there is a semipermanent to permanent water source, you are apt to encounter this turtle species. Adult females may barely exceed 15 inches (males are somewhat smaller) in carapace length, but a more usual size is 9–12 inches for both sexes.

Because of the distinctive yellow(ish) hairpin-shaped marking on each side of the head (the open ends extend well onto the neck) this is an easily identified turtle. The peninsula cooter is usually somewhat less wary than the river cooters. Its carapace is dark (often olive brown). Rather than a backward-directed C on the second costal scute, there is a light, broad, irregular, vertically oriented bar. This may be forked or in the shape of a Z at top and bottom. The carapace is deepest at, or just anterior to, the midpoint. The submarginals bear either solid oval spots or ocelli. The yellow plastron is unmarked. Hatchlings are a much brighter green than the adults. Mature males have elongated claws. This turtle has neither notch nor cusps on the upper jaw.

## 28. Alabama Red-bellied Cooter

*Pseudemys alabamensis*

**Abundance/Range:** This uncommon turtle is designated as federally endangered. It occurs only in the vicinity of Mobile Bay, Alabama.
**Habitat:** This beautiful turtle may be found in vegetated creeks, rivers, and backwaters. Like other species of this genus, the Alabama red-bellied cooter often basks on exposed snags and rafts of floating plants and logs. Wary while basking, it slides into the water at the slightest disturbance.
**Size:** At 12 inches in shell length, females are the slightly larger sex. Hatchlings are about 1¼ inches in length.
**Identifying features:** The carapace varies from light olive brown to dark olive brown, usually with at least some evidence of a broad vertical orange bar in each costal scute. The carapace of the adult Alabama red-bellied cooter is usually prominently greaved (bearing tiny, profuse, but irregular grooves) and the posterior marginals are serrate. The head, neck, and limbs are of the same ground color as the carapace but marked with yellow lines. The interorbital bar, in conjunction with a yellow marking at the tip of the nose, forms an arrow. The plastron is variably orange to orange yellow. Juvenile Alabama red-bellies often have a dark central plastral figure. Other than some dark spotting, hatchlings are a rather bright green above.

28a. Alabama red-bellied cooter, adult

28b. Alabama red-bellied cooter, juvenile

**Similar species:** Range, along with plastral color, should differentiate the Alabama red-bellied cooter from all other species.

**Comments:** The Alabama red-bellied cooter is fully protected by law. It should not be collected or harassed in any manner.

## 29. Florida Red-Bellied Cooter

*Pseudemys nelsoni*

**Abundance/Range:** This is a common turtle over most of peninsular Florida and immediately adjacent southeastern Georgia. A disjunct population occurs in the Apalachicola region of the Florida panhandle.

**Habitat:** The Florida red-bellied cooter occurs in nearly any permanent body of fresh water.

**Size:** This is a thick-shelled turtle that is rather highly domed and occasionally exceeds 12 inches in length. Females are the larger sex. Hatchlings are about 1¼ inches in length.

**Identifying features:** The green hatchlings are busily patterned with darker markings. Their plastron is often a bright orange to red orange with large but

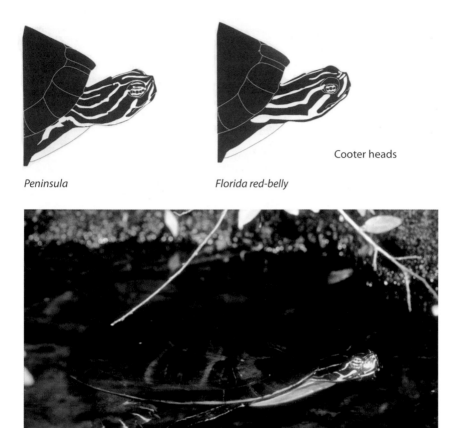

Cooter heads

*Peninsula*                    *Florida red-belly*

29. Florida red-bellied cooter

dark spots along the seams of some scutes. Adults are olive brown to nearly black, often with vertical orange bars in each costal. The turtle typically dulls with advancing age. The plastron of many old adults is patternless orange yellow or yellow. Submarginal markings are entirely dark rather than ocelli. Although usually discrete these markings may join and form continuous areas of black. The posterior marginals are weakly serrate. Adult males may be more brightly colored than adult females. There are few yellow lines on the dark head. The most constant identifying mark is the arrow with the shaft between the eyes. The point contours the snout. A medial notch is present in the upper jaw. This is edged on each side by a downward-projecting cusp. Adult males have long foreclaws.

**Similar species:** When this turtle is in hand or within suitable binocular distance, the yellow arrow between the eyes is a good diagnostic tool. The red-orange, orange, or orange-yellow plastron and vertical orange costal bars should further assist in a positive identification.

## 30. Northern Red-bellied Cooter

*Pseudemys rubriventris*

**Abundance/Range:** This beautiful turtle ranges from northeastern North Carolina northward to eastern West Virginia, southeastern Pennsylvania, and central New Jersey. There is a disjunct population in eastern Massachusetts. In abundance, this turtle varies from common in some locations to uncommon in others.

**Habitat:** This is a basking turtle of permanent marshes, ponds, lakes, oxbows, and rivers. It is known to enter estuarine areas. It chooses rafts of floating plants, exposed snags, and, occasionally, sloping banks on which to bask.

**Size:** This big turtle may attain 16 inches in shell length, but 10–14 inches is the more normal size. Females are slightly larger than the males. Hatchlings are about 1¼ inches in length.

**Identifying features:** Hatchlings are dark green with a busy dark carapacial pattern. The plastron is often a bright orange to red orange with large but discrete dark spots along the seams of some scutes. Adults are olive brown to nearly black with vertical orange bars in each costal. The plastral pattern and color often fade as the turtle grows and ages. The plastron is then an unrelieved orange yellow or yellow. Submarginal markings are entirely dark rather than ring-like ocelli and are most strongly outlined anteriorly. The posterior marginals are weakly serrate. A suffusion of melanin sometimes largely obscures the colors of old red-bellies of both sexes. There are few yellow lines on the dark head. The most constant identifying mark is the arrow. The shaft is between the eyes and the point contours the snout. The presence of a cusp-flanked medial notch in the upper jaw is typical of the members of the red-bellied group. Adult males have long foreclaws.

**Similar species:** Neither of the other red-bellied cooters occurs near the range of *P. rubriventris*. The notched and cusped upper jaw, arrow between the eyes, and coral, orange, or orange-yellow plastron and vertical orange costal bars should afford a positive identification.

30. Northern red-bellied cooter

**Comments:** The population of red-bellied cooters in eastern Massachusetts was long considered a recognizable subspecies. Once designated as the Plymouth red-bellied turtle, *P. rubriventris bangsi*, it has now been synonymized with the northern red-bellied cooter.

### Sliders, genus *Trachemys*

Like the cooters, the sliders are persistent baskers. The females are often larger than the males. The males of some have elongated front claws that are used during their aquatic courtship rituals.

Babies are brightly colored (usually green with darker markings dorsally), and adults are usually less so. Old adult males become suffused with pattern-obscuring melanin and may look virtually black or olive black.

The heads and necks of juveniles, females, and young males are strongly striped.

Because of the release of unwanted pets, the popular red-eared slider, *Trachemys scripta elegans*, has become the most widely distributed turtle in the world. Besides the Mississippi drainage (to which it is native), it occurs virtually throughout the United States as well as in France, Japan, Australia, Mexico, and other countries.

Hatchlings and young sliders eat a high percentage of animal matter—insects, fish, snails, and carrion. Larger specimens tend toward herbivory.

### 31. Big Bend Slider

*Trachemys gaigeae*

**Abundance/Range:** This "red-eared" slider occurs in the Big Bend region of Texas, adjacent Mexico, and central New Mexico. It is restricted in distribution to portions of the Rio Grande and its drainage and adjacent stock watering tanks and ponds. It is a common but wary turtle.

**Habitat:** This slider requires permanent water but may wander from pool to pool as the rivers become lower and pools evaporate during dry periods. It may be seen sunning on banks as well as on exposed rocks, snags, and plant mats.

**Size:** One of the smaller sliders, the Big Bend slider is adult at 4½–8 inches in carapace length. Adult males are usually smaller, less highly domed, and more elongate than the females. Hatchlings are about 1 inch in length.

**Identifying features:** Hatchlings of the Big Bend slider have carapaces of olive gray patterned with numerous *curved* lines. As they age, the carapace becomes olive green. Two red spots, a small postocular and a larger usually oval or rounded temporal spot, are present on the face. The olive-green head, neck, and limbs are vividly striped with yellow. The plastron has a large central figure

31a. Big Bend slider, adult

31b. Big Bend slider, hatchling

that follows nearly the entire midline and has outward-extending arms along the scute seams.

Colors and pattern dull with age. Because of an encroachment of dark pigment, adult males are often duller than females of a similar age. Old males can be entirely devoid of pattern and nearly a uniform dark olive to olive black in color.

Sexually mature males do not develop elongated front claws.

**Similar species:** This slider was long confused with the red-eared slider and was initially thought to be a subspecies of the latter. Most researchers now consider the Big Bend slider a full species. Throughout most of their range, red-eared sliders have only a single, broad, elongate, red ear stripe. In South Texas, where the ear stripe is apt to be broken into a small postorbital and a larger temporal marking, the red-eared slider has discrete plastral ocelli (rather than the large central figure) and vertical bars (rather than curved lines) on the carapacial scutes.

**Comments:** The courtship sequence of the Big Bend slider differs markedly from that of the superficially similar red-eared slider. Lacking the elongated foreclaws with which the male red-ear vibrates and strokes the face of the female, the male Big Bend slider merely chases the female and nips at her shell, tail, and hind legs before mounting.

## 32. Yellow-Bellied Slider

*Trachemys scripta scripta*

**Abundance/Range:** This abundant turtle ranges southward in the coastal plain and southern piedmont from southeastern Virginia to northern Florida and its panhandle.

**Habitat:** The yellow-bellied slider prefers heavily vegetated ponds, lakes, canals, ditches, slowly flowing rivers, and marshes. This turtle and its subspecies may be found in surprisingly small bodies of water.

yellow-bellied
red-eared
Cumberland

**Size:** Typically these pretty turtles attain an adult length of 5–8 inches. Some exceed 10 inches. Adult males are usually somewhat smaller than females. Hatchlings are about 1¼ inches in length.

**Identifying features:** The coloration of this slider varies with age and other more complex factors. Hatchlings have dark and light markings on a greenish carapace. The green head bears large yellow cheek blotches and diagonal yellow lines from the snout to the chin. The limbs are also greenish and bear several narrow stripes (forelimbs) or spots (rear limbs) of yellow. The skin on each side of the tail is vertically striped with green and yellow.

With growth this turtle darkens to an olive drab or olive black and many of the markings are obscured. Old examples may be almost uniformly black. The yellow facial markings are the last to dull.

*Chicken turtle*

*Yellow-bellied slider*

Turtle leg stripes

32. Yellow-bellied slider, subadult

Juveniles, subadults, and young adults have prominent, dark, rounded markings on the lower surface of the marginals and on the anterior scutes of the plastron. Most sexually mature males have elongated front claws.

**Similar species:** This is the only one of our turtles to have prominent yellow cheeks. The various river cooters lack strong vertical, light carapacial markings. The various red-bellied cooters have orange rather than yellow vertical markings on their carapace and lack the yellow facial patch. The chicken turtle has an extraordinarily long neck and only a single yellow stripe on the front of its forelimbs.

### Additional Subspecies

33. The Red-eared Slider, *Trachemys scripta elegans*, once a turtle of the Mississippi River drainages, is now widespread throughout much of the United States (and indeed, the world). The range extensions are the result of the release or escape of pet turtles. Unwanted pet specimens should be placed in caring foster homes, never released into the wild. Intergrades between this and the yellow-bellied slider or the Cumberland slider, *Trachemys scripta troosti*, are often encountered.

Hatchlings of the red-eared slider have carapaces of green patterned with numerous narrow lighter and darker, primarily vertically oriented lines. The submarginal and plastral scutes are patterned with irregular dark ocelli or spots.

33a. Red-eared slider, adult

33b. Red-eared slider, hatchling from Texas

The green face and limbs are striped with yellow. The very broad red temporal stripe, from which this turtle takes its name, is usually prominently evident but may be relatively narrow, rarely absent, or, in southern Texas, broken into two spots. Males are often duller than females of a similar age and size. Old males can be entirely devoid of pattern and nearly a uniform dark olive to olive black in color. This species attains a carapace length of 7 to nearly 12 inches. Sexually mature males have elongate front claws.

34. Cumberland slider

34. The Cumberland Slider, *Trachemys scripta troosti*, is restricted in distribution to eastern Tennessee and western Virginia. It lacks a yellow cheek patch or broad red ear stripe. Instead, the ear stripe is relatively narrow and orange, yellow, or yellow green. Facial and limb stripes are relatively broad, hence fewer in number than on the yellow-bellied and red-eared sliders. The yellowish plastron bears an ocellus on each of the scutes, but these may obscure with growth. The submarginal spots are narrow. Hatchlings are a rather bright green with dark and light vertically oriented carapacial markings. Larger specimens dull to olive green and melanism may occur.

## Pond Turtles, genera *Clemmys* and *Glyptemys*

Until very recently, this was a single genus with four species, three of them of eastern distribution. These three are the spotted, the bog, and the wood turtles. The fourth, the Pacific pond turtle, is a declining resident of our Pacific states and Baja California.

Recently, taxonomic reassessment has retained the spotted turtle in the genus *Clemmys* and erected the genus *Glyptemys* for both the wood and the bog turtles. (The Pacific pond turtle was placed in the genus *Actinemys*.)

Of the three eastern species, the spotted is the most aquatic, inhabiting weedy ponds. The wood turtle is the most terrestrial. The bog turtle is a secretive resident of acidic shallow-water bogs that often do not require much swimming prowess to successfully negotiate. All hibernate in the water.

These are all considered "cool weather" turtles. They become active very early in the year, may become largely inactive during the hottest days of summer, and are again active in the autumn.

The clutch size of all is relatively small. The spotted turtle and the bog turtle have 2–4 (rarely to 6 or 7) eggs and have been known to double-clutch. The wood turtle has a single clutch of 6–10 (rarely to 18) eggs. The incubation period is 58–85 days.

Wild populations of all species of pond turtles have diminished noticeably over the last few decades. This may be attributed to, among other things, habitat fragmentation and reduction, collection for scientific purposes, and collection for the pet trade. The bog turtle and the wood turtle are now largely protected throughout their ranges, but legislation protecting the spotted turtle is lagging in many key states.

POND TURTLES

## 35. Spotted Turtle

*Clemmys guttata*

**Abundance/Range:** This is the most common of the various pond turtles, but because it is secretive, it is seldom seen. It ranges southward along the Atlantic coastal plain from central Maine to central peninsular Florida. It also occurs in Piedmont habitats from Virginia to Georgia and in a wide swath around the Great Lakes. Disjunct populations occur in the Carolinas, Indiana, Quebec, and Ontario.

**Habitat:** This is a species of shallow, vegetated, mud-bottomed ponds, swamps, marshes, and bogs. It may wander far from water but is far less terrestrial than other pond turtles.

**Size:** At a length of 3½–4¼ inches (rarely to 4¾ inches), this pretty turtle is one of North America's smallest. The sexes are about equal in size. Hatchlings are just over 1 inch long.

**Identifying features:** The overall ground color of this turtle is black. The head and carapace are usually liberally spotted with yellow dorsally. Females have yellowish or orange jaws, snout, and chin. The corresponding facial areas of adult males are suffused with dark pigment. Spots on the sides of the head, neck, and legs are usually orange, but may be yellow. The skin at the apices of all limbs and on the neck is orange. Males usually have brown eyes; females have yellow

35. Spotted turtle

or orange irises (irides). The orange plastron is smudged with dark pigment. Hatchlings often have only a single yellow spot on each carapacial plate.

**Similar species:** The bog turtle has orange blotches (not small discrete spots) on the back of its head, lacks carapacial spots, and has a vertebral keel. The Blanding's turtle is larger, more highly domed, and more elongate and it has a hinged plastron.

## 36. Wood Turtle

*Glyptemys insculpta*

**Abundance/Range:** Once relatively common, the wood turtle is now uncommon to rare throughout most of its range, and protected in all states where it is occurs. This pretty turtle ranges southward from Nova Scotia to northern Virginia and westward in the region of the Great Lakes to extreme eastern Minnesota.

36. Wood turtle

**Habitat:** Despite its propensity for wandering well away from water and for foraging extensively on land, the wood turtle is actually a riverine species that occurs in greatest densities in sunny river-edge glades and stream-edge clearings.

**Size:** This is a fairly large turtle. It is not uncommon to find adults 7–8 inches in carapace length, and an occasional example may be 9 inches long.

Hatchlings are about 1½ inches long.

**Identifying features:** Despite not being of particularly bright color, the wood turtle is one of the most distinctive North American species. The prominently sculptured carapace is mud-brown in color. The plastron and submarginal scutes are yellow with a smudge of dark pigment at the outer rear edge of each scute. The head is brown. The neck and apices of the forelimbs (and, to a lesser degree, the tail) vary from yellow green (westernmost populations) to bright orange (easternmost populations). The intensity of this color may vary seasonally. The posterior marginal scutes are strongly serrate. The top of the head is dark brown to black.

Hatchlings are grayish-brown and do not have the brilliant flash colors. Their tail is very long and slender.

**Similar species:** None. Although the shell of the bog turtle may be similarly colored, the bog turtle (usually) has prominent yellow to orange blotches on each side of the rear of the head.

**Comments:** The wood turtle has been observed "stomping" for worms. Although the stomping often involves only the forefeet, at times the plastron is also smacked against the surface of the ground. It is thought the low level vibrations (perhaps reminiscent of those created by activity simulating raindrops) induce the worms to surface, whereupon the turtle eats the worms.

No state in which the wood turtle is indigenous allows collecting for commercial purposes. Commercial collecting and subsequent transportation across state lines for the purpose of sale constitutes a federal violation. Commercialization of captive-bred wood turtles from legally collected adults is allowed.

## 37. Bog Turtle

*Glyptemys muhlenbergi*

**Abundance/Range:** This is the most infrequently seen of the various pond turtles. It requires very precise habitats, and even when conditions are ideal, the turtle is present only in small numbers. It is found in isolated areas of New York, Pennsylvania, western Massachusetts, western Connecticut, New Jersey, Maryland, and Delaware, then again in western Virginia, the western Carolinas, and immediately adjacent northeastern Georgia. It is federally protected.

**Habitat:** This is a species of shallow, spring- or creek-fed, vegetated, mud-bottomed bogs and swampy meadows and pastures. It is one of the most

37. Bog turtle

secretive turtles of North America. It constructs and follows trails through the sphagnum habitats it prefers, may forage either in or out of the water, and more often walks than swims along the bottoms of shallow rivulets.

**Size:** At a length of 3½–4¼ inches (rarely to 4½ inches), the bog turtle is another tiny North American species. Males are often slightly larger than the females. Hatchlings are only about 1 inch in length.

**Identifying features:** Although the skin and shell of the bog turtle are usually obviously of some shade of rich to dark brown, occasionally they near black in color. Typically, the growth rings on each carapacial shield are well defined but with advancing age these may be worn smooth. The areolae are often slightly lighter than the surrounding shell; from these, faint lighter marks may radiate outward. A low medial keel is present. The plastron is usually predominantly dark, occasionally with a central light area. The head is dark with lighter reticulations. The mandibles often bear vertical alternating dark-and-light bars. A large, (usually) orange to (rarely) yellow blotch is present on each side of the rear of the head and may extend well down toward the throat and onto the soft skin of the neck. The forelimbs often have an orangish overwash.

**Similar species:** Occasional specimens of the spotted turtle may lack most spots and have orange head blotches. However, they tend to be black (rather than rich brown) above, and to have a predominantly yellow (with black smudges) plastron instead of a predominantly black one with a yellowish centerline, and to lack a vertebral keel. Box turtles are more highly domed and have a hinged plastron. The wood turtle has serrate posterior marginal scutes.

**Comments:** Collection of bog turtles from the wild for any purpose is prohibited except by permit.

## Map Turtles, genus *Graptemys*

Most of the map turtles prefer the moving water of rivers and large streams. They are adept at negotiating quite considerable currents. Among the wariest of basking turtles, they are best identified at a distance with binoculars.

There are two primary groups—those with narrow heads and those with broad heads. Both males and females of the narrow-headed map turtle species eat aquatic insects. Juveniles and males of the broad-headed group also eat insects. However, the females of this latter group develop enormously enlarged heads as they age and become mollusk eaters.

Females of the larger species are slow maturing, apparently requiring a dozen or more years to attain sexual maturity. On the other hand, males reach sexual maturity in about 4 years.

Growth rings (annuli), visible on each of the carapacial scutes for the first few years of a map turtle's life, often obscure with advancing age. This is especially true of the females.

The adult males of all map turtles are smaller than the adult females. Most males develop elongated foreclaws at sexual maturity.

There are 12 species (a total of 15 subspecies) in this genus, all found in the eastern and central United States. Many are restricted in distribution to streams and rivers on the Gulf Coastal Plain.

Two of the smaller species are federally endangered, and other forms are offered protection from overexploitation by state laws or regulations.

Because of their very prominent middorsal keeling, three of the smaller forms—the black-knobbed map turtle, the yellow-blotched map turtle, and the ringed map turtle—are often referred to as sawbacks.

Map turtles employ an elaborate courtship involving head movements and/or forelimb tickling. Females may lay up to 6 clutches of 2–20 eggs (smaller species lay the fewest eggs) annually. Sandbars and sandy, secluded, river-edge situations are the preferred nesting sites. Incubation normally takes 60–80 days.

The perceived relationships of the Ouachita, the Sabine, the false, and the Mississippi map turtles are problematic. The Ouachita map turtle has very variable head markings, and some specimens resemble the false and Mississippi map turtles. Consider range when identifying these examples. Map turtles agilely climb snags and balance upon relatively slender branches projecting steeply from the water. The climbing abilities of this group of turtles belie the image of clumsiness usually ascribed to these creatures.

## 38. Barbour's Map Turtle

*Graptemys barbouri*

**Abundance/Range:** Locally common, the Barbour's map turtle occurs in the Apalachicola and Ochlocknee river drainages of Florida's central panhandle, Georgia's Flint River drainage, and the Chattahoochee River drainage of western Georgia and eastern Alabama.

**Habitat:** The Barbour's map turtle is a persistently aquatic species that is not known to migrate over land. This map turtle is found in stretches of rivers and creeks having limestone bottoms and abundant snags on which it can haul out to bask.

**Size:** This species is tremendously dimorphic; i.e., the sexes differ in size, with females up to 12 inches in length and males rarely larger than 4½ inches. Hatchlings are about 1¼ inches in length.

38a. Barbour's map turtle, female

38b. Barbour's map turtle, juvenile male

**Identifying features:** Dorsally, this is a gray to olive brown turtle. A prominent black vertebral keel is present, and this is particularly prominent and sawlike on juveniles and males. Juveniles and males have numerous yellow maplike lines in all carapacial scutes. Old females may be nearly unicolored. The plastron is cream to yellow olive and each scute outlined with dark pigment. The olive to olive gray head bears a very broad yellow-green blotch behind each eye. This may curve up onto the snout between the eyes or break behind the eyes, leaving the interorbital marking a discrete blotch. A broad curving yellow bar on the chin parallels the lower jaw line. The olive-gray neck and limbs bear many thin greenish yellow lines. Adult females have a very enlarged head and massive crushing jaws.

**Similar species:** Range alone will disqualify all look-alike species. The lack of a curved chin bar should differentiate the other bigheaded map turtles of the Southeast.

## 39. Cagle's Map Turtle

*Graptemys caglei*

**Abundance/Range:** Cagle's map turtle is one of several species that have been collected extensively for the pet trade. Although it is still locally common, it can now be difficult to find. It is now protected by the state of Texas. This turtle is found only in the Guadalupe River drainage in central southeastern Texas.

**Habitat:** Cagle's map turtle is persistently aquatic. It is not known to migrate over land. This species seems most common where the current is moderate or relatively slow and where basking snags are plentiful.

**Size:** Despite its being one of the smaller species of map turtles, Cagle's map turtle is noticeably dimorphic. Females of this species attain a carapace length of somewhat more than 7½ inches while adult males are often not more than half that length. Hatchlings are about 1¼ inches in length.

**Identifying features:** The carapacial ground color is greenish to olive brown. The very intricate maplike pattern of yellow lines is best seen on juveniles of both sexes and on adult males. Carapacial markings may become obscured on old females. A prominent vertebral keel is present on Cagle's map turtles of all ages, but is particularly prominent and sawlike on juveniles and males. The plastron is cream to yellow olive with each scute having a rather extensive amount of seam-following dark pigment. The black head, neck, and limbs are intricately marked with yellow. Outward projections from the arms of a prominent, rearward-pointing yellow (often incomplete) V may form a crescent behind the

39. Cagle's map turtle

eyes. One or two additional yellow lines may parallel the crescent. A series of crescent-shaped yellow bars are present on the chin.

**Similar species:** Range, color and carapacial keel will identify this turtle. The Texas map turtle, found in the Colorado River system, has an orange J behind the eye rather than a crescent.

## 40. Escambia Map Turtle

*Graptemys ernsti*

**Abundance/Range:** This turtle is found in drainages of Florida's Escambia and Yellow Rivers, and Alabama's Conecuh and Shoal Rivers. It is locally distributed but not uncommon.

**Habitat:** The Escambia Map Turtle prefers stretches of river with a sand or gravel bottom and many exposed basking snags and logs.

**Size:** Females attain a carapace length of 11 inches. Males are adult at about 4½ inches. Hatchlings are about 1¼ inches in length.

**Identifying features:** Carapace, face, and limbs are olive gray, gray, or olive brown. A maplike pattern of dark-edged, light lines is present on all carapacial scutes. The pattern, best defined on juveniles and males, may be all but obscured on old females. A black vertebral keel is present. This is most prominent on

40a. Escambia map turtle, adult

40b. Escambia map turtle, juvenile male

juvenile and male specimens. The plastron is yellow but dark pigment is present along the seams of the scutes. The yellow-olive postocular and interorbital blotches are discrete. There are light lines on the neck and limbs. There is a light chin blotch at each outermost edge of the lower mandible.

**Similar species:** Barbour's map turtle has a broad, curved bar on the chin paralleling the lower jaw line. Both the Alabama and the Pascagoula map turtles have the large head blotches joined.

## 41. Yellow-blotched Map Turtle

*Graptemys flavimaculata*

**Abundance/Range:** This small map turtle is federally endangered. Despite this listing, it is of variable abundance (quite common in some stretches) in Mississippi's Pascagoula River system, and quite rare in others.

**Habitat:** Like the other map turtles, the yellow-blotched map turtle is persistently aquatic and, in most areas, very wary. However, around commercial boat ramps or canoe rental facilities, wherever boat traffic is fairly heavy but turtles have not been molested, they may allow reasonably close approach before becoming frightened. This map turtle is most common where the current is moderate to strong, and where basking snags are plentiful.

**Size:** Females of this species attain a carapace length of 6–7 inches; adult males are often not more than 3½ inches long. Hatchlings are about 1¼ inches in length.

**Identifying features:** This map turtle lacks the light maplike carapacial markings so typical of most members of this genus. The carapacial ground color is greenish to olive brown. Juveniles of both sexes and males of all ages have a yellow blotch in the center of each carapacial scute and, once growth has begun, very prominent growth rings. The posterior marginals are strongly serrate. Both growth rings and yellow blotching may become obscured on old females. A prominent vertebral keel is present, and the keels are black tipped. The plastron is cream to yellow olive; each scute has rather extensive seam-following dark pigment. The olive to almost black head, neck, and limbs are intricately marked with yellow. A prominent postorbital marking in the form of an irregular rectangle is present. This is connected dorsally to a broad, rearward projecting, yellow stripe.

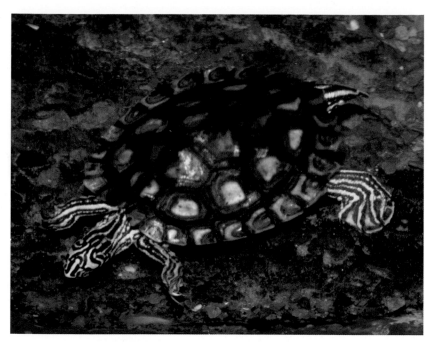

41. Yellow-blotched map turtle

**Similar species:** Range, the yellow carapacial blotches, and carapacial keel will identify this turtle.

## 42. Northern Map Turtle

*Graptemys geographica*

**Abundance:** This widespread turtle is found in many river systems, impoundments, and associated lakes from southern Quebec and northern Vermont to central Minnesota, Arkansas, and central Alabama. The former name, common map turtle, seems apropos since this is overall a common species.

**Habitat:** This riverine turtle seems to prefer slow-moving waters, avoiding rapids and riffles. It is considered a

42a. Northern map turtle

42b. Northern map turtle

large-river and large-lake species. This is the northeasternmost species of map turtle. It prefers areas having many exposed snags and logs where it can bask.

**Size:** Females attain lengths of up to 11 inches; males are normally about half that size. Hatchlings are about 1¼ inches in length.

**Identifying features:** Carapace color is olive brown to brown with a variably distinct maplike pattern of yellow to orange lines. All markings often become obscured with age and are more easily seen when the turtle's shell is wet. Dark ocelli are present on each marginal scute (often on the posterior portion) and the posterior marginals are strongly serrate. There is no vertebral keel. The plastron is cream to olive cream (adults) to yellow orange (juveniles). Dark pigment is present along the seams of the plastral scutes. Juveniles and males have more extensive plastral markings than adult females. The limbs, neck, and head are olive black to black. All are strongly striped with yellow. Two small groupings of circular lines are present on each side of the face. One is behind the eye, the other below the eye at the rear of the jaw. A small (often triangular) discrete yellow blotch is present behind each eye. The chin is patterned with yellow stripes.

**Similar species:** Range will differentiate the Sabine map turtle from the northern map turtle. The postorbital blotch of the Ouachita map turtle, false map turtle, and Mississippi map turtle is connected to a neck stripe.

## 43. Pascagoula Map Turtle

*Graptemys gibbonsi*

**Abundance/Range:** The range of this broad-headed map turtle includes the drainages of the Pearl and Pascagoula Rivers of Mississippi. The turtles are fairly common where river conditions are suitable.

**Habitat:** This riverine species occurs in swiftly flowing waters of fairly large rivers and creeks. A powerful and agile swimmer, it prefers stretches with a sand or gravel bottom and many exposed basking snags and logs.

**Size:** Females, by far the larger sex, may attain a carapace length of 11 inches. Males are adult at about 5½ inches.

**Identifying features:** Carapace color is olive gray to olive brown. A maplike pattern of dark-edged, broad light lines is present on all carapacial scutes, including marginals. The pattern is best defined on juveniles and males and may be all but obscured on old adult females. A black vertebral keel is present. This is most prominent on juveniles and males. The plastron is yellow but dark pigment is present along the seams of the scutes. The yellow-olive postocular and interorbital blotches are joined. Broad yellow lines adorn the head, neck, and

43. Pascagoula map turtle

limbs. There is a light chin blotch at each outermost edge of the lower mandible.

**Similar species:** Use range as an identification tool. Neither the Barbour's map turtle nor the Alabama map turtle occurs in the same rivers as the Pascagoula map turtle.

## 44. Black-knobbed Map Turtle

*Graptemys nigrinoda nigrinoda*

black-knobbed
Delta

**Abundance/Range:** This is the only of the three "sawbacks" that is not on the federal endangered species list. It is a wary inhabitant of the upper stretches of the Tombigbee-Black Warrior river drainages of western Alabama and eastern Mississippi. It remains quite common in suitable stretches of these rivers.

**Habitat:** Like the other map turtles, the black-knobbed map turtle is persistently aquatic. This map turtle is most common where the water is deep and the current running at moderate to strong pace over sand and clay bottoms. It basks on snags, rafted plants, accumulated brush, and fallen trees.

44. Black-knobbed map turtle

**Size:** Females of this species attain a carapace length of 6–7 inches; adult males are often not more than 3½ inches long. Hatchlings are about 1¼ inches in length.

**Identifying features:** Although this map turtle has some of the light maplike markings on the carapace for which the genus is known, the most conspicuous markings are usually dark-edged light circles or rings. The carapacial ground color is warm brown to olive brown. Growth annuli are usually visible. The posterior marginals are strongly serrate. All markings are best defined on young turtles. Very prominent black vertebral knobbing is present (it is from these that turtles derive their names). The submarginals bear well-defined ocelli. The plastron is cream to yellow olive with a variable amount of dark pigment following each transverse scute-seam. The olive to almost black head, neck, and limbs are intricately marked with yellow. The soft parts are predominantly light. A yellow Y is present on the top of the head. A prominent postorbital J-shaped marking or crescent is present and usually in contact with at least one other facial stripe.

**Similar species:** Range, the yellow postocular J and the well-defined carapacial rings should separate this turtle from the Alabama map turtle. The postocular blotch of the ringed map turtle (another of the sawbacked forms) is usually discrete.

45. Delta map turtle

### Additional Subspecies

45. The Delta Map Turtle, *Graptemys nigrinoda delticola*, is found in the same river systems as the nominate species but closer to the coastline. It is a darker turtle than its more northerly relative, having the soft parts predominantly black and a very extensive dark figure on the plastron. The two races readily intergrade where the ranges abut.

### 46. Ringed Map Turtle

*Graptemys oculifera*

**Abundance/Range:** This is a federally endangered species that inhabits the Pearl River system of western Mississippi and eastern Louisiana. Despite its designation, it can be fairly common where habitat remains ideal.

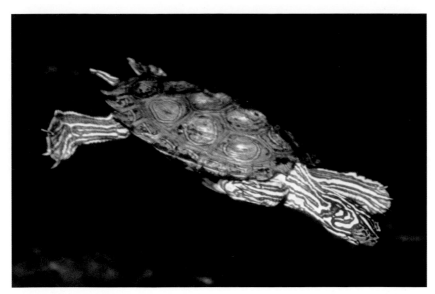

46. Ringed map turtle

**Habitat:** Like the other map turtles, the ringed map turtle seldom leaves the safety of the water except to bask on emergent debris. This map turtle is most at home where the current is running at moderate to strong pace over a sand or clay bottom. It may be seen, sometimes in numbers, basking on snags, rafted plants, accumulated brush, and fallen trees.

**Size:** Females of this species attain a carapace length of up to 8½ inches (but most are an inch or so smaller); adult males are often not more than 3½ inches long. Hatchlings are 1¼ inches in length.

**Identifying features:** This is another of the sawbacked map turtles. The ringed map turtle lacks most of the light maplike markings on the carapace for which the genus is known. It has instead a dark edged light O (or a ring) in each scute. A well-defined, light crescent is present in each supra- and submarginal scute. The carapacial ground color is warm brown to olive brown. Once growth has begun, at least a few annuli are visible. Lateral marginals are weakly serrate; posterior marginals are strongly so. All markings are best defined on young turtles. Very prominent black vertebral knobbing is present. The plastron is cream to yellow olive with a variable amount of dark pigment following the scute seams. The olive to almost black head, neck, and limbs are prominently patterned with broad yellow stripes. The prominent postorbital marking may be oval, rectangular, round, or shaped like a teardrop, and is usually not in contact with the interorbital stripes.

**Similar species:** When attempting to identify this turtle, consider range, the shape of the carapacial markings, and the shape of the postorbital marking. The black-knobbed map turtle has a Y on the top of the head and reversed Js as postorbital markings. The yellow-blotched map turtle has large yellow markings on each carapacial shield. The Alabama map turtle has a nonstriped green(ish) crown that touches the very large postorbital markings.

## 47. Ouachita Map Turtle

*Graptemys ouachitensis ouachitensis*

Ouachita
Sabine

**Abundance/Range:** This widespread turtle ranges northward from eastern Texas and northern Louisiana to southwestern Wisconsin and adjacent Minnesota. It is an abundant chelonian.

**Habitat:** A riverine species, this map turtle occurs in swiftly flowing waters of fairly large rivers and creeks. It may also be found in oxbows, lakes, and associated swamplands. Like other species of map turtles, the Ouachita map has a fondness for rather heavily vegetated waters with many exposed snags and logs on which it can bask.

**Size:** Females attain a length of 11 inches. Males are adult at about half that size. Hatchlings are 1¼ inches in length.

**Identifying features:** Carapace color is olive brown to brown. Each costal scute contains both a dark blotch and a maplike pattern of light lines. All markings can become obscured with age and are more easily seen when the turtle's shell is wet. The light lines and some indistinct dark smudging are present on the supramarginal scutes. The submarginals bear distinct ocelli. The posterior marginals are very serrate. A black vertebral keel is present. This is most prominent on juvenile and male examples. The plastron of adults is cream to olive cream but dark pigment is present along the seams of the scutes and occasionally as smudges on the scute interiors. Juveniles and males have more extensive plastral markings than adult females. Ouachita map turtles have extensive light striping on their dark-colored limbs, neck, and head. The leg striping may be less contrasting than that on the head and neck. Posterior to the eye, the uppermost neck stripe thickens and drops downward, often forming a prominent (but variable) squared or rectangular blotch, and 1–3 of the uppermost neck stripes of-

47. Ouachita map turtle

ten reach the orbit. A yellow spot (sometimes a continuation of a mustache-like nose stripe, or sometimes discrete) occurs beneath each eye and another is on each side of the chin.

**Similar species:** The false map turtle has a much smaller postorbital blotch and lacks both the mustache and prominent subocular spots. The Mississippi map turtle usually has a prominent postorbital crescent. The postocular marking of the Northern map turtle is discrete.

### Additional Subspecies

48. The Sabine Map Turtle, *Graptemys ouachitensis sabinensis*, is restricted in distribution to the Sabine River drainage of eastern Texas and western Louisiana.

This map turtle is very similar to the Ouachita map turtle, but has a proportionately smaller, discrete, rounded or oval postorbital blotch. The Sabine map turtle has 4–9 neck stripes extending forward to the orbit between the postocu-

48. Sabine map turtle

lar and the subocular blotches. Range will separate the Sabine map turtle from the northern map turtle.

## 49. False Map Turtle

*Graptemys pseudogeographica pseudogeographica*

**Abundance/Range:** The range of this turtle follows more northerly sections of the Missouri and Mississippi drainages. The spidery fingers of the range extend southward from south central North Dakota and western Wisconsin to Missouri and Illinois.

false
Mississippi

**Habitat:** The false map turtle is more of a habitat generalist than many of its congeners. Besides the riverine habitats in which map turtles are so often found, this turtle occurs in rather heavily vegetated oxbows, lakes, large ponds, and streams. It is also more apt to move overland than many other map turtles.

49. False map turtle

It may be seen in considerable numbers, sometimes piled high, on branches, snags, floating logs, and rafts of aquatic vegetation.

**Size:** This is one of the larger map turtles, and females occasionally attain a 10-inch carapace length. Males are about half that length. Hatchlings are about 1¼ inches in length.

**Identifying features:** Although certainly not brightly colored, the combination of grays, browns, yellows, and black produces an attractive appearance. The false map turtle has a carapace of olive to olive gray or olive brown. There may be smudges of darker pigment at the rear of each carapacial scute, including the supramarginals. It also has black vertebral projections and prominently serrate rear marginal scutes. Dark-edged light lines are present on each carapacial scute. Carapacial markings may become obscured on old females. The plastron of an adult false map turtle is cream to yellow olive with vague darker markings that follow the scute seams. The plastron of young turtles is very extensively marked with a dark figure of intricate outline. The dark head, neck, and limbs are intricately marked with yellow or orange. Behind each eye a blotch (that is often teardrop-shaped) projects downward. Below this blotch several of the neck stripes reach the orbit. Head and neck markings often contrast more strongly than leg markings. The lower jaw has a medial spot and the chin is striped.

**Similar species:** The Ouachita map turtle has much more prominent postorbital blotches, a mustache, and prominent subocular spots. The Mississippi map turtle usually has a prominent postorbital crescent. The postocular marking of the northern map turtle is discrete.

**Additional Subspecies**

50. The Mississippi Map Turtle, *Graptemys pseudogeographica kohnii*, is even better known than the related false map turtle. It, too, has a strong black vertebral keel and dark smudges on a carapace of gray, olive gray or olive brown. The rear marginals are prominently serrate. Dark-edged light lines, best seen on juveniles and males, are present on each carapacial scute. Carapacial markings may become obscured on old females. The plastron of adult Mississippi map turtles is cream to yellow olive with vague darker markings. The plastron of young turtles is very extensively marked with a dark figure of intricate outline. The dark head, neck, and limbs are busily marked with yellow or orange. An elongate postorbital crescent paralleling the rear of each orbit prevents any neck stripes from reaching the orbit. Head and neck markings often contrast more strongly than leg markings. The lower jaw has a medial spot and the chin is striped. Large females have a moderately enlarged head and feed extensively on mollusks. This abundant turtle ranges northward from southern Texas and Louisiana to Missouri and Illinois.

50. Mississippi map turtle

## 51. Alabama Map Turtle

*Graptemys pulchra*

**Abundance/Range:** This is a beautiful, somewhat variable map turtle that inhabits many of the Alabama and Georgia rivers draining into Mobile Bay. It is common to abundant in many areas of its range.

**Habitat:** This is a riverine species, but it may also be found in impoundments and oxbows. Males often occur in fairly shallow water, habitats shunned by the larger females. The Alabama map turtle occurs in swiftly flowing waters of fairly large rivers and creeks. A powerful and agile swimmer, it prefers stretches with a sandy or gravel bottom and basks on exposed snags, brush piles, and logs.

**Size:** The 11-inch adult females are often more than twice the length, and several times the bulk, of the 5½-inch males. Hatchlings are 1¼ inches in length.

**Identifying features:** Carapace color is olive to olive brown. A maplike pattern of dark-edged, broad light lines is present, but may be difficult to discern. Each supramarginal scute bears several light crescent markings. The pattern is best defined on juveniles and males and may be virtually obscured on old adult females. A black vertebral stripe and keel are present. The plastron is yellow

51. Alabama map turtle

but dark pigment is present along the seams of the scutes. The yellow-olive postocular and interorbital blotches are joined. There may be a hint of old rose on the posterior edges of the postocular blotches. There are broad light lines on the neck and limbs.

**Similar species:** This is the only large, broad-headed map turtle with the interorbital and postocular blotches joined and also found in the rivers draining into Mobile Bay. The Pascagoula map turtle, the species most similar in appearance, has only a single broad yellow bar on each supramarginal scute.

## 52. Texas Map Turtle

*Graptemys versa*

**Abundance:** This once common turtle is becoming increasingly uncommon along many of its more readily accessible riverine habitats. It is restricted in distribution to the Colorado River drainage on the Edwards Plateau.

**Habitat:** The Texas map turtle is a riverine species that seldom migrates over land. This species seems most common where the current is moderate, where aquatic vegetation is plentiful, and where basking snags are abundant. However, it is also present in oxbows and lakes associated with the river system.

**Size:** Like all map turtles, the Texas map turtle is noticeably dimorphic. Females of this species attain a carapace length of somewhat more than 7½ inches, while adult males are often only half that length. Hatchlings are 1¼ inches in length.

52. Texas map turtle

**Identifying features:** The carapacial ground color is olive to olive brown. All markings tend to be more orange than yellow. A prominent vertebral keel is present, but it lacks the black tipping so commonly seen among many other species of map turtles. The keel is particularly well developed on hatchlings and juveniles. The posterior marginals are serrate, but not as strongly as on certain other species. All carapacial scutes bear intricate orange markings; those on very old females may be dulled. The plastron is yellow(ish) and unmarked except for dark seaming. The bridge bears 5 or 6 thin dark lines. The olive head, neck, and limbs are intricately marked with orange. Many specimens display a prominent but variable orange J, with the straight portion directed posteriorly and the crook behind each eye, on each side of the head (on some specimens this marking may look more like an L or a U than a J). The chin is often marked with a central, and two lateral, light spots but may be longitudinally striped. Old females have a moderately enlarged head and apparently include mollusks in their diet.

**Similar species:** Range, coupled with the very noticeable nonblackened vertebral keel and J-shaped head marking, should identify this turtle in the field.

## Diamond-backed Terrapins, genus *Malaclemys*

The single species of diamond-backed terrapin contains 7 variable subspecies that are difficult to differentiate. Knowing the origin of a specimen and checking the relative shape of the carapace from above may help. All diamondbacks are restricted to salt and brackish water habitats. All are predominantly gray and black in color.

Diamond-backed terrapins are rather closely related to the freshwater map turtles.

Diamondbacks usually show prominent carapacial growth annuli. Dark pigmentation may follow the ridges of these annuli.

These turtles are now much reduced in numbers; one, the mangrove terrapin(s) of the Florida Keys, seems particularly difficult to find.

Diamondbacks lay rather small clutches of 4–8 eggs, but females may nest several times during each season. Incubation duration varies from 60 to 85 days depending on both soil temperature and nest depth.

Diamondbacks are wary turtles that are quick to flee and difficult to observe. By using binoculars, one may occasionally see them basking on, or walking between, oyster beds and mudflats.

## 53. Northern Diamond-backed Terrapin

*Malaclemys terrapin terrapin*

**Abundance:** Once so common that they supplied a thriving food industry, diamond-backed terrapins are now far less so. They are protected by many of the states in whose coastal waters they occur. This, the northernmost race, may be encountered in scattered pockets of habitat from Cape Cod, Massachusetts, southward to the Albemarle region of North Carolina.

**Habitat:** This turtle is a resident of brackish and saltwater marshes, estuarine areas, coastlines, and similar habitats.

**Size:** Females of the northern diamond-backed terrapin attain a length of 6–8½ inches. Males are smaller, often being only 4½–5½ inches long. Hatchlings are 1–1½ inches in length.

53a. Northern diamond-backed terrapin

53b. Northern diamond-backed terrapin

**Identifying features:** When viewed from above, the carapace of the northern diamond-backed terrapin will be seen to be wider posteriorly than anteriorly. The coloration of both the shell and the skin is immensely variable. Some examples are so dark overall that they appear almost black, while others have a light gray carapace with darker growth rings and gray skin speckled with black dots and dashes. The upper mandible is often white to light gray and stands out boldly against the darker skin. Hatchlings and juveniles may have a dark vertebral line and a low vertebral keel. Adult females usually have a proportionately larger head than males. The plastron is dark and may be smudged with dark pigment.

**Similar species:** The various diamondbacks are the only turtles in saltwater habitats that are gray(ish) in color and have normal feet (not flippers). The map turtles, many of which are also gray, are creatures of freshwater habitats and have yellow or orange facial markings.

**Comments:** Several things have contributed to today's reduced populations of diamond-backed terrapins. The collecting of these turtles for food led to the extirpation or near extirpation of many populations. Many of these turtles drown in crab traps. Today, hatchlings are collected for the pet trade. It now takes a concerted search, or more than a modicum of luck, to find a turtle of this species.

### Additional Subspecies

The sizes of all of the races are similar to those of the northern diamond-backed terrapin.

54. The Carolina Diamond-backed Terrapin, *Malaclemys terrapin centrata*, ranges southward from northern North Carolina to southern Flagler County, Florida. It is a variable and pretty turtle. The carapace may be medium gray or very dark gray. Carapacial growth annuli are prominent. The head and limbs are light gray spotted with black. The sides of the carapace are nearly parallel when viewed from above. This race does not have a prominent dark middorsal line and keel but, if the carapace is light in color, the vertebral tubercles are usually darker than the surrounding shell.

55. The Texas Diamond-backed Terrapin, *Malaclemys terrapin littoralis*, is the westernmost race of this turtle. Its population statistics remain unknown. It may be found northward from Corpus Christi, along the Texas coast, to a point immediately east of the Texas-Mississippi state line. The Texas diamondback is one of the darker races. It has a gray(ish) to black carapace, normally devoid of any significant brighter highlights. The plastron is very light and may be smudged with dark pigment. Dark, blunt, vertebral keeling is present. The gray (sometimes with a pale greenish tinge) skin of head, neck, and limbs may be profusely or sparsely dotted with black. Females usually have a proportionately

54. Carolina diamond-backed terrapin

55. Texas diamond-backed terrapin

larger head than males. The eyes are black. Some hatchlings have rather prominent vertebral keeling. Depend on range and habitat to identify this variable
turtle.

56. The Ornate Diamond-backed Terrapin, *Malaclemys terrapin macrospilota*,
is the brightest of the races in color. Restricted to Florida's Gulf Coast, this subspecies occurs roughly from the panhandle's Choctawatchee Bay to Key Largo.
Typically, this turtle has a gray(ish) carapace with orange scute centers and a
gray skin that is profusely or sparsely dotted with black. Adults have a dark low
vertebral keel. The keel is more prominent on juveniles and males. Aged females

56. Ornate diamond-backed terrapin

57. Mississippi diamond-backed terrapin

have a proportionately larger head. The plastron may be orange, yellowish, or gray and is often smudged with dark pigment.

57. The Mississippi Diamond-backed Terrapin, *Malaclemys terrapin pileata*, is found from Choctawatchee Bay, Florida, westward to a point just east of the Texas-Louisiana state line. The carapace of this race is grayish black to charcoal.

58. Mangrove diamond-backed terrapin

59. Florida east coast terrapin

The vertebral tubercles are often at least slightly darker than the surrounding shell color. The skin of the head, neck, and limbs is light to dark gray and may be spotted or almost unicolored. The top of the head is often very dark. The upper mandible is dark, giving the appearance that the turtle is wearing a mustache.

58. The Mangrove Diamond-backed Terrapin, *Malaclemys terrapin rhizophorarum*, is restricted in distribution to the Florida Keys. It is a rather dark, but variable, race. The carapace is blackish and there is a vertebral keel. The plastral seams are often broadly edged with black pigment. The top of the head is black, the head and neck spots are coalesced into irregular black stripes and the upper mandible is dark. The sides of the face and the neck are light gray.

59. The Florida East Coast Terrapin, *Malaclemys terrapin tequesta*, usually has a grayish carapace that lacks the dark rings outlining the prominent annuli. The center of each carapacial scute may be lighter than the rest of the shell. A weak vertebral keel is present. The raised tubercles *may* be darker than the surrounding shell. The sides of the head, neck, and limbs are light gray and the facial pattern is usually of large black spots. The center of the head is dark and a variably dark mustache is usually present. This subspecies is found from Miami-Dade County northward to Flagler County.

Chicken Turtle, genus *Deirochelys*
Blanding's Turtle, genus *Emys*
Box Turtles, genus *Terrapene*
Spotted-legged Wood Turtle, genus *Rhinoclemmys*.

We have grouped these four genera together merely for the sake of convenience, not because they are closely allied.

The chicken and Blanding's turtles are pond and marsh dwellers that often wander far from water. The spotted-legged wood turtle, a South American species, is found only in South Florida in remnants of the Everglades. All of the above have webbed feet.

Depending on the species, the box turtles may be either damp woodland or aridland turtles. The forefeet of the box turtles are stubby and short; the rear feet are rather typical but unwebbed.

The box and Blanding's turtles have comparatively highly domed carapaces, although on the two races of the western box turtle this is often centrally flattened.

The plastron of adult box turtles and the Blanding's turtle is prominently hinged crossways and attached at the bridge by tough cartilage. The hinge is nonfunctional at hatching but fully functional by the time the turtles are half grown.

Chicken turtles and the Blanding's turtle are primarily carnivorous, eating fish, crayfish, and aquatic insects. They usually eat while in the water. The ornate and western box turtles and the spotted-legged wood turtle eat mushrooms, berries, worms, and insects and feed while on land.

These turtles breed seasonally. Clutch sizes vary from 1 or 2 eggs (the spotted-legged wood turtle) to 20 or more (Blanding's turtle). Female box and chicken turtles may produce more than a single egg-clutch each year. The Blanding's turtle nests only once a year, and may occasionally skip a year. Nothing is known about the breeding biology of the spotted-legged wood turtle in Florida. Incubation varies from as little as 52 days to more than 100 days.

## 60. Eastern Chicken Turtle

*Deirochelys reticularia reticularia*

**Abundance/Range:** The eastern chicken turtle is fairly common but it is

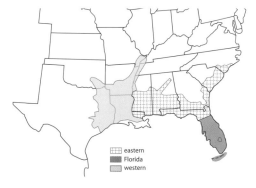

eastern
Florida
western

60. Eastern chicken turtle

very secretive. This turtle ranges from north central Florida to eastern Louisiana in the west and central North Carolina in the north. Two apparently disjunct colonies exist, one in central southern North Carolina and the other in southeastern Virginia.

**Habitat:** The chicken turtle is typically associated with quiet, heavily vegetated bodies of water. Such habitats as grassy ditches, shallow canals, weedy ponds, and equally weedy lake edges are among the preferred habitats. However, chicken turtles wander widely and may be found a mile or more from water. They bury themselves, sometimes on dry land, during adverse weather.

**Size:** Although most specimens of this narrow-shelled turtle are adult at 5–7 inches, occasional examples may slightly exceed 9 inches in length. Hatchlings are 1 to 1¼ inches long.

**Identifying features:** The carapace varies from dark olive drab to dark olive green. Dull yellow carapacial markings form a busy reticulum. Fine longitudinal linear rugosities are on all carapacial scutes and to a lesser degree near the midline of the plastral scutes. When viewed from above, the carapace is edged in yellow. The elongate, smooth-edged carapace is narrowest anteriorly and broadest above the rear legs. The plastron is a rather bright, unmarked yellow. The neck of the chicken turtle is long and the head is narrow. Both are green(ish) striped with yellow. The upper jaw is notched, not beaked. A *broad* yellow stripe is on the front of each forelimb. The dark skin posterior to each forelimb and on each side of the tail bears vertical yellow markings. Hatchlings and juveniles are more brightly colored than adults.

**Similar species:** The various sliders all have proportionately shorter necks and broader heads. Only the chicken turtle has a combination of a *single broad* stripe on the anterior of the forelimbs, *vertical barring* on each side of the tail, and *no* large yellow blotch or broad red(dish) stripe on the side of the head.

### Additional Subspecies

61. The Florida Chicken Turtle, *Deirochelys reticularia chrysea*, ranges southward from north central Florida to the southern tip of peninsula Florida. It is very similar in appearance to the eastern chicken turtle, but has broader and brighter carapacial lines.

62. The Western Chicken Turtle, *Deirochelys reticularia miaria*, ranges westward from southeastern Louisiana to eastern Texas and northward to central Oklahoma and southeastern Missouri. The carapace bears a busy reticulum of rather broad markings but the markings do not contrast sharply with the carapacial color.

61. Florida chicken turtle

62. Western chicken turtle

## 63. Blanding's Turtle

*Emydoidea blandingii*

**Abundance/Range:** Although it is becoming uncommon over much of its range, the Blanding's turtle cannot yet be considered rare. Isolated populations may be found in Nova Scotia, eastern New England, Pennsylvania, South Dakota, and Missouri. The main range is from south central Quebec and northern New York to western Nebraska.

**Habitat:** Although it often wanders far afield (especially in the spring of the year) this is primarily a turtle of marshes, vegetated ditches, lakes, and, more occasionally, streams. It is often seen while basking on protruding snags or muddy banks. Hatchlings seek refuge in floating rafts of vegetation.

**Size:** This is a fairly large turtle with a high-domed, narrow shell. Occasional adults may barely exceed 10¾ inches in length, but 6–8 inches is the more normal size. Hatchlings are 1–1¼ inches long.

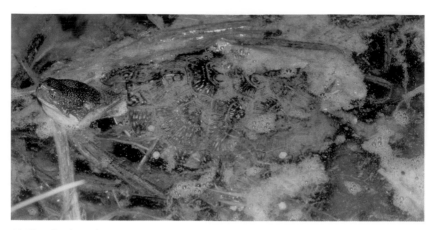

63. Blanding's turtle

**Identifying features:** This is one of the more distinctive of the North American turtles. Adults have an elongate, nonkeeled, high-domed, dark-colored carapace and a functionally hinged plastron. The carapace may be strongly or sparsely patterned with light, elongate, teardrop-shaped markings. The throat and chin are bright yellow. The top and sides of the head are reticulated, olive on slate gray. The upper jaw is notched, not beaked. The neck is proportionately long, and when the turtle is basking in the sunlight or swimming with its head extended well above the water, the yellow chin stands out like a semaphore. The plastron may be predominantly yellow or nearly all black. If yellow, there is usually a black smudge at the outer posterior corner of each scute. Hatchlings are less high domed, not strongly patterned, and have a low medial keel.

**Similar species:** None. The notched upper jaw, yellow throat, hinged plastron, and elongate carapace are distinctive.

BOX TURTLES

## 64. Eastern Box Turtle

*Terrapene carolina carolina*

**Abundance/Range:** Many populations of this once common turtle are now seriously reduced. This box turtle ranges westward and southward from eastern Massachusetts to western Illinois and

[ ] eastern
[ ] Florida
[ ] Gulf Coast
[ ] three-toed

64. Eastern box turtle

extreme northeastern Florida. Habitat degradation (including fragmentation, which often brings the turtle in contact with vehicles) and collecting for the pet trade have accounted for the removal of many box turtles of all races from the gene pool.

**Habitat:** The eastern box turtle may be found in open mixed woodland, in damp pasture and meadow edges, and near swamps and marshes. These terrestrial turtles may enter shallow water but seldom actually swim.

**Size:** Males attain a carapace length of a little more than 7½ inches. Females are somewhat smaller. Hatchlings are about 1 inch long.

**Identifying features:** The eastern box turtle is high domed, roughly of oval shape (when viewed from above), and of variable color. The carapace, head, neck, and limbs of the eastern box turtle are usually of some shade of brown. The carapace is adorned with irregular olive, orange, or yellow markings. The large scales on the anterior of the forelimbs are often yellow or orange. Depending on the color scheme, some examples may be quite dull in coloration while others are very bright. The plastron may be of a color similar to the carapace, or be somewhat differently colored. Males often have bright red irises; the irises of the females are buff or brown. Males, which are the larger sex and which have a variable degree of flaring to the rear marginal scutes, have a prominent concavity in the rear lobe of the plastron. Hatchlings are usually an olive brown with a single pale yellow spot on each carapacial scute. This race usually has 4 toes on the hind feet.

**Similar species:** Other than the box turtles, only the Blanding's and mud turtles have strongly hinged plastrons. Both are strongly aquatic. The Blandings turtle is smoothly domed but elongate and has a notched (not beaked) upper jaw. The plastron of the mud turtles has two hinges and does not form a complete cover for the head, limbs, and tail.

### Additional Subspecies

65. The Florida Box Turtle, *Terrapene carolina bauri*, has a narrow, highly domed carapace with the highest point posterior to midpoint. Its color is deep brownish black to black with radiating yellow lines and a yellow vertebral keel. There are two yellow stripes on the sides of the face, which is rather light in color. The skin of the leg apices and neck is also light. The plastron is yellow with variable dark markings. An adult size of 5½–7½ inches is attained. Hatchlings are colored like the adults, but the yellow carapacial radiations are broken into irregular spots. The vertebral keel is yellow. The eyes of both sexes are dark. This race is found throughout the Florida peninsula and immediately adjacent southeastern Georgia. Most Florida box turtles have only 3 toes on each hind foot. Adult males have a prominent concavity in the rear lobe of their plastron. This helps them remain positioned atop the female for breeding.

65. Florida box turtle, female with eggs

66. Gulf Coast box turtle

66. The Gulf Coast Box Turtle, *Terrapene carolina major*, is the largest and most aquatic of these interesting turtles. Males commonly attain a carapace length of 7½ inches, and more rarely may reach 8½ inches. It may occasionally be seen walking or foraging on the bottom of ponds, puddles, or canals, and also forages terrestrially. This big dark box turtle is a resident of the woodlands, stream and canal edges, pinewoods, and marshes of Florida's southern panhandle. It readily intergrades with box turtles of abutting subspecies.

The ground color of the Gulf Coast race is brown or black, and the variable carapacial markings are yellowish or olive. Males often have red irides; those of the females are dark. The carapace of this race is depressed centrally. The plastron is usually darkest anteriorly and males have a prominent concavity in the rear lobe. This race usually has 4 toes on each hind foot. The posterior marginals of aged male Gulf Coast box turtles flare prominently. Old males often have a variable amount of white on their faces. This may be restricted to the anterior chin and mandibles or so extensive that it involves the whole head.

67. The Three-toed Box Turtle, *Terrapene carolina triunguis*, ranges westward from central eastern Alabama to eastern Texas and eastern Kansas.

This is one of the least colorful of the box turtles. The carapacial ground color is horn, olive, tan, or buff, with or without lighter radiations or teardrop-shaped

67. Three-toed box turtle

markings. Both males and females have brownish red eyes. The plastron is yellowish or olive and devoid of markings. Males often lack the rear-lobe plastral concavity that is so prominent in other races. Red and/or white facial markings are often present. Males may attain 6¼ inches in total length, but females are seldom more than 4–5 inches in carapace length. The marginals do not flare significantly. This race usually has three toes on each hind foot.

## 68. Ornate Box Turtle

*Terrapene ornata ornata*

**Abundance/Range:** This beautiful turtle is found in semiarid habitats from western Louisiana and most of the Texas plains northward to western Indiana, Illinois, and South Dakota. Where its habitat has been fragmented by now-busy roadways and wandering "boxies" run over, its numbers are reduced. In rural areas, it remains abundant.

**Habitat:** The ornate box turtle is associated with grasslands, cactus/succulent habitats, and open scrub areas. It burrows into the earth, often against the trunk of a shrub, to partake of shade and to slow moisture loss. During the hottest

68. Ornate box turtle

weather, these turtles typically forage early in the day and at dusk. Showers may activate them at any time.

**Size:** Adult ornate box turtles measure 4–5 inches in carapace length, rarely attaining 6 inches.

**Identifying features:** The adult ornate box turtle has a deep brown to olive-black or black carapace with 5–9 yellowish radiating lines on the second costal. All other carapacial costal scutes are also prominently patterned with radiating lines. This race is invariably well patterned and the pattern does not fade with age. The carapace is highly domed but flattened centrally. The top of the head and the cheeks may be quite dark. The neck is usually lighter. The cheeks and neck are patterned with lighter markings. The mandibles and chin are light; yellowish to orange scales are usually present on the limbs. Males often have red eyes and those of the females are yellowish. The plastron is usually dark with many light lines. The plastral hinge is well developed. Adult males have a plastral concavity on the rear lobe. The tiny tail may be yellow dorsally. Adult males have the innermost toe on each hind foot thickened and affixed at an angle to the other claws. Males may have a bright red iris while that of the female is often brown. Hatchlings have dark brown to black carapacial scutes spotted with yellow. A yellow vertebral stripe is present.

**Similar species:** The carapace of the three-toed box turtle is fully domed and the turtle is not prominently patterned. Mud turtles have 2 plastral hinges.

69. Desert box turtle

### Additional Subspecies

69. The adult Desert Box Turtle, *Terrapene ornata luteola*, has an olive brown, olive tan to yellowish carapace with variably discernible lighter (10–16 on the second costal) radiating markings on each costal scute. If present, the light markings may obscure with advancing age. The carapace is highly domed but flattened centrally. The top of the head may be quite dark, but the cheeks and neck are usually lighter and contain tan to yellowish markings. The mandibles and chin are light and yellowish scales are usually present on the limbs. Males often have red eyes; those of the females are yellowish. The plastron reverses the carapacial colors, being predominantly light with many dark lines. The plastral hinge is well developed. Adult males have a plastral concavity on the rear lobe. Adult males have the innermost toe on each hind foot thickened and affixed at an angle to the other claws.

Hatchlings of the desert box turtle have a poorly defined pattern on their tan to brown carapace, a relatively low dome, and an undeveloped plastral hinge. They are shy and seldom seen in nature.

This turtle ranges westward from the Big Bend area of Texas to the grasslands of eastern Arizona and southward into northern Mexico.

## 70. Spotted-legged Wood Turtle (introduced species)

*Rhinoclemmys punctularia punctularia*

**Abundance/Range:** This introduced turtle has been present in southern Miami-Dade County, Florida, for about ten years. It is of rare occurrence. Its population statistics in Florida are unknown, but its status is thought to be precarious.

**Habitat:** In Florida this turtle occurs near canals. It can swim, readily enters the water, and often walks along the bottom in shallow-water situations. Most Florida specimens have been found at the edges of parking lots and roads on the Miccosukee Indian Reservation.

**Size:** Although in South America this turtle may attain a length of up to 10½ inches, those in Florida seem to top out at a carapace length of about 8 inches. Hatchlings are about 1½ inches long.

**Identifying features:** This turtle has a well-domed brown to nearly black carapace and a well-developed vertebral keel. The plastron is usually predominantly dark (brown to near black) but may have a significant amount of yellow peripherally and along the scute seams. The forelimbs have black-spotted yellow and/or red scales anteriorly. The head is dark but strongly patterned with broad red stripes. The most noticeable pair of these extend forward from the nape to converge (and sometimes touch) between the eyes. Another pair is on the rear of the crown, and a third pair runs from the nostrils to the eyes.

70. Spotted-legged wood turtle

**Similar species:** None. This is the only very dark turtle with narrow red markings on its head. Red-eared sliders have the red present as a broad stripe in back of the eye.

---

A half-dozen kids stood on the banks of a South Miami canal, holding nets in various states of disrepair. I (RDB) was driving by, in the area to check on a population of introduced whiptail lizards, and had been just about to access the fast lane when the nets caught my eye. Instead I swerved up onto the right-of-way and stopped. The kids eyed me warily as I dug my net out of the back of the truck. As I walked to the canal they started to disperse, but when they saw that I was about to begin dip netting they stopped and watched. As luck would have it, in the first netful I had several species of introduced tropical fish, so I walked back to the car to get a bucket. The kids came closer to watch, close enough for me to ask what they had caught.

Their answer of "tortugas," (turtles) was of interest.

"What kind?" I asked.

"Yellow heads" was their answer.

That left me pondering. What was a yellow head? The turtles of that area have yellow stripes on their faces, necks, and legs, but none have a yellow head.

"Can I see one?" I asked.

"No. We took them home."

Just then, in a netful of water lettuce, I caught a baby red-bellied cooter.

"Like this?" I asked, sure that I had solved the mystery.

The kids came over to take a closer look then replied, "No, Señor, yellow-heads!"

Apparently I was no closer to the answer than before. In fact, I was even further away, for I had just eliminated the species I had thought they were talking about.

"C'mon," I pleaded, "please let me see them."

The kids looked at one another, and then one of them loped off to the neighborhood across the street from the canal. He returned a few minutes later with a bucket, and when I saw the contents, I almost fell over in surprise. On the bottom of the bucket were ten little yellow-spotted river turtles, a South American species that I hadn't seen in Miami canals in more than thirty-five years.

That they had just hatched was apparent from the caruncle (egg tooth) still on the snout and the fact that their facial coloring was still yellowish white rather than the bright yellow to orange of larger juveniles.

My trip had just taken an upturn in interest and the children had provided me with a new research project.

---

## Afro-Neotropical Side-necked Turtles, family Pelomedusidae

This is a family of primarily aquatic turtles that are distributed in Africa, Madagascar, and the Neotropics. Only one representative of these turtles is currently found in the United States.

### River Turtles, genus *Podocnemis*

This is the federally endangered yellow-spotted river turtle, a species that ranges naturally over much of northern South America. It is rare in the United States and restricted to a few canals in Miami-Dade County, Florida. Its presence is probably attributable to the release or escape in the 1960s and 1970s of pet trade specimens. It often swims or floats with only its nose and eyes above the water surface.

This is a pretty and graceful turtle that undergoes quite considerable age-related changes of the facial color and pattern. It feeds primarily on aquatic vegetation but also accepts some animal matter and filters edible particulate matter from the water.

The breeding biology of this turtle in Florida is unknown, but hatchlings have been found in June. In the Amazon Basin an adult female produces two clutches of up to 25 eggs a year. The nests are dug in river-edge sandbars or, sometimes, other sandy areas some distance from the water. Incubation takes 50–65 days.

A second species, an African mud turtle of the genus *Pelusios*, has also been reported from two areas of Florida. We have not been able to find examples in the wild.

## 71. Yellow-spotted River Turtle (introduced species)

*Podocnemis unifilis*

**Abundance/Range:** Endangered in its native northern South America, this turtle is rare and local in some canals in southern Dade County, Florida.

**Habitat:** Persistently aquatic, this introduced turtle leaves the water only to bask on emergent objects or muddy banks, or to lay eggs.

**Size:** Adult females may occasionally attain 2 feet in length. Males are seldom more than a foot in length. Hatchlings are about 1¾ inches in carapace length.

**Identifying features:** There are considerable ontogenetic (age related) color changes in this species. Hatchlings emerge from the egg with pale (almost translucent) white facial spots. Within two months these have changed to a rich yellow or yellow orange; this color remains until sexual maturity is reached. Adult

71a. Yellow-spotted river turtle, adult female

71b. Yellow-spotted river turtle, juveniles

males may retain a rather well-defined facial pattern, but the female's spots pale and merge until her head and face are merely suffused with a gray paler than that of the neck and limbs. The carapace is olive brown to light gray when the turtle is small, but becomes a darker olive or brown with growth. The plastron is yellow but often becomes suffused with dark pigment as the turtle grows. The limbs are gray and the feet are fully webbed.

**Similar species:** None. The clownlike facial markings will identify juveniles of both sexes and most males. The very large size, oval carapace with only moderate doming, and flaring nonserrate posterior marginals will identify adult females.

**Comments:** In the 1960s and early 1970s this turtle was imported annually by the tens of thousands for the American pet trade. Periodic reports of babies and adults being found in the Dade County, Florida, canal system occurred in the 1970s and 1980s but gradually died out. That this turtle is still breeding in southern Dade County was confirmed again in 1999 and 2000.

TORTOISES AND SOFT-SHELLED TURTLES

## Tortoises, family Testudinidae

Although this is a fairly large family, only three species are found in the United States, and only two are east of the Sonoran Desert. Both of these (plus the western species and a single northern Mexican form) are in the genus *Gopherus*.

Both the eastern and the central species—the gopher tortoise and the Texas tortoise—are depleted in numbers but still seen with some regularity.

Most of the time in our reptile hunts all we see of tortoises is burrows or sleeping pallets. But some trips are more productive.

Ahead of me on a sandy South Texas road I (RDB) could see no fewer than four Texas tortoises ambling determinedly from right to left. What, I have wondered ever since, made that left side so desirable? Both sides looked the same to me—typical Texas thorn scrub of the kind that made me want to stay far, far away. That morning I was to see nearly a dozen of these chelonian tanks, most plodding slowly across the road, but a few eating roadside grasses and scrub.

Occasionally the gopher tortoises of the east will be similarly active, most in a colony exiting their burrows almost simultaneously to forage. I'm not quite sure yet what brings about this spate of activity, for on other mornings—mornings that look and feel identical to me—nothing but the burrows, their sandy aprons punctuated by the tracks left by tiny tortoise feet on previous days, are to be seen.

### Gopher Tortoise and Texas Tortoise, genus *Gopherus*

Both of these tortoises have flattened forefeet with which they make burrows or sleeping depressions. The hind feet are stubby and elephantlike. The carapace is high domed and often strongly sculptured with growth annuli in each scute. A gular extension—an anterior projection used to batter and overturn rivals in territorial disputes—is present on both species, but particularly well developed on the Texas tortoise.

The gopher tortoise digs a long burrow where it spends inclement weather, but the Texas tortoise usually digs shallow sleeping pallets against the trunk of a shrub or other desert plant. More rarely it may construct a short burrow or utilize the burrow of a desert mammal.

Both species are terrestrial and predominantly vegetarian.

As the temperatures change seasonally, so, too, do the activity patterns of these tortoises. They are active even at midday during moderate weather, but usually only during the morning or afternoon hours during periods of excessive heat. They may hibernate, or become periodically dormant, during the worst of the winter cold.

Tortoises are slow to reproduce and have high hatchling mortality. Males are very territorial, and during the breeding season lengthy skirmishes may occur. Combat between males can last for nearly a half an hour and may result in the

72. Texas tortoise

weaker (or unluckier) male being overturned. If this happens in an open area on a sunny day it may result in the death of the overturned tortoise before it can right itself. Breeding male tortoises produce a clucking sound. June, July, August, and September are the principal months for nesting. The gopher tortoise often digs her nest into the apron of sand at the mouth of the burrow. Although up to 12 eggs may be laid by old, healthy female gopher tortoises, Texas tortoises produce only 1–3 eggs. The female Texas female tortoise may soften the sun-baked soil by releasing water from her bladder. Two nestings in a season have been documented. Incubation takes 3–4 months.

These tortoises are colonial. All have a home territory.

Longevity is known to be more than a half-century.

An upper respiratory ailment (called an URD, for upper respiratory disease) of unknown origin, but seemingly readily spread, is now afflicting many wild gopher tortoises. The seriousness of this disease is not yet fully understood.

## 72. Texas Tortoise

*Gopherus berlandieri*

**Abundance/Range:** Once common throughout most of southern Texas, the Texas tortoise is now far less frequently seen. Habitat fragmentation causes many of these placid animals to try to cross rural roadways, an often-fatal endeavor. They were once collected extensively for the pet trade, but are now protected by Texas law. The range of this tortoise continues southward from Texas well down into eastern Mexico.

**Habitat:** Sandy open scrub, semidesert, and desert habitats are favored. Mesquite, acacia, prickly pear, and arid-adapted grasses are typical plants in the tortoise's habitat.

**Size:** At a maximum size of 8¾ inches (most adults are an inch or two smaller), the Texas tortoise is the smallest member of the genus. The carapace is highly domed and each scute is usually strongly sculpted by growth rings. The hatchlings can vary in size, but average about 1 5/8 inches in carapace length. They are tan (or light brown) with cream to orange overtones at hatching.

**Identifying features:** Adult Texas tortoises are merely moderately sized brown to almost black turtles (sometimes with lighter scute centers) that usually show prominent carapacial growth annuli. The nonhinged plastron is somewhat lighter in color than the carapace. The gular scutes are greatly developed and protrude forward noticeably. Adult males have a plastral concavity. This species is relatively short and proportionately very high domed. The head is wedge shaped and the nose is rather pointed. Mental (chin) glands are present and well developed. Head, neck and limbs may be brown to yellowish brown. The forefeet are broad, flattened, and spadelike, with stout claws. The rear feet are clublike. The legs are strong and the turtle walks with its shell well elevated above the ground. The hatchlings are tan (or light brown) with cream to orange overtones at hatching.

**Similar species:** Use range to separate this from the more easterly gopher tortoise. Box turtles, the only other terrestrial turtle with a highly domed carapace, have a hinged plastron.

## 73. Gopher Tortoise

*Gopherus polyphemus*

**Abundance/Range:** The gopher tortoise may be found from extreme southern South Carolina, southward through Florida, and westward to extreme eastern Louisiana. It is now of spotty distribution.

**Habitat:** Look for this Coastal Plain species in sandy open scrub habitats. Areas dominated by turkey oak–longleaf pine associations, sandy vegetated coastal dunes, and other well-drained habitats with ample low herbaceous growth are utilized.

73. Gopher tortoise

**Size:** This tortoise has a high-domed but flat-topped carapace. Length is normally 10–13 inches, with a confirmed record of 15 inches. The hatchlings average about 1⅝ inches in carapace length.

**Identifying features:** Although adult gopher tortoises are often an unrelieved brown, hatchlings have a yellowish head and limbs and dark-edged carapacial scutes with peach or yellowish centers. When young, gopher tortoises show prominent growth annuli. The plastron is usually somewhat lighter in color than the carapace. The head is rounded, the neck is fairly short, the digging forefeet are broad, flattened, and spadelike with stout claws, and the rear feet are clublike.

**Similar species:** Use range to separate the gopher from the Texas tortoise. Box turtles, the only other terrestrial turtle with a highly domed carapace, are smaller and have a hinged plastron.

**Comments:** Habitat degradation and other pressures have reduced the numbers of this tortoise. The communicable respiratory ailment mentioned earlier is present in many tortoise colonies. This apparently can be spread by humans handling tortoises, and perhaps by animals moving between colonies.

## Soft-shelled Turtles, family Trionychidae

Three species of soft-shelled turtles occur in eastern North America. There is a remarkable sexual dimorphism in all, with the females often being twice the length of the males. Female Florida soft-shelled turtles, the largest North American species, are known to attain a weight of more than 70 pounds; it is suspected that they may occasionally exceed 100 pounds. This is the largest soft-shelled species in North America.

### American Soft-shelled Turtles, genus *Apalone*

Soft-shelled turtles are almost fully aquatic. They are powerful and agile swimmers with fully webbed feet. Two of the three species often bask in shallow water or clamber onto water-surrounded rocks and snags (the Florida softshell comes ashore to bask). Collectively, softshells have a long neck and a Pinocchio nose.

Softshells have the shell covered with a thick, leathery skin rather than keratinized scutes. Although the center of the shell is comparatively rigid, the edges of the carapace are flexible. There are only 3 claws on each of the fully webbed feet. Males have a greatly enlarged tail that extends well beyond the edge of the carapace. The tail of the female is so tiny that it is usually not visible from above.

Females may lay several (actually, up to 5) clutches of 10–30 (occasionally more) eggs per clutch each season. The nest is constructed in a sandy location, often near the water, but occasionally some distance away. Incubation takes somewhat more than 2 months.

Softshells are seldom defensive when in the water, but may strike and bite savagely if molested while on land. The long neck and strong jaws are to be carefully reckoned with. Besides the jaws, the raking claws of a carelessly handled specimen can leave deep scratches.

◇◇◇◇◇◇◇◇◇◇◇◇◇◇◇◇◇◇◇◇◇◇◇◇◇◇◇◇◇◇◇◇◇◇◇◇◇◇◇◇◇◇◇◇◇◇◇◇◇◇◇◇◇◇◇◇◇◇◇◇◇◇◇◇◇◇◇◇◇◇◇◇

The log, easily seen while driving across the bridge, projected obliquely and far out of the water. It was packed to full capacity by basking northern spiny soft-shelled turtles. Every square inch bore some part of some turtle, and some were stacked two and three deep to partake of the early morning sunshine. Should I stop for a better look? No, I knew that there would be no better look, for I had tried before and almost before the car had stopped every turtle had plunged into the river, leaving only fast-fading ripples behind.

I had seen the same phenomenon in western Texas. On warm sunny mornings every rock projecting above the surface of the Rio Grande often hosts one or two Texas soft-shells. And as the temperature warms the soft-shells are joined on the rocks by Big Bend sliders.

Both are memorable sights, sights of the kind for which we watch as we motor the byways of the nation, but sights of the kind that are so ephemeral that they are often not caught on film.

◇◇◇◇◇◇◇◇◇◇◇◇◇◇◇◇◇◇◇◇◇◇◇◇◇◇◇◇◇◇◇◇◇◇◇◇◇◇◇◇◇◇◇◇◇◇◇◇◇◇◇◇◇◇◇◇◇◇◇◇◇◇◇◇◇◇◇◇◇◇◇◇

*Trionyx muticus*        *Trionyx ferox*        *Trionyx spiniferus*

*Trionyx muticus    Trionyx ferox*
*Trionyx spiniferus*

Softshell snouts and shells. Illustration by Dale Johnson.

## 74. Florida Soft-shelled Turtle

*Apalone ferox*

**Abundance/Range:** This turtle is common throughout Florida, adjacent Alabama, southern Georgia, and southeastern South Carolina. It has been introduced into ponds on the campus of the University of Texas at Arlington.

**Habitat:** This is the only species of North American softshell to preferentially choose nonflowing waters for its home. The Florida soft-shelled turtle is common to abundant in ponds, lakes, canals, ditches, swamps, marshes, cypress heads, and other such habitats.

**Size:** Females regularly exceed 12 inches in carapace length and the largest female specimen confirmed to date measured 24¾ inches. Males most often measure 6–10 inches in length at maturity, but many have been found that were substantially larger. One male had a length of 18 inches when measured over the curve of the carapace. The hatchlings measure about 1½ inches in carapace length.

**Identifying features:** These are dark-colored turtles. Both sexes have a carapace color of olive tan to olive brown, but males are more apt than females to retain some of the juvenile pattern, described below. This is especially true of the facial

74a. Florida soft-shelled turtle, adult depositing eggs

74b. Florida soft-shelled turtle, juvenile

markings. When viewed from above, the carapace is oval. The anterior edge of the carapace is studded with low hemispherical tubercles. There is a horizontally oriented ridge on the nasal septum. Hatchling Florida softshells are patterned with numerous large dark carapacial spots that are separated by a lighter reticulum. A yellow to olive-yellow band edges the carapace. The plastron is dark olive gray and the dark head busily spotted and striped with yellow.

**Similar species:** The other species of softshells are more rounded when viewed from above, have a light carapace with dark spots, and have well-defined light lines on the sides of the face. The two races of the smooth softshell lack the horizontal ridge on the nasal septum.

## 75. Midland Smooth Soft-shelled Turtle

*Apalone mutica mutica*

**Abundance:** The midland smooth soft-shelled turtle is a common but seldom seen turtle. Following the river systems south from south central North Dakota and west from western Pennsylvania, the range of this

midland
Gulf Coast

75a. Midland smooth soft-shelled turtle, adult

75b. Midland smooth soft-shelled turtle, juvenile

species extends to the Gulf Coast of Texas. A disjunct population occurs in central eastern New Mexico.

**Habitat:** This turtle is most common in rivers with moderate currents and extensive, open sandbars.

**Size:** This is the smallest of the softshells. Females reach slightly more than 12 inches in carapace length; the much smaller males are adult at 4–6 inches. The hatchlings measure about 1½ inches in carapace length.

**Identifying features:** Juveniles and males of this species have an olive-tan to light olive-brown carapace. The carapace is patterned with a variable number of small black dots and dashes and edged with a lighter marginal color that is bordered on the inside with a single black line. The color atop the head, neck, limbs, and tail is similar to that of the carapace. The upper surface of the limbs may be streaked with dark pigment (especially near the apices), but often is not, and the top of the neck may be peppered with fine black dots. The top of the head usually lacks black markings. The undersides of the head, neck, tail, and limbs are cream, yellow(ish), or light tan. Facial markings are often not well defined, but consist of a dark-bordered light diagonal line extending downward from the eye to the neck and a light and dark marking, extending onto the snout from each eye. The plastron is usually lighter in color than the brownish underside of the carapace and may be white or gray. The anterior edge of the carapace lacks bumps and spines, and there is no horizontal ridge on the nasal septum (do keep in mind that if you are close enough to any large softshell to determine this latter, you are probably close enough to be bitten!).

The entire dorsal surface of adult female smooth softshells darkens and assumes a variable blotchy pattern that is difficult to describe, on an olive brown to olive slate ground color.

The hatchlings of the midland smooth soft-shelled turtle are of delicate, almost translucent appearance. The anterior edge of the carapace may fold down and in when the head is withdrawn, and the ribs may often be seen in outline.
**Similar species:** The Florida softshell is big, dark, and strongly oval when viewed from above. The various spiny softshells have either tubercles or spines on the anterior edge of the carapace and a horizontal ridge on the nasal septum.

## Subspecies

76. The Gulf Coast Smooth Soft-shelled Turtle, *Apalone mutica calvata*, is the southeastern representative of this species. It is found from central eastern Mississippi and adjacent Alabama to the Gulf Coast of eastern Louisiana and western Florida. Females of this soft-shelled turtle reach 10½ inches (rarely a little more); the smaller males vary, measuring 4–6 inches in carapace length. The olive-tan to light olive-brown carapace has numerous, well-separated, large dark spots. A single black line follows the carapace near the rim. The plastron is lighter in color than the brownish underside of the carapace. There is a dark-edged yellow line on each side of the head. The forelegs are not strongly patterned. Males tend to retain the carapacial spots of babyhood. The carapacial spots become obscured on large female specimens.

76. Gulf Coast smooth soft-shelled turtle

## 77. Eastern Spiny Soft-shelled Turtle

*Apalone spinifera spinifera*

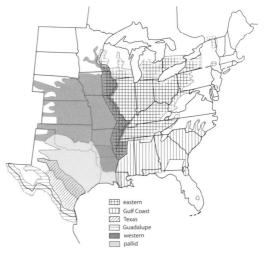

eastern
Gulf Coast
Texas
Guadalupe
western
pallid

**Abundance/Range:** This turtle is common to abundant throughout much of its range in the northeastern United States. It occurs also in extreme southern Ontario. Disjunct populations exist in New Jersey, New York, and Vermont.
**Habitat:** This is a riverine species that may also occur in lakes and large ponds.
**Size:** Like other softshells, this species and its five subspecies are strongly dimorphic. Females commonly attain a carapace length of 7–12 inches and occasionally grow to 17+ inches. Adult males are about half that size.
**Identifying features:** The carapacial color of the eastern spiny softshell is tan to olive brown. There are dark ocelli in the central area of the carapace and dark spots closer to the edge. The plastron is about the same color as the underside

77a. Eastern spiny soft-shelled turtle, adult female

77b. Eastern spiny soft-shelled turtle, juvenile (photo by James Harding)

of the carapace. A single (often broken) dark line borders the edge of the carapace. There are two (usually) nonconvergent dark-edged yellow lines on each side of the face. The feet and neck are heavily spotted and streaked. A horizontal ridge is present on the nasal septum. The anterior of the carapace bears conical spines.

**Similar species:** The midland smooth soft-shelled turtle lacks conical spines on the anterior edge of its carapace and also lacks a horizontal septal ridge.

### Additional Subspecies

78. The Gulf Coast Spiny Soft-shelled Turtle, *Apalone spinifera aspera*, is the southeasternmost representative of this species. It is found from extreme northern Florida to eastern Louisiana, northern Mississippi, and eastern North Carolina. It is a common turtle. Females commonly attain a carapace length of 7–12 inches and occasionally grow to 16 inches. Adult males are about half that size. This race differs from the nominate form principally in being slightly smaller, having somewhat less heavily patterned limbs, having the 2 facial stripes converge at the rear of the head, and having 2 narrow dark stripes paralleling the rear of the carapace.

79. The Texas Spiny Soft-shelled Turtle, *Apalone spinifera emoryi*, is the common race of spiny softshell in the Rio Grande and Pecos Rivers and in the ponds, lakes, and resacas associated with those river systems. Beyond Texas, the Texas softshell occurs in restricted areas of Utah, New Mexico, Arizona, southeastern California and south of the international boundary in northern Mexico. Fe-

78. Gulf Coast spiny soft-shelled turtle

79. Texas spiny soft-shelled turtle

males, twice as large as the males, commonly attain a carapace length of 10–15 inches and occasionally grow to 16 inches.

Dichromatism (sexual differences in color) exists. The carapacial color of males and young females of the Texas spiny softshell is tan to olive brown. There are usually tiny white spots on the rear one-third of the carapace. These may or may not be (partially) encircled with dark pigment. The light carapacial marginal band is much wider posteriorly than along the sides. This is often edged inside with a single dark line. Aged females lose the white spots, the contrast between the marginal marking and the ground color lessens, the carapace darkens and becomes blotchy. The underside of the carapace, tail, limbs, neck, and chin are white or cream. The dark-edged light ocular stripe is present but may fragment on the cheek. The feet are spotted distally and the legs are streaked at the apices. The top of the head and neck may bear tiny black flecks.

80. The females of the Guadalupe Spiny Soft-shelled Turtle, *Apalone spinifera guadalupensis*, also attain a length of about 16 inches. The males are adult at about half that size. The Guadalupe differs slightly from the Texas softshell in having tiny white spots covering virtually the entire carapace. Each spot is narrowly ringed with black. The carapacial ground color of this race tends to be olive to brown—in other words, darker than the ground color of the Texas softshell. The dark-edged light marginal band is present; it tends to be wider posteriorly than on the sides. With ageing, females lose the white spots and assume

80. Guadalupe spiny soft-shelled turtle

a blotchy carapacial color. This race occurs in the drainages of the Guadalupe, Nueces, and San Antonio Rivers.

Spiny softshells in the Colorado River drainage are apparently intergrades between the Guadalupe and pallid races.

81. The Western Spiny Soft-shelled Turtle, *Apalone spinifera hartwegi*, lacks white carapacial dots, but has small black carapacial spots or flecks. The light carapacial band is usually strongly in evidence and bordered on the inside by a thin black line. The typical dark-edged light facial markings are prominent and the forelimbs are streaked with black. In general, this race is darker in color, and has smaller dark carapacial markings than the other subspecies. Old females, which can attain an 18-inch carapace length, are usually blotched or mottled and lack most, if not all, contrasting markings. Males are smaller (seldom more than 7 inches long) and may retain some of the juvenile pattern. This is the spiny softshell found in most of our central states.

82. The Pallid Spiny Soft-shelled Turtle, *Apalone spinifera pallida*, is the largest race of the spiny softshell. The record size for this big softshell is 21¼ inches, but most specimens are considerably smaller. Lacking black markings, this is also the palest of the spiny softshells. When young, tiny white dots are often present

81. Western spiny soft-shelled turtle

on the posterior half of the carapace. Old females lose the white markings and assume a blotchy mottled appearance. Both the dark-edged cheek markings and the marginal carapacial band are usually prominent. This subspecies has a wide distribution in northeastern Texas. It is also known from southern Oklahoma, eastern Louisiana, and extreme southeastern Arkansas.

82. Pallid spiny soft-shelled turtle

MARINE TURTLES

## Sea Turtles, family Cheloniidae

Four members of this family occur along the eastern and Gulf coasts of North America. These tropical turtles are most common in Caribbean waters. If they do stray northward, unless they return south prior to the onset of the cooler days (and waters) of autumn, they will succumb (see note on the leatherback, account 87).

All of these turtles have flipperlike limbs. Some species have pored scutes on the bridge, where the carapace and plastron meet. The term "pored" refers to a single pit near the posterior edge of each scute.

Two, the loggerhead and the green turtle, are of threatened status; the hawksbill and Kemp's ridley are federally endangered.

Only two decades ago, the chance of seeing a marine turtle of any kind in the United States was difficult. Today (2004), marine turtles of three species and two families are becoming increasingly easy to observe, though there are numerous legal hoops through which you must jump (because all are federally protected) to be near one. Marine turtles usually nest at night, and the use of flashlights on nesting beaches is prohibited. However, federally sanctioned, guided "turtle walks" are organized by many sea turtle protection groups. By availing yourself of one of these services, you may have a chance to see wonderfully impressive chelonians. Among those organizations hosting turtle walks are the Caribbean Conservation Corporation of Gainesville, Florida, and the Marine Life Center of Juno Beach, Florida.

Loggerhead Sea Turtle, genus *Caretta*
Green Sea Turtle, genus *Chelonia*
Atlantic Hawksbill Sea Turtle, genus *Eretmochelys*
Ridley Sea Turtles, genus *Lepidochelys*

After uncountable years of exploitation for meat, eggs, and shell, the numbers of all sea turtles are reduced. Recent protection (including protection of eggs, lighting regulations at the laying beaches, and use of turtle excluders in traps and nets), however, seems to have stabilized or bolstered the numbers in many populations. Several species are breeding on our Atlantic and Gulf Coast beaches in increasing numbers. The loggerhead, the green turtle, and the Kemp's ridley now regularly nest on southern and Gulf beaches; the hawksbill is of accidental occurrence.

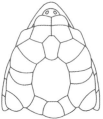

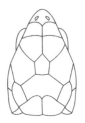
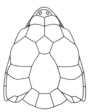

*Caretta caretta*        *Chelonia mydas*        *Eretmochelys imbricata*    *Lepidochelys kempii*

Sea turtles. Illustration by Dale Johnson.

Females nest only every second or third year, but in breeding years lay several clutches of 50–100+ eggs at intervals through the summer. Nesting and emergence of the hatchlings from the nest usually occur at night. Prior to the actual nesting, a body pit is dug with the forelimbs. Then the egg chamber is dug with the hind limbs. Incubation lasts for 2–3 months. Bright, unshielded beachfront lighting confuses hatchlings and they crawl away from rather than toward the water.

Besides shellfish, crustaceans, coelenterates, fish, and myriad other marine creatures, sea turtles eat turtle grasses (*Zostera*) and other vegetation.

## 83. Loggerhead Sea Turtle

*Caretta caretta*

**Abundance/Range:** This gigantic turtle is still relatively common but considered a threatened species. It may be seen during warm weather anywhere from Canada southward to southern Latin America; in our region it is most common from the Carolinas to Texas.

**Habitat:** Tropical and subtropical oceans.

**Size:** The loggerhead is the third largest of the marine turtles. Large adults attain a carapace length of more than 3½ feet and have been known to weigh more than 400 pounds. Hatchlings have a carapace length of 1¾–2 inches.

**Identifying features:** Clean adult loggerheads are reddish brown with tan highlights. When they are on land their color is often obliterated by beach sand. Additional clues that will help identify this species are:

83a. Loggerhead sea turtle, nesting female

83b. Loggerhead sea turtle, immature

83c. Loggerhead sea turtle, hatchlings

- there are normally 5 costal scutes on each side
- the first costal scute always touches the nuchal scute
- there are usually 3 nonpored scutes on the bridge
- there are 2 pairs of prefrontal scales (between the eyes)

Hatchlings are dark brown.

**Similar species:** Hawksbills are darker brown or have calico carapacial scutes, and they have 4 costal scutes. Green turtles have only a single pair of prefrontal scales and 4 costals. Ridleys are comparatively small, olive gray or gray in color, and have 4 pored bridge scutes.

## 84. Green Sea Turtle

*Chelonia mydas*

**Abundance:** This is the second most commonly seen sea turtle of our eastern waters. A hulking, hard-shelled turtle, the green sea turtle may be encountered in summer from Cape Cod, Massachusetts (rarely a little further north), to Texas and southward to southern South America. It is a federally threatened species.

84. Green sea turtle, very large

**Habitat:** This is a species of tropical and subtropical oceans. It is often seen in shallow flats where it feeds on eelgrass.

**Size:** Only the leatherback exceeds this turtle's size. Green turtles attain a shell length of 3–4½ feet and have been known to attain 5 feet. They may weigh more than 500 pounds. Hatchlings have a carapace length of 1¾–2 inches.

**Identifying features:** Adults have a light to dark brown carapace. Radiating dark lines may be visible on the costal scutes of some of the lighter specimens. There are 4 costal scutes on each side. The first costal is not in contact with the nuchal scale. The venter is light. Hatchlings are dark brown to nearly black with the flippers edged neatly in white. This species has only a single pair of prefrontal scales (the scales between the eyes).

**Similar species:** All other sea turtles of this family found in the western Atlantic or Gulf waters have two pairs of prefrontal scales.

**Comments:** In recent years green turtle populations have been plagued by rapidly developing viral fibropapillomas. Despite a great deal of research being directed toward this problem, a cure has not yet been found.

## 85. Atlantic Hawksbill Sea Turtle

*Eretmochelys imbricata imbricata*

**Abundance/Range:** This endangered sea turtle is a distinct rarity in the waters of the continental United States. Only occasionally does it nest on our eastern beaches.

**Habitat:** This is a species of the open oceans.

**Size:** Adults range 28–32 inches in length, with a record size of only 36 inches, and weigh 100–175 pounds. Hatchlings have a carapace length of 1½–1¾ inches.

**Identifying features:** The carapace of the hawksbill is brown(ish), only occasionally with a prominent tortoiseshell pattern. There is a vertebral keel. Carapacial scutes are noticeably imbricate (overlapping) on young turtles but become less so as the turtle grows and ages. The rear marginals are quite serrate. The plastron is cream to light yellow in color. Young are quite similar to adults in color but usually have a more vividly contrasting pattern. Hatchlings are very

85. Atlantic hawksbill sea turtle

dark brown to nearly black and lack a carapacial pattern. This species has a narrow hawklike beak. Yellow interstitial skin is visible between the head scales.
**Similar species:** Kemp's ridley is gray in color and almost round. The loggerhead has 5 costals on each side. The green turtle has only 2 prefrontal scales.
**Comments:** The carapacial scutes of this turtle were once used extensively in the manufacture of tortoiseshell for eyeglass frames and other items for which plastic is now largely used.

### 86. Kemp's Ridley Sea Turtle

*Lepidochelys kempii*

**Abundance/Range:** This once abundant sea turtle is now considered an endangered species. However, its numbers appear to have stabilized. It is most common in the Gulf of Mexico and also seen in the South Atlantic.
**Habitat:** This is an oceangoing species.
**Size:** Kemp's ridley is adult at 20–25 inches. Its record size is only 29½

86a. Kemp's ridley sea turtle, adult

86b. Kemp's ridley sea turtle, hatchling

inches. Its average weight is about 90 pounds. Hatchlings have a carapace length of 1½–1¾ inches.

**Identifying features:** When viewed from above, this species is nearly circular. Hatchlings are gray with a lighter stripe on the trailing edge of each front flipper. Adults are olive green to gray above and yellowish ventrally. There are 5 costals, 2 pairs of prefrontal scales, and either 4 (usually) or 5 (rarely) pored scutes on the bridge. The first costal touches the nuchal scute.

**Similar species:** Adults of all other sea turtles now known to occur in the waters of the United States and Canada are larger. Green turtles have only one pair of prefrontal scales. The Atlantic hawksbill has 4 costals on each side, the first of which does not touch the nuchal scute. The loggerhead has only 3 scutes (non-pored) on the bridge.

**Comments:** The Olive Ridley, *Lepidochelys olivacea*, originally an Old World species, now breeds on South American shores, and occasional specimens have been found in coastal Cuba and Puerto Rico. The olive ridley is similar in size to Kemp's ridley, but is more olive in color and has 6–9 costal scutes on each side of the carapace.

Kemp's ridley once appeared in vast nesting arribadas on the Gulf coast of northern Mexico. Head start programs have been in place for some time now, but their exact benefit to the species remains uncertain.

## Leatherback, family Dermochelyidae

This gigantic oceangoing chelonian is the largest extant turtle. A carapace length of more than 6 feet and a weight of more than a ton have been recorded. Like all marine turtles, the leatherback has flipperlike limbs. Because of a complex circulatory system, this turtle is the most cold tolerant of the ocean-dwelling chelonians. This family has been erected solely for this unusual turtle.

This immense turtle nests above the tide line on open beaches. A female may nest only every 2–4 years. Several clutches of 150+ eggs are laid by a female during her nesting year. Incubation takes 2½–3½ months.

This is a wide-ranging turtle that is capable, because of circulatory system modifications, of sustaining a warm body temperature in very cold waters. Leatherbacks are immensely powerful and extreme care should be used when observing them. Nesting and the dispersal of the hatchlings from the nest both occur under cover of darkness. Occasional females nest during the hours of daylight.

## 87. Leather-backed Sea Turtle

*Dermochelys coriacea*

**Abundance:** This rare sea turtle is now increasing in numbers in American waters. It is still (perhaps understandably) rare in Canadian waters. Although it is somewhat more common in its primary Latin American and Malaysian breeding grounds, it is listed as an endangered species.

**Habitat:** This is a pelagic marine species about which little is known.

**Size:** Most specimens seen are in the 3½–4½-foot carapace range; 74¼ inches is the record carapace length. It has been known to attain a ton in weight. Hatchlings are about 2¾ inches in carapace length.

**Identifying features:** The overall predominating dorsal color of this turtle is slate blue to black. There are no keratinized scutes on the carapace. There are usually scattered white, yellowish, or pinkish markings. The carapace has 7 pro-

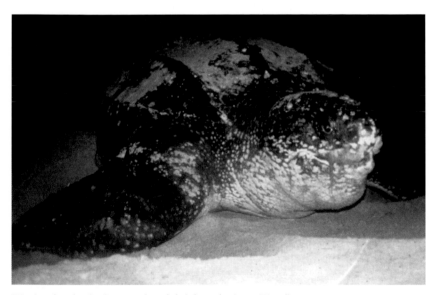

87a. Leather-backed sea turtle, adult (photo by Larry Wood)

87b. Leather-backed sea turtle, hatchling

nounced longitudinal keels. The plastron is somewhat lighter in color than the carapace and bears 5 keels. Males have concave plastrons. The front flippers are proportionately immense. Hatchlings have a ground color much like the adults but have numerous small (often white) scales (which are later shed), white keels, and white outlining both front and rear flippers.

**Voice:** Leatherbacks are capable of emitting sounds that are reminiscent of a human belch.

**Similar species:** None.

**Comments:** Jellyfish are the unlikely diet of this, the largest turtle in today's world. Deaths of even large individuals have occurred after the turtles have mistakenly ingested discarded clear plastic bags.

**4**

WORM LIZARDS, SUBORDER AMPHISBAENIA

# Amphisbaenids

The amphisbaenids or worm lizards are burrowing, legless, practically eye-less lizard relatives that are morphologically distinct enough to be placed in their own suborder within the order Squamata. (Lizards, suborder Sauria, and snakes, suborder Serpentes, are also placed within Squamata.) There are four families of amphisbacnids, one of which is found in the United States; its only known representative occurs in Florida.

Despite the fact that they are not true lizards, the amphisbaenids have long been referred to as such. Perhaps a more appropriate common name would be "amphisbaenians" (am-fis-BAY-nee-ans). These are specialized burrowers with the scales arranged in rings (annuli) that make the creatures look superficially like earthworms. However, their skin is dry, they have a very discernible mouth, and the scales on their head are easily seen. No amphisbaenid has functional eyes.

The worm lizards are well represented in other subtropical and tropical parts of the world. Rumors, long existing and continuing, refer to a second species having been found in both Arizona and Florida. This creature purportedly has forelimbs like some well-known Mexican species. Thus far, neither Arizona nor Florida specimens have reached museum collections or herpetologists.

I was at home in Tampa, Florida, gardening in a bed of perennials in the front yard. Actually, I was just trying to remove a year's accumulation of dead leaves without disturbing the plants unduly, so was raking gently. Things were going well. Progress was being made. At least progress was being made until I glanced down at an area of cleared soil just in time to see a strangely annulated pink creature disappearing from sight into a pencil-sized burrow. I grasped its tail and fortunately the loosened soil gave way as the creature squirmed vigorously. I found myself holding a foot-long Florida worm lizard, the first live one I had ever seen.

Since that time we have been fortunate enough to find several other individuals of this interesting reptile, the sole representative of the family known with certainty to exist in the United States. Most have been in loose sandy soil beneath surface debris.

## Florida Worm Lizards, genus *Rhineura*

These specialized burrowers are occasionally found by raking fallen leaves from a sandy substrate or by sorting through sand and debris from near the base of sand-scrub plants.

Little is known about the breeding biology of the worm lizard. It lays eggs; females with up to 3 fully formed oviducal eggs (eggs still in the oviducts) have been found in the summer.

The diet consists of tiny burrowing insects and, perhaps, earthworms. Captives feed upon the larvae of tenebrionid beetles and termites. Except when forced to the surface by heavy rains, the worm lizard is seldom seen. They seem to construct their burrows closer to the ground surface during the cool days of spring and summer than when the temperatures are really hot.

## 88. Florida Worm Lizard

*Rhineura floridana*

**Abundance/Range:** The population statistics of these creature are difficult to assess. Although uncommon in some regions, in areas of prime habitat they are quite common. Worm lizards were long thought to range northward from just north of Lake Okeechobee to just south of the Florida-Georgia state line. However, the finding of a single specimen in extreme southern Georgia has raised the possibility that the range may extend beyond Florida.

**Habitat:** Sandy, easily burrowed soils are preferred by this species.

**Size:** Although 6–12 inches is the size of the majority of specimens found, worm lizards are known to occasionally attain a 16-inch length.

**Identifying features:** This annulated "lizard" varies from pale sandy pink to a very bright pink. This species lacks limbs, openings, and functional eyes. The head is wedge-shaped, and the short tail studded dorsally with conical tubercles. The lower jaw is countersunk.

**Similar species:** None. The sand skink has tiny but visible eyes and limbs. Glass lizards have shiny scales, are not annulated, and have functional eyes and ear openings. All Florida and Georgia snakes (except the tiny introduced Braminy blind snake, which is never pink) have well-developed eyes.

88. Florida worm lizard

# 5

## Lizards, suborder Sauria (Lacertilia)

Worldwide, the suborder Sauria contains more than 3,800 species distributed in all but Arctic and Antarctic regions. Diverse in habitats, habits, and appearance, these creatures are contained in 400 genera in 24+ families.

All have scales, most have functional limbs with clawed feet (but some are legless), and most have functional eyes with lids. Others have functional eyes protected by a transparent, spectacle-like brille rather than by lids and yet others lack functional eyes. The tails of lizards as a group may be short and broad, short and slender, or long and tapered. Many lizards have tails that break (autotomize) if stressed and some do so with rather remarkable ease. To facilitate breakage, the tail (caudal) vertebrae may possess fracture planes—weakened areas—in the bone.

Lizards vary in size from the massive girth and 9-foot length of the Komodo dragon to the soda-straw thickness of some 1½-inch geckos.

Lizards are well represented in eastern and central North America. There are 14 families that contain 96 species and 117 recognized subspecies, listed here in alphabetical order.

- Old World Agamas, family Agamidae (3 species)
- Glass Lizards and Alligator Lizards, family Anguidae (5 species)
- Eyelidded Geckos, family Eublepharidae (2 species)
- Typical Geckos, family Gekkonidae (16 species)
- Iguanas and relatives, family Iguanidae (40 sFpecies)
- Old World Wall Lizards and Green Lizards, family Lacertidae (3 species)
- Skinks, family Scincidae (12 species)
- Racerunners and Whiptails, family Teiidae (14 species)
- Monitors, family Varanidae (1 species)

Most of our lizards are of very typical overall appearance (long bodied, four legs, and a long tail), but a few types diverge from the norm. Although most of our lizards have ear openings, a few species do not. Some have legs so short that they are hardly noticeable and a few species lack legs entirely. The various horned lizards look like animated pincushions. Most lizards are diurnal to crepuscular in their activity patterns, but many of the geckos are primarily nocturnal.

## Agamids, Family Agamidae

Agamidae is a huge grouping of Old World lizards, two species of which are now found in Florida. In form and habits many of the members seem to roughly parallel the New World iguanian lizards. However, none of the agamids attain the large size of the true iguanas and none of the iguanians have distensible rib membranes that allow long gliding flights (like the flying dragons).

Two agama species have become established in Florida. Both are pet trade species. (The presence of a third species has been reported.) One, the red-headed agama, dwells naturally amid rocky aridland habitats in Africa. The habitat of the second, the variable tree agama, is indicated by this lizard's common name. It is an Asian species.

When suitably warmed and if healthy, both species are very alert, very active, very fast, very difficult to approach, and most colorful.

The bobbing red head of a displaying male agama is a field mark that can be neither missed nor mistaken. It was along the periphery of a field in Broward County, Florida, on some construction rubble, that I (RDB) saw my first example of this species in the wild. These lizards, in one subspecies or another, are now also present near Lake Okeechobee and in Charlotte County, Florida. They prefer disturbed areas, such as construction sites, parking lots with curbs, and bridge abutments. The populations are not large, but seem self-sustaining. These lizards are wary, fast, and adept at avoiding capture should that be what an observer has in mind. Look for them after the sun has begun to warm the cement structures the lizards call home.

### Agamas, genera *Agama*, *Calotes*, and *Leiolepis*

### Indochinese Tree Lizard, genus *Calotes*

In Florida these African and Asian lizards are associated with disturbed habitats. Both species are pet trade staples. These lizards may often be seen foraging on the ground but both climb well and readily in pursuit of food or to avoid predators. As a component of their territoriality displays, sun-warmed males often indulge in stylized pushups and head bobbing.

Females in Florida produce clutches of 5–18 eggs. Hatchlings are commonly seen in late summer.

# 89. African Red-headed Agama

*Agama agama* ssp. (introduced species)

**Abundance/Range:** An East African species, the red-headed agama is known from Broward, Charlotte, Miami-Dade, Martin, and Seminole counties, Florida, in the United States.

**Habitat:** These lizards may be seen climbing trees, on the cinder block walls of houses and property barriers, amid construction rubble, and on bridge abutments.

**Size:** Adult males attain a robust 12 inches in length. Females are slightly smaller. Hatchlings are 3–3½ inches in length.

**Identifying features:** When they are warm, dominant, nonstressed males in nuptial coloring have brilliant orange heads, a bluish gray to charcoal dorsum, an orange vertebral stripe of slightly enlarged scales, a blue tail, and a light belly. When they are cool or stressed the lizards are less colorful. Females and juveniles are tan to brown and may have traces of dorsal bars. Breeding females may have an orangish or a bluish blush to the head and a bluish blush on the limbs.

**Similar species:** Use range to separate this from other lizards. There are no similar lizards in Florida.

**Comments:** Some populations of the red-headed agamas in Broward and Miami-Dade counties are *A. a. agama*, as described above. However, both in the above counties and in Martin, Charlotte, and Seminole counties, the subspecies present is *A. a. africana*. This race differs in having the distal half of the tail black.

89b. Red-headed agama, nonbreeding male

89a. Red-headed agama, male in breeding colors

### Tree Agamas, genus *Calotes*

This is a fairly large genus of Asian agamids. Only a single species, the angular, slender, very long-tailed Indochinese tree agama occurs in Florida. Although it has been present in its restricted habitats for about twenty years, it does not seem to have spread far from its points of release. Despite being largely arboreal, this agamid can often be seen sitting on sidewalks and curbs.

## 90. Indochinese Tree Agama

*Calotes mystaceus* (introduced species)

**Abundance:** This lizard is known only in Okeechobee and Glades counties, Florida.
**Habitat:** These lizards display and bask in trees, on fence posts, and even on curbstones.
**Size:** This slender lizard attains 15 inches in overall length. Hatchlings are about 3½ inches in length.
**Identifying features:** Males have a grayish body and a variably blue head. During the breeding season, the throat may become orangish. Females tend to be brownish and have darker crossbars, longitudinal dorsolateral stripes, and a black shoulder spot. A prominent vertebral crest is present.
**Similar species:** This species could be mistaken for a baby iguana or a female northern brown basilisk. However, iguanas are usually bright green and lack contrasting head color, and the basilisk is brown with yellow shoulder markings.

90. Indochinese tree agama

## Butterfly Lizards, genus *Leiolepis*

This is a small genus of Asian lizards typified by brightly colored sides that the males flare when displaying. They typically return to a home burrow of their own making each evening. These lizards are quite inactive in cloudy, rainy, or cool weather.

### 91. Butterfly Lizard

*Leiolepis belliana* ssp. (introduced species)

**Abundance/Range:** This lizard has been present in Kendall, Miami-Dade County, Florida, for almost a decade.

**Habitat:** This is a terrestrial lizard that digs home burrows in gardens and lawns. It basks on sunny days.

**Size:** Males attain a total length of about 16 inches; females are smaller.

**Identifying features:** This is a large and easily identified lizard. Warm males are the most intensely colored. The back is olive brown in coloration. There is a broken olive-tan stripe along each upper side as well as a broken tan vertebral stripe. Between these on each side is a row of well-separated light spots. Each side is adorned with a series of alternating bright orange and black vertical bars.

91. Butterfly lizard (photo by Kevin Enge)

When basking or displaying, the males flatten the body, making the orange sides very evident. There are light spots on the top and blue spots on the anterior surface of each thigh. The upper forelimbs are banded with black and pale orange. The lower forelimbs are spotted. The belly is light in color. The long tail is flattened toward the base. Females are not as brightly colored as the males. **Similar species:** None. The orange and black barred sides are distinctive.

## Glass Lizards and Alligator Lizards, family Anguidae

The lizard family Anguidae is represented in eastern and central North America by four rather similar appearing legless species, the glass lizards, and by the attenuate but prominently limbed Texas alligator lizard. It may be necessary to have the glass lizard in hand, where you can check the positioning of the dark stripes and count scales along the lateral groove to be sure of the species. Three of the four species are rather well known. The fourth, the mimic glass lizard, has only recently been described.

All anguid lizards within the scope of this guide are oviparous. Females usually care for their eggs throughout the incubation period.

Although they are rather common, anguid lizards can be hard to find. They are quite secretive but occasionally emerge from their places of hiding to bask in the morning sun or at a few minutes before dusk to forage or change home territories.

By accident, I (RDB) have seen Texas alligator lizards crawling across mountain trails in Texas, but when I have decided to actually look for the lizards I have been unable to find one.

Glass lizards, those legless creatures of the southeastern and south central lowlands that are so often mistaken for snakes, are a little easier to find.

By laying boards in an out of the way place in our yard we have provided secure hiding places for several eastern glass lizards, including one female that used the cover to lay and protect her eggs.

On warm, humid spring evenings, island glass lizards could be found crossing a paved road near the Fort Myers, Florida, airport. I never found the species elsewhere in that area of Florida, even though I searched diligently.

And there are certain roads from Florida to Texas on which you might expect to find a crossing slender glass lizard, but to happen across one in the field is almost unheard of.

Are these lizards common?

Probably.

Are they easily found?

No. But when you do succeed you feel that the result is worth the effort.

These lizards have a longitudinal expansion fold from nape to vent. This allows a degree of expansion after eating. Because they have osteoderms (bony plates beneath each epidermal scale), the glass lizards lack the sinuosity and suppleness of snakes. There are other important differences as well. Glass lizards have functional eyelids and ear openings (snakes have neither), and the glass lizards do not have the enlarged belly scales so characteristic of most snakes.

All of our anguids have proportionately long tails. The alligator lizard and three of the four species of glass lizards have caudal fracture planes (a weakened area in a caudal vertebra to facilitate ready breakage). Fracture planes are absent in the tail of the island glass lizard. The tail of those species with fracture planes regenerates well and almost fully. The tail of the island glass lizard does not.

It is from the ease with which the tail is broken that the name "glass lizard" (these lizards are also referred to as glass "snakes" in error) has been derived. Legend erroneously relates that if broken by a predator, once danger has passed, the tail sections of a glass lizard will rejoin.

In fact, the shortened but not fatally injured lizard seeks a place of hiding while a predator is distracted by the writhing, broken tail. Eventually a new tail will be regenerated.

## Eastern Alligator Lizards, genus *Gerrhonotus*

These lizards are primarily insectivorous, but may occasionally eat nestling rodents or birds.

Females produce up to 31 eggs, but most clutches contain 8–20 eggs. Not too surprisingly, larger females have the largest clutches. Gravid females preferentially choose an area that will hold at least a small amount of ground moisture for deposition. A site beneath a fallen trunk or a flat rock may prove ideal. Following deposition the female remains with the clutch through the 50–70 days of incubation.

If threatened the alligator lizard will inflate its body (distending the lateral groove), and gape its jaws. The bite is strong but not dangerous. We have seen these lizards crossing trails in the morning and sunning amid rocks near canyon springs in the late afternoon.

## 92. Texas Alligator Lizard

*Gerrhonotus infernalis*

**Abundance:** This secretive lizard is rather generally distributed in central and western Texas. Its range extends far southward into Mexico.

92a. Texas alligator lizard, adult

92b. Texas alligator lizard, juvenile

**Habitat:** Look for this alligator lizard in well-drained, rock-strewn regions bearing oak or oak-scrub overstory. It favors wooded canyons, wooded rocky slopes, and rocky stream or spring side locations. It also persists in some numbers along ditches, canals, and creek beds in urban areas, providing surface rocks or debris are present for cover.

**Size:** The tail of this slender lizard is about twice the length of its head and body. Adults range 12–15 inches in total length. The record size is 20 inches. Hatchlings are about 4 inches long.

**Identifying features:** This species undergoes considerable age-related (ontogenetic) pattern and color change. Hatchlings are a deep metallic brown and their white cross bands are narrow and precisely defined. With growth the dorsal coloration lightens to yellowish, buff, olive brown, warm brown, or reddish brown. The edges of the cross bands diffuse and the contrast between band and ground color lessens considerably. Adults have cross banding of tan or gray weakly edged with brown. Very old specimens may be only vaguely crossbarred and stippled. Back and side scales are prominently keeled. The belly is gray(ish), variably mottled with a lighter gray and, occasionally, with some indication of darker markings. The lateral groove is well developed and graphically separates the dorsum from the venter. The scales in the groove are very tiny. The head is lance shaped and covered dorsally and laterally with prominent overlapping scales. All four legs are well developed, but appear proportionately short.

**Similar species:** Skinks are shiny, have smooth, unkeeled scales, and lack a lateral groove.

**Comments:** When startled into motion, the alligator lizard folds its legs against its body and progresses in an undulating serpentine movement. When in the open it is alert and moves quietly to safety as a disturbance nears. These lizards can climb well and use their tail to steady themselves. The tail is strong and prehensile enough to easily support the entire weight of the lizard, yet it autotomizes easily.

### Glass Lizards, genus *Ophisaurus*

This genus is represented in Asia, Mexico, Europe, and North America.

A clutch of 3–20 eggs is laid. The chosen moisture-retaining nesting site is often beneath clumps of fieldgrass or wiregrass, beneath logs, or beneath man-made debris. The female attends the clutch throughout the 48–65-day incubation. The hatchlings of many species are strongly striped or saddled, patterns that some species retain into adulthood.

These alert lizards often allow close approach but will thrash wildly if actually restrained. Glass lizards may often be seen crossing sandy or paved country roadways in the late afternoon or early evening, or during or following daytime showers.

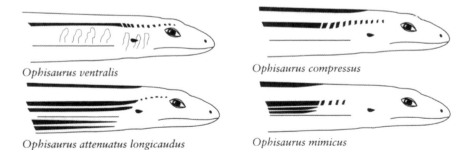

*Ophisaurus ventralis*

*Ophisaurus compressus*

*Ophisaurus attenuatus longicaudus*

*Ophisaurus mimicus*

Glass lizards. Illustration by Dale Johnson.

## 93. Western Slender Glass Lizard

*Ophisaurus attenuatus attenuatus*

western
eastern

**Abundance/Range:** This secretive lizard is common over much of its range. It may be found from western Louisiana and central Texas northward to southern Nebraska and Wisconsin. This is the only glass lizard present west of the Mississippi River.

**Habitat:** This is a species of sandy, yielding soils. It occurs in open pine and oak scrub woodlands. It often hides beneath rocks, logs, or other surface debris at field edges and in grasslands. It may be found near water but requires well-drained habitats. Although it is fully capable of burrowing, it does so less persistently than other glass lizards.

**Size:** Adult western slender glass lizards range in size from 2 to 3 feet. The record size for this glass lizard is an even 3½ feet. Hatchlings are 8–9½ inches in total length.

**Identifying features:** The dorsal color of adults is a warm sandy brown; the venter is lighter. A heavy, dark vertebral stripe and equally heavy, dark dorsolateral stripes are usually very apparent. Thin lateral and ventrolateral stripes are also present. With advancing age the pattern of longitudinal lines may fade and be replaced anteriorly by dark-edged, light dorsal crossbarring. The crossbars often run between the two dorsolateral stripes. As the lizards continue to age, light

93. Western slender glass lizard

stippling infiltrates dark fields and may eventually produce a nearly overall salt-and-pepper effect. Males are more prone than the females to these ontogenetic changes. There are a series of (usually) dark-outlined, light vertical bars, often numbering 7–9, beginning beneath the eye and continuing onto the neck and anterior body. The ventrolateral stripes may be more poorly defined than those above the groove, but they are present. The length of the tail is more than twice, but less than 2½ times that of the head and body. There are more than 97 scales along the edge of the lateral groove. There are prominent ear openings.

**Similar species:** All of the glass lizards are confusingly similar, but range alone will identify the western slender glass lizard. However, confusion in identifying the eastern subspecies will occur. Please see the species accounts for the mimic, the island, and the eastern glass lizards. All snakes lack eyelids and ear openings.

### Subspecies

94. The Eastern Slender Glass Lizard, *Ophisaurus attenuatus longicaudus*, ranges eastward from coastal eastern Louisiana and central Kentucky to eastern Virginia and Florida. It is absent from wetlands. Adult eastern slender glass lizards range 2–3½ feet in size. The eastern slender glass lizard is similar to its western relative in all respects except proportionate tail length. The length of the tail of the eastern race is 2½ or more times the combined length of the lizard's head and body.

94. Eastern slender glass lizard

## 95. Island Glass Lizard

*Ophisaurus compressus*

**Abundance/Range:** This locally common glass lizard is secretive and seldom seen. It occurs in suitable
habitat throughout peninsular Florida, in the coastal
regions of the eastern Florida panhandle, and northward along the coast to central South Carolina.

**Habitat:** This is a resident of sandy, relatively dry,
pine-oak scrubland. It is often found near ephemeral ponds.

**Size:** The island glass lizard is adult at 16–22 inches long. Hatchlings are 6½–7½
inches in total length.

**Identifying features:** Like most glass lizards, the adults of the island glass lizard
are darker in color and less precisely patterned than the young. Young specimens are prominently striped (usually 3 stripes) for their entire length. All
stripes are above the lateral groove. Older specimens develop a pattern of vague
crossbars and stippling. Young specimens have a series of 7–10 prominent *dark*
(not dark-edged) vertical markings posterior to the ear opening. This species
lacks caudal fracture planes. Although the tail will break, it does not readily do
so and tail regeneration is comparatively imperfect.

**Similar species:** See species accounts for the eastern slender glass lizard, mimic
glass lizard, and eastern glass lizard. The legless Florida worm lizard is pinkish
and has no functional eyes. Snakes lack eyelids and ear openings.

95. Island glass lizard

## 96. Mimic Glass Lizard

*Ophisaurus mimicus*

**Abundance/Range:** This small glass lizard ranges eastward along the coastal plain from extreme eastern Louisiana through northern Florida and adjacent southern Georgia to coastal central North Carolina.

**Habitat:** This glass lizard prefers sandy habitats. It is a species of sandy but seasonally wet pine flatwoods as well as of open damp meadows and woodlands.

**Size:** The mimic glass lizard measures 16–25½ inches in length when adult. Hatchlings are 6½–8 inches in total length.

**Identifying features:** The ground color of this species is olive tan to brown. It has an immaculate off-white belly. A vertebral stripe may be present along with 3 or 4 dark side stripes above the lateral groove. The uppermost of these is the most prominent. There is one very poorly defined stripe below the lateral fold. There are 95 or fewer scale rows along the lateral groove. About 7 vertical bars occur posterior to the ear opening. The bars are predominantly dark but may have narrow white centers. There are also bars or spots between the eye and the ear opening. The tail vertebrae have fracture planes and the tail autotomizes readily.

**Similar species:** The slender glass lizard has multiple stripes (some rather well defined) below the lateral groove. Besides its vertebral stripe, the island glass

96. Mimic glass lizard

lizard has only 1 stripe on each side. Eastern glass lizards of all ages lack a well-defined vertebral stripe. The Florida worm lizard has no functional eyes.

**Comments:** It is because of its similarity of appearance to other species of glass lizards that this species was given the epithet of *mimicus*—the mimic glass lizard.

## 97. Eastern Glass Lizard

*Ophisaurus ventralis*

**Abundance:** This is the most widely and generally distributed of our glass lizards. It ranges southward in the coastal plain and Piedmont provinces from extreme southeastern Virginia to eastern Louisiana.

**Habitat:** The eastern glass lizard may be found in both moist and dry habitats in areas as diverse as suburban yards, woodlands, and wetlands.

**Size:** This is the bulkiest of the glass lizards, as well as marginally the longest. Most examples seen are in the 19–28-inch range. Very occasional specimens near 36 inches in length, and the record size is 42⅝ inches. Hatchlings are 7–8½ inches in total length.

**Identifying features:** Babies are pleasingly colored and contrastingly marked. They are olive tan with two prominent dark dorsolateral lines; the vertebral stripe that is so prominent on other species of glass lizards is either indistinct or lacking on this one. The venter is yellowish. With growth, colors dull and pat-

97a. Eastern glass lizard

97b. Eastern glass lizard

97c. Eastern glass lizard

terns obscure. Old adults lose even vestiges of the stripes and become suffused with turquoise or green dorsally. The belly turns a rather bright yellow. Dark spots develop on the rear of the dorsal scales and light spots on the lateral scales. There are no dark lines below the lateral fold. The tail is very easily broken.

**Similar species:** This is the only one of our glass lizards to appear turquoise or greenish when adult. Old adults of other species are fawn or brown. The smaller Florida worm lizard has an annulated body, lacks functional eyes, and is pinkish. Snakes lack eyelids and ear openings.

## Gekkonid Lizards: Geckos with and without eyelids
## Eyelidded Geckos, family Eublepharidae

This is a small family of lizards that is represented in the New World by only the single genus *Coleonyx*. Two species occur in our central states. Because of the rather standardized body pattern these small, delicate-appearing lizards have when young, they are often referred to colloquially as banded geckos. With advancing age the pattern becomes diffuse. The New World representatives are terrestrial and nocturnal, have functional eyelids, and lack expanded toepads. All have vertically elliptical pupils.

Male geckos in this family have pheromone-releasing preanal pores that are arranged in a V anterior to the anus.

Tail scalation is arranged in rings (whorls) and the tail autotomizes very easily.

These nocturnal geckos are insectivores. One, the Texas banded gecko, is widely distributed and well known whereas the reticulated gecko is of restricted distribution and rarely seen.

### Banded Geckos, genus *Coleonyx*

The members of this genus are primarily terrestrial in habits, but one member, the reticulated gecko, is adept at climbing boulders and cliff faces.

These geckos usually produce eggs in pairs but, rarely, a clutch may consist

Moonset had been an hour earlier but the hill shaded the roadway anyway. It was almost four o'clock in the morning and it had been a while—quite a while—since I had seen a reptile on the road. An occasional Couch's spadefoot was still being encountered and deer and peccaries remained active. Big Hill was now far behind me and the road transected an immense boulder field. A movement on the sandy shoulder caught my attention—a pocket mouse or a kangaroo rat, perhaps? I quickly pulled onto the shoulder, trying to avoid the tire-puncturing thorns of mowed mesquites, grabbed the flashlight and camera and walked back, carefully scanning the roadside as I went. Hmmmm—it seemed that this was just about where I had seen the motion. A mournful hoot from the darkness disclosed that a great horned owl was still up and active.

There! There on the edge of the road! No mouse this. It was a lizard, and I could already see by its size and the way that it held its tail that it was precisely the lizard I had hoped to see. I was looking at a Big Bend gecko, a species restricted to this area of Texas and adjacent Mexico, a lizard for which I had looked unsuccessfully on a dozen earlier occasions. Pictures were taken and I left with a smile.

of only a single egg. The soft-shelled eggs are placed beneath a sheltering object where there is some degree of ground moisture. Incubation can take 40–60 days.

Both of these geckos are secretive and terrestrial. When moving rapidly, or when hunting, they often raise and writhe the tail. The tail is easily autotomized, but quickly regenerates. Regenerated tails have scaling noticeably different from the original. Seen in the glow of car headlights as they dart across the road like diminutive, low-slung, tail-writhing mice, these geckos appear silvery.

## 98. Texas Banded Gecko

*Coleonyx brevis*

**Abundance:** This is a common gecko that ranges widely in southern and western Texas, southeastern New Mexico, and northern Mexico.
**Habitat:** The Texas banded gecko favors semiarid to arid natural areas with ample ground cover. It is particularly common in areas where its favored cover, flat rocks and succulent vegetative debris, is found. Hillsides, canyonlands, and creviced escarpments are typical habitats. It may also be found near human habitations where it seeks seclusion beneath boards, discarded roofing tins, and other debris.
**Size:** This is the smallest member of this widespread genus. Texas banded geckos are adult at 3½–4 inches in total length. They very seldom exceed 4½ inches. The tail is about equal in length to the length of the head and body. Hatchlings are about 1¾ inches long.
**Identifying features:** This pretty little gecko lacks enlarged tubercle-like scales.

98. Texas banded gecko

When young, the Texas banded gecko is strongly and precisely banded with bands of warm brown and creamy yellow. As the gecko ages the edges of the bands diffuse and are infiltrated by the adjacent color. Old adults may appear mottled (or reticulated) rather than banded. Black spots occur in both the dark and the light fields. This gecko lacks expanded toepads. The pupils are elliptical. These geckos are often lighter in color at night than during the day.

**Voice:** If frightened, restrained, or involved in territorial disputes, male Texas banded geckos may produce barely audible squeaks.

**Similar species:** Although their patterns may be similar, the much larger reticulated gecko has tuberculate scales scattered among the smooth scales of its back and sides. Texas banded geckos are differentiated from the more westerly *Coleonyx variegatus* ssp. by the arrangement of the preanal pores. The pores of the Texas banded gecko form an incomplete V, the apex being separated at the midline.

**Comments:** Inexplicably and erroneously, some people believe this harmless species, one of the most innocuous of all lizards, to be venomous!

## 99. Reticulated Gecko

*Coleonyx reticulatus*

**Abundance:** Because it lives in such a remote area, the population statistics of this gecko are quite unknown. Certainly this gecko is infrequently seen, but whether it is rare, just secretive, or both, has not been ascertained. It is thought that the main population of the reticulated gecko occurs in Brewster County, within the confines of Big Bend National Park, Texas. Additional specimens have been found in neighboring Presidio County. This species is protected both by the state of Texas and, if in Big Bend National Park, by federal decree.

**Habitat:** Limestone canyonlands, boulder-strewn hillsides, and plots of rock-strewn land are the favored habitats of the reticulated gecko. It occurs, seemingly also in disjunct colonies, in northern Mexico. It is occasionally seen at night on paved roads in the Big Bend region of Texas.

**Size:** This is the largest member of the genus in our area of coverage. Fully grown male reticulated geckos may attain 6½ inches in total length. The tail is equal to the head and body in length. Besides being large, the reticulated gecko is relatively heavy bodied. Hatchlings are about 3 inches in total length.

**Identifying features:** Hatchlings of this large and poorly understood gecko are prominently banded when hatched. This is the only terrestrial gecko in Texas to have a scattering of prominently enlarged tubercular scales among the small scales on the back. Although the overall pattern of the reticulated gecko soon

99. Reticulated gecko, adult

obscures and changes, some indication of banding is often retained. Adults have both the light and the dark fields suffused with discrete dots and streaks. The ground color is pinkish to cream, the dark banding is a rather pale brown. Functional eyelids are present and the pupils are elliptical. There are no expanded toepads.

**Voice:** As with most other geckos, males of this species are able to produce weak squeaking notes. These are given during times of stress or during territorial disputes.

**Similar species:** The much smaller Texas banded gecko lacks tuberculate scales on the dorsum.

## Typical Geckos, family Gekkonidae

With a single exception, the typical geckos of the eastern United States are of introduced status. The majority of the 16 species are found only in the state of Florida; of these, many are restricted in distribution to the southern one-third of the peninsula and the Florida Keys. One species is found only on Galveston Island, Texas. Some of these lizards have arrived on our shores unbeckoned, stowaways in shipments of imported products. The presence of others seems to be associated with the pet trade, populations having been established by either escapees or deliberately released individuals. The only typical gecko now considered native to the eastern United States is the tiny Florida reef gecko, *Sphaerodactylus notatus notatus*.

Understandably, because of their proximity to humans, it is the several species of "house-dwelling" geckos that are best known. These nocturnal wraiths may be found in and on buildings and include species as diverse as the Mediterranean house gecko (and its relatives), the rough-tailed gecko, two species of wall geckos, and the big tokay gecko.

Although the Cuban ashy gecko and reef gecko also congregate on illuminated walls to hunt the insects drawn there, they are more often encountered beneath the loosened bark of dead trees, amid leaf litter, and under human-generated surface debris.

Three species of geckos in the east are diurnal. These are two species of day gecko and the yellow-headed gecko.

Most typical geckos have distended toepads, which allow them to climb even smooth surfaces agilely. The toepads are not simple "suction cups" as is often thought, but much more complex than they might seem. The pads are transversely divided into a series of lamellae that contain vast numbers of tiny bristlelike keratinized setae. The setae are tipped with an equally vast number of microscopic, nonskid spatulae with rounded ends. The spatulae and the smooth surface on which the gecko is climbing form weak attractive forces. To fully appreciate the complexity of these climbing devices, simply watch the way a slowly moving gecko curls its toes upward when disengaging a foot.

Typical geckos lack functional eyelids, their eyes being instead protected with a clear spectacle (the brille).

It is because of sensitivity to low temperatures that these lizards are restricted to the southernmost United States.

Geckos are among the few lizards with a voice. These range in volume from the difficult-to-hear squeaks of the tiny house geckos to the loud, two-syllabled advertisement calls of the foot-long tokay.

All geckos have an easily broken tail. Some species are capable of autotomizing the tail with little, if any, external help. Regenerated tails always differ in scalation and appearance from the originals.

Male geckos are territorial at all times, but are especially so during the breeding season. Serious skirmishes can occur if two males meet and one does not back down quickly. A gecko's skin is thin and can be easily torn free, often permitting an attacked gecko to escape a predator. A gecko's skin also heals quickly.

All geckos within the scope of this book are oviparous. Females of most species usually lay two eggs per clutch and produce several clutches a year. The females of the yellow-headed, reef, and Cuban ashy geckos produce only a single egg at a time. The eggs have a hard shell that may be adhesive when they are first laid, effectively cementing the clutch against vertical surfaces.

Most geckos are capable of changing colors. The lizards are darker and (often) more strongly patterned during their activity periods than when resting.

〰〰〰〰〰〰〰〰〰〰〰〰〰〰〰〰〰〰〰〰〰〰〰〰〰〰〰〰〰〰〰〰〰〰〰〰〰〰〰〰〰〰〰〰〰〰〰〰〰〰〰

"You can find those geckos on the big tamarind tree in the schoolyard," we had been told. We were now in Key West hoping that our information had been correct. Our search was for the dusky yellow-headed gecko, a tiny creature that seemed to be becoming more difficult to find in Florida. Led to it by its raucous calls, we had already found and photographed the big tokay gecko the night before. Amid a copse of Australian pines we had also found ashy geckos and reef geckos. We were on the countdown now. Only yellow-headed and ocellated geckos remained on our "I want to photograph" list.

"There's one," Patti exclaimed. Sure enough, almost invisible behind an ascending Virginia creeper, head downward in a crevice of the tamarind was a female yellow-headed gecko. Now, could we find a male?

The answer on that trip proved to be no, but on a subsequent trip, on some big shady olive trees, we did succeed, leaving the ocellated gecko (now thought to have been extirpated from Florida) as our sole gekkonid target in the state.

Well, that quest provides us with an occasional reason to travel to Key West.

〰〰〰〰〰〰〰〰〰〰〰〰〰〰〰〰〰〰〰〰〰〰〰〰〰〰〰〰〰〰〰〰〰〰〰〰〰〰〰〰〰〰〰〰〰〰〰〰〰〰〰

One species, the ocellated gecko, *Sphaerodactylus argus*, native to the West Indies but long established on Florida's two southernmost keys, was thought to have been extirpated in the state but has been refound.

## Typical Geckos, subfamily Gekkoninae

### Flat-tailed Gecko, Genus *Cosymbotus*

This is a small house gecko that in the United States is restricted to the walls of a few warehouse complexes. It descends at night from its hiding places high in the eaves but darts quickly back upward at the slightest disturbance.

The tail is somewhat flatter than that of the house geckos of the genus *Hemidactylus* and has serrate edges.

## 100. Flat-Tailed Gecko

*Cosymbotus platyurus* (introduced species)

**Abundance/Range:** In the United States this Asian gecko occurs in Alachua, Pinellas, Dade, and Lee counties, Florida. It has been established for more than twenty years.

**Habitat:** This is essentially a house gecko.

**Size:** This arboreal gecko is adult at about 3½ inches in overall length. Hatchlings are 1¼ inches long.

**Identifying features:** The lateral skin flanges make this gecko appear quite flat-

100. Flat-tailed house gecko

tened. Its broad tail has serrate edges. The toes are partially webbed and the toepads are large. The pupils are vertically oriented. This gecko is darkest by day but may appear a uniform pasty cream color at night.

**Voice:** When restrained or involved in territorial disputes male flat-tailed geckos produce clicks or high-pitched squeaks.

**Similar species:** Most house geckos of the genus *Hemidactylus* have scattered tuberculate scales on their body or are yellow to orange ventrally. They also have less extensive webbing on the feet.

## Bow-footed Geckos, genus *Cyrtopodion*

Although a saxicolous (rock dwelling) species in its native Egypt, in Galveston, Texas, this small and inconspicuous nocturnal gecko acts like a house gecko. It hides in darkened areas behind or beneath materials, or in the rafters by day, but hunts its insect prey in the glow of lightbulbs at night. It probably arrived on our shores as a stowaway in imported commercial goods.

## 101. Rough-tailed Gecko

*Cyrtopodion scabrum* (introduced species)

**Abundance/Range:** This gecko is now a common resident of many of the extensive warehouse complexes on Galveston Island, Texas.

**Habitat:** Look for this gecko on the upper walls of dockside buildings.

**Size:** A total length of 3¼–4¼ inches is attained by this species. Males appear to be the larger sex. Hatchlings are about 1¼ inches in total length.

101. Rough-tailed gecko

**Identifying features:** This nocturnal gecko lacks eyelids and has vertically elliptical pupils. The back and sides are a light sandy color. Irregular, often paired dark spots are present on the back and tail. The belly is white. The tail scales are enlarged and keeled. The toes are long, bent upward near the tip, and lack noticeably expanded pads. Except for their smaller size, hatchlings are identical to the adults.

**Voice:** Males involved in territorial disputes produce weak clicks.

## Tropical Asian Geckos, genus *Gekko*

Like so many other Old World geckos, this genus is represented in the United States by only a single species, the tokay gecko. It is known to be established only in South Florida, but it is speculated that it may occur in the vicinity of Brownville, Texas, as well. On spring and summer nights, the calls of this nocturnal lizard can be heard emanating from the hollows of roadside trees in Greater Miami and in various areas on the Florida Keys. This gecko can and will bite painfully if it is carelessly restrained. The tokay gecko has been purposely released in many areas of the country in the futile hope that it would rid homes of roaches. Many geckos escaped, but only those in the subtropical area of Florida are long-term survivors.

## 102. Tokay Gecko

*Gekko gecko* (introduced species)

**Abundance/Range:** This very arboreal gecko seems firmly established and quite common in many areas of South Florida. It is particularly common in the vicinity of Miami International Airport and on the lower Florida Keys. Isolated specimens have been seen in Cameron County, Texas. The tokay gecko is of Asian origin.

**Habitat:** The tokay gecko is often seen on buildings, shade trees, palms, and power poles. It is particularly common on trees with hollows or deep crevices where it can hide safely during the day.

**Size:** This is the largest gecko now found in the United States. In fact, at a foot in length, it is one of the largest species in the world. The young are a bit more than 3 inches long at hatching.

102a. Tokay geckos

102b. Tokay gecko, eggs

**Identifying features:** The gray body has orange and white markings and many tuberculate scales. The protuberant eyes may vary from yellow green to orange. The pupils are complex and vertically elliptical. The toepads are large and easily visible.

**Voice:** Males produce a loud, sharp "to-kay, to-to-to-kayyyyy, to-kay" call. They vocalize most persistently on warm spring and summer nights.

**Comments:** Communal nests, some containing hundreds of eggs, are common. If threatened with capture, tokays open their mouths widely, "growl" with a drawn out "tooooookk" and may actually jump toward an offending object, such as a hand, in an effort to bite. They will retain their grip with a bulldog-like tenacity.

### House Geckos, genus *Hemidactylus*

This genus is a huge assemblage of nocturnal, arboreal, Old World geckos. Four species are now known to occur in the southern United States. They are so adept at seeking cover during the cold days of winter that two species have been able to expand their range far to the north and west of areas colonized thus far by other gecko species. The geckos in this genus have expanded toepads and, as indicated by their common name, are firmly associated with the walls of houses and other buildings. They may often be seen on warm nights hunting for insects that are drawn to windows and walls by house lights.

The common Indo-Pacific house gecko is an all-female parthenogenetic species.

### 103. Common House Gecko

*Hemidactylus frenatus* (introduced species)

**Abundance/Range:** Unknown. This gecko occurs on the zoo grounds in both Dallas and Fort Worth, Texas, as well as in Lee and Monroe counties, Florida. It is native to tropical Asia, but is now a tropicopolitan (cosmopolitan in the tropics) species.

**Habitat:** This arboreal gecko is most commonly seen high on the walls of dwellings and warehouses.

**Size:** The common house gecko seldom exceeds 4 inches in overall length. The hatchlings are 2 inches long.

**Identifying features:** By day this gecko has a dorsal color of ashy gray with an irregular pattern of obscure darker pigment. It becomes very light at night. Ven-

103. Common house gecko

trally it is nearly white. A gray lateral line *may* be present. The scales of the body are mostly smooth, but there are six rows of strongly keeled scales on its tail.
**Voice:** Fighting males produce barely audible squeaks.
**Similar species:** The Indo-Pacific gecko has a bright yellow (often lemon) belly. Both the Mediterranean and the Amerafrican house geckos have tuberculate skin. The rough-tailed Gecko has a spiny tail and lacks noticeably expanded toepads. The flat-tailed gecko has a flattened, flanged tail.

## 104. Indo-Pacific House Gecko

*Hemidactylus garnotii* (introduced species)

**Abundance:** This is a very common gecko now found in Florida, southern Georgia, Alabama, Mississippi, Louisiana, southeastern Texas, and the Dallas–Fort Worth metroplex. It continues to expand its range.
**Habitat:** Most common on dwellings, the Indo-Pacific house gecko may also be seen on live and dead trees, on wooden fences, on masonry security walls, and amid construction rubble.
**Size:** This gecko is adult at 3¾–5 inches in total length. The hatchlings are 2 inches long.
**Identifying features:** Dorsally, this gecko varies from a medium dark grayish brown during the day to a nighttime color of translucent flesh white. There may

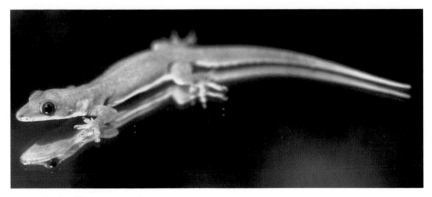

104. Indo-Pacific house gecko

or may not be indications of darker or lighter spotting. The belly is yellowish and the underside of the tail is often a rich orange. The body is covered with tiny nontuberculate scales. The sides of the tail appear vaguely flanged.

**Voice:** This is a vocal gecko, but the weak squeaking sounds it produces may be easily overlooked.

**Similar species:** No other gecko of the eastern United States has a yellowish to orange venter. The rough-tailed gecko lacks greatly dilated toepads. The common house gecko, which can be of very similar coloration dorsally, has a white to very pale yellow venter.

## 105. Amerafrican House Gecko

*Hemidactylus mabouia* (introduced species)

**Abundance/Range:** This house gecko is expanding its range by leaps and bounds. It has already become one of the most abundant species throughout most of the southern half of Florida and is now found as far north as Seminole, Orange, Polk, and Hillsborough counties.

**Habitat:** This species may be seen on buildings, trees, ornamental rock fixtures, and piles of debris.

**Size:** This robust gecko is marginally the largest of our four introduced *Hemidactylus* species. It commonly attains 4 inches in total length and may occasionally attain 5 inches. Hatchlings are about 2 inches in total length.

**Identifying features:** Like most geckos, this one is much darker in color and more strongly patterned during the day, when its colors may vary from tan to gray or olive brown. There are usually several darker, rearward-pointing dorsal markings in the shape of chevrons. Tuberculate scales are liberally scattered over the dorsum and especially abundant laterally. The venter is light. At night Amerafrican house geckos often appear an unpatterned, ghostly white.

105. Amerafrican house gecko

**Voice:** Males click and squeak quite audibly if restrained or when involved in territorial disputes.

**Similar species:** Indo-Pacific house geckos, common house geckos, and flat-tailed geckos lack tuberculate scales. The Mediterranean house gecko is smaller, has more prominent tubercules, and does not have chevron-shaped dorsal markings.

## 106. Mediterranean House Gecko

*Hemidactylus turcicus*
(introduced species)

**Abundance/Range:** Once the most common gecko in Florida, this species is being replaced in many areas by the Amerafrican house gecko. However, the Mediterranean house gecko remains common in north Florida. It is now abundant in eastern and southern Texas and found in small colonies in Arkansas, South Carolina, New Mexico, California, Nevada, Arizona, Oklahoma, Louisiana, Mississippi, Alabama, and Georgia.

**Habitat:** This gecko is strongly tied to human habitations but has now expanded its range to tree trunks, piles of debris, and dumps.

**Size:** This species occasionally nears 5 inches in total length. The hatchlings are nearly 2 inches long.

106. Mediterranean house gecko

**Identifying features:** The dorsal tubercles are prominently large and most abundant on the upper sides. Those on the tail are conical. Mediterranean house geckos are normally gray with darker markings during the day and almost white at night. The venter is white.

**Voice:** Fighting or restrained males produce clicks and squeaks.

**Similar species:** At the time of this writing (2004) any warty arboreal gecko found outside of Florida is probably this species. This and the Amerafrican house gecko occur in southern Florida; of the two, the Mediterranean house gecko has larger, more conspicuous tubercles. The dorsal markings of the Amerafrican house gecko are chevron shaped, whereas those of the Mediterranean house gecko are less precisely defined and never shaped like chevrons.

### African Wall Geckos, genus *Pachydactylus*

A small population of a single species, *P. bibroni*, has existed in a residential area of Manatee County, Florida, for more than twenty-five years and seems to be neither expanding nor dying out. These nocturnal South African geckos have broadly distended toepads and are persistently arboreal. They seem primarily restricted to walls, but are occasionally seen in trees and on power poles.

## 107. Bibron's Gecko

*Pachydactylus bibroni* (introduced species)

**Abundance/Range:** This gecko is a native of South Africa. It was introduced to Manatee County, Florida, in the 1970s, and small numbers still persist on dwellings and warehouses.

**Habitat:** Although normally a rock-dwelling gecko, in Florida, a state largely without rocks, Bibron's gecko is seen usually on the outer walls of dwellings and on nearby power poles and trees.

**Size:** This is a heavy-bodied gecko. Although known to attain an adult size of 8 inches, few in Florida measure more than 5½ inches. Hatchlings are about 2½ inches long.

**Identifying features:** This big-headed gecko is tan to buff or light brown dorsally. The many keeled tuberculate scales are separated by flat, granular scales and give the dorsum an almost sandpapery texture. Scales encircling the original (nonregenerated) tail are particularly spiny. The tuberculate body scales often form weakly defined dark bars bordered posteriorly by white tubercles. Scattered lateral scales are also white. Occasional examples are very dark and lack most contrasting markings. The venter is white. Like most geckos, Bibron's geckos are lighter in color at night than during the day.

**Voice:** Males produce squeaking clicks as an advertisement mechanism as well as to indicate aggression and fright.

107. Bibron's gecko

**Similar species:** Young Moorish geckos have scalation very similar to that of Bibron's gecko but usually have a weaker pattern. The ranges of the two in Florida are widely separated at present. The white-spotted wall gecko has smoother scales and 4 white spots on the shoulder. House geckos are much smaller and more slender.

## Day Geckos, genus *Phelsuma*

At least two species of this large Madagascan and East African gecko genus have occurred in South Florida for more than ten years. One is a small species and one is large. Besides insects the day geckos feed on sap and pollen. Most are clad in skin of a vivid kelly green with highlights of blue, yellow, and rust. Despite having been present in Florida for more than a decade, there is some evidence that the populations continue to be bolstered by escapees from the pet trade. Were this augmentation to cease, it is not known whether the populations would be self-sustaining or would eventually die out. Although these geckos may be found on buildings, they are more adapted to life among the greenery surrounding the buildings.

Adult, gravid females of the geckos in this genus have an endolymphatic (chalk) sac on each side of the neck. It is thought that the calcareous material contained therein is important to the formation of the egg shells.

## 108. Gold-dust Day Gecko

*Phelsuma laticauda laticauda* (introduced species)

**Abundance/Range:** A native of Madagascar, this small, beautiful, diurnal gecko is rare and locally distributed in South Florida (including Key Largo). It is known from Lee, Collier, Broward, Miami-Dade, and Monroe counties, usually in the proximity of reptile dealerships.
**Habitat:** This gecko may be seen on banana trees, bamboos, palms, and other trees near buildings, and on the buildings themselves.
**Size:** This small day gecko is adult at about 4½ inches in length. The hatchlings are 1½ inches long.
**Identifying features:** The ground color of this gecko is a bright green. A dusting of gold lies over the nape, shoulders, and anterior trunk. Transverse orange bars are present on the top of the head. An orange bridle crosses the bridge of the nose, and the ends extend almost to each eye. Some turquoise shading is often present near each eye. Orange spots and longitudinal bars are present from midback to above the hind legs. Bruises and tears in the delicate skin will show dull green until fully healed. The belly is whitish. Fright or cold temperatures

108. Gold-dust day gecko

will cause the lizard to assume a much darker, less pleasant green. The large, lidless eyes have round pupils. The toes are broadly expanded. This gecko is an agile and persistent climber.

Hatchlings are usually a dull olive green.

**Voice:** Sparring males often voice weak squeaks.

**Similar species:** Green anoles are more slender and lack both the dusting of gold and the orange dorsal spots. The giant day gecko is much larger, lacks the gold dusting on the shoulders, and has better defined, transverse, orange dorsal markings.

### 109. Giant Day Gecko

*Phelsuma madagascariensis grandis* (introduced species)

**Abundance/Range:** This is a tenuously established species. It has been found on several occasions in Lee County, Florida, but colonies are apparently present in Broward and Miami-Dade counties. It is more solidly established on several of the Florida Keys. It is native to Madagascar.

**Habitat:** In Florida this gecko may be seen on the trunks of palms and shade trees, as well as on the walls of buildings.

**Size:** Males may near 12 inches in length but are usually several inches shorter. Females are the smaller sex. Hatchlings are 2½ inches long.

**Identifying features:** This heavy-bodied lizard is somewhat flattened in appearance. Adult giant day geckos are predominantly a bright kelly green both

109a. Giant day gecko, adult

109b. Giant day gecko, hatchling

dorsally and laterally. Transverse-oriented spots or blotches of brilliant orange are often present dorsally. An orange stripe extends on each side of the snout from nostril to eye, and the arms of an anteriorly directed orange V may extend anteriorly from each eye and meet on the top of the snout. Except for the stripes from the nostril to the eye (which are always present), the amount of orange is very variable and may be lacking entirely. Bruises and tears in the skin will show dull green until fully healed. The belly is greenish white. The lizard is darker green when frightened or otherwise stressed. The scales of the back and sides are granular. The large eyes are lidless and have round pupils. Toepads are strongly developed. Hatchlings are usually a dull olive green but soon brighten.

**Voice:** Although capable of making sounds, this gecko is less vocal than many species.

**Similar species:** Knight and Jamaican giant anoles lack orange markings and tend to be compressed somewhat from side to side rather than flattened from top to bottom.

## Wall Geckos, genus *Tarentola*

Only two species of this sizable genus of nocturnal geckos occur in the United States. Both are restricted to southern Florida and it is probable that both were introduced by the pet trade. These are heavy-bodied, strong-jawed, predatory geckos that may occasionally include a smaller gecko among their more normal insect repast. They have broadly dilated toetips and in Florida (a geographic region sorely lacking in the cliff faces and ruins these lizards usually call home) they are associated with walls and piles of building rubble.

## 110. White-spotted Wall Gecko

*Tarentola annularis* (introduced species)

**Abundance/Range:** Unknown. This gecko is found in Broward, Lee, and Miami-Dade counties, Florida.

**Habitat:** Normally a rock-dwelling species, in Florida this noc-turnal species is a "house" gecko. Where present, it is seen on the outside walls of dwellings and warehouses.

**Size:** Males, the larger sex, attain a total length of 6 inches. Hatchlings are about 2 inches long.

**Identifying features:** This is a sandy gray to dark gray gecko. It is easily iden-tified by the 2 pairs of white spots on the shoulders. These spots are poorly

110. White-spotted wall gecko

developed on hatchlings. Large, weakly keeled scales are scattered among the tiny dorsal scales. Belly scales are smoother than dorsal scales. The toepads are very prominent.

**Voice:** Males produce clicking squeaks that serve as advertisement calls. Females are also capable of emitting weak calls.

**Similar species:** None. This is the only gecko in Florida having white shoulder spots.

## 111. Moorish Wall Gecko

*Tarentola mauritanica* (introduced species)

**Abundance/Range:** Unknown. This newly established gecko is found in isolated warehouse areas in Lee, Broward, and Miami-Dade counties, Florida. It is now also known from San Diego, California.

**Habitat:** In the United States, this rock-dweller has become a "house" gecko. It may be seen on the walls of dwellings and warehouses as well as in construction rubble.

**Size:** This heavy-bodied, big-headed gecko attains a total length of about 6 inches. Hatchlings are about 2 inches long.

**Identifying features:** Adults have a variable but never brilliant color. The dorsal color varies from sandy tan to olive gray. Crossbars may be present. The dorsal scales, which are large and roughened, dictate the alternate name of "crocodile gecko." Young specimens have dark transverse bands. Tail scales are spinose, especially along the tail edges. These geckos are paler at night than during the day. Toe pads are prominent.

**Voice:** Males emit clicking squeaks during courtship, during territorial disputes, or when the lizard is restrained.

**Similar species:** Bibron's gecko has rough sandpapery dorsal and lateral scales and a less spinose tail. At present, Bibron's geckos are known only from Manatee County, Florida. The white spotted wall gecko has smoother scales and 4 white spots on the shoulders. House and flat-tailed geckos are slimmer and smaller.

112. Moorish wall gecko

## Neotropical Bent-toed and Dwarf Geckos, subfamily Sphaerodactylinae

### Neotropical Bent-toed Geckos, genus *Gonatodes*

The many species in this genus are native to the Neotropics including the West Indies. A single introduced species may be found on Key West, Florida, where it is now uncommon. It was once also found on the southern tip of the Florida peninsula. This species of gecko lacks toepads, but readily climbs trees and walls.

### 112. Dusky Yellow-headed Gecko

*Gonatodes albogularis fuscus* (introduced species)

**Abundance/Range:** In the United States, the yellow-headed gecko continues to exist only on the southernmost Florida Keys. It is native to the West Indies and Latin America,

**Habitat:** These geckos are most often seen hanging from the underside of low, large-diameter, rough-barked, horizontal limbs.

**Size:** This tiny gecko is adult at only 3¼ inches in total length. Hatchlings are about 1¼ inches long.

**Identifying features:** This diurnal gecko has round pupils. Despite lacking toepads they are agile climbers. Males have a dark ground color overlain with a bluish sheen and a yellow-ochre head. They also have a dark shoulder spot that is sometimes outlined with blue. The male's tail may also be yellowish and if not

112a. Dusky yellow-headed gecko, male

112b. Dusky yellow-headed gecko, female

regenerated will have a white tip. Breeding males are most brightly colored. The females are grayish brown with a vague reticulated pattern and a pronounced lighter collar. Hatchlings are quite like the female but have yellowish bands.

**Voice:** No vocalizations have been noted.

**Similar species:** Other geckos lack a yellow head or a well-defined collar and have expanded toepads.

## Dwarf Geckos, genus *Sphaerodactylus*

This is a large genus of lilliputian, primarily West Indian geckos. One species, the Florida reef gecko, is considered native to Florida. Two additional species have been introduced into that state probably as stowaways in imported commercial shipments. These geckos have expanded toepads but are more often than not found on the ground beneath surface debris. They may ascend the walls of buildings at night to hunt tiny insects at the outer perimeter of halos cast by porch lights.

## 113. Ocellated Gecko

*Sphaerodactylus argus argus* (introduced species)

**Abundance/Range:** This tiny gecko is a native of Jamaica. It has been established on Key West and Stock Island (where it is uncommon) for several decades.

113. Ocellated gecko. Photo by R. W. Van Devender

**Habitat:** This primarily terrestrial gecko hides behind the loosened bark of both standing and fallen trees as well as beneath ground-surface debris including fallen leaves. It may occasionally climb.

**Size:** The ocellated gecko is adult at a total length of 2⅜ inches.

**Identifying features:** This secretive gecko is of rather uniform coloration. It is primarily olive brown; adults usually have a decidedly orange tail that is brightest distally. There is a profuse peppering of tiny light spots on the back and sides. There may be several pairs of light spots on the nape. The body scales are keeled. Toepads are well developed.

**Voice:** None

**Similar species:** The reef gecko has larger keeled dorsal and lateral scales and usually lacks orange on the tail. The Cuban ashy gecko has nonkeeled scales.

## 114. Cuban Ashy Gecko

*Sphaerodactylus elegans elegans* (introduced species)

**Abundance/Range:** This Cuban native is established on the lower Florida Keys.

**Habitat:** This gecko is predominantly crepuscular and nocturnal. It hides behind the loosened bark of both standing and fallen trees as well as beneath ground-surface debris and is also found on the walls of buildings.

**Size:** The Cuban ashy gecko is adult at a total length of 2¾ inches. Males are the larger sex. Hatchlings are just over 1 inch in total length.

**Identifying features:** This smooth-scaled gecko undergoes marked ontogenetic changes. Hatchlings are jade green with dark cross bands and orange tails. These

114a. Cuban ashy gecko, adult

114b. Cuban ashy gecko, juvenile

colors gradually fade until the adult coloration of light spots, dots, and streaks against a dark ground color is assumed. Colors are lightest at night.

**Voice:** None

**Similar species:** The reef gecko has keeled dorsal and lateral scales.

## 115. Florida Reef Gecko

*Sphaerodactylus notatus notatus*

**Abundance/Range:** This tiny gecko is the more common and the more widely distributed of the two dwarf geckos now found in Florida. It may be found in coastal areas on the southern mainland in Palm Beach, Broward, Dade, Monroe, and Collier counties.

**Habitat:** Reef geckos are found beneath leaf litter and trash. They can be abundant amid tidal wrack just above the high tide line and amid construction rubble.

**Size:** This gecko is adult at a total length of about 2 inches. Hatchlings are just over 1 inch in total length.

115. Florida reef gecko

**Identifying features:** This is a dark-colored gecko. Males are flecked with dark brown specks against a slightly lighter ground color. Females are similar but have dark stripes on the head and usually bear a pair of light ocelli in a dark shoulder spot. The brown tail may be tinged with orange. Body scales are large and keeled.

**Voice:** None.

**Similar species:** The very uncommon ocellated gecko occurs on Key West and Stock Island. The ocellated gecko has dorsal scales that are noticeably smaller than the scales on its sides. It usually bears several pairs of light ocelli on the nape, *light* lines on the head, and a decidedly orange tail. The scales of the larger Cuban ashy gecko are not keeled.

## Iguanid Lizards

## Typical Lizards, family Iguanidae

These lizards are distributed not only in the American East and the central states, but also in the west and in Latin America, the West Indies, and Madagascar and on some Pacific Islands as well.

## Casque-headed Lizards, subfamily Corytophaninae

Although no lizards of this Neotropical family are native to the United States, a single species is now established in southern Florida and a second species is occasionally seen there. Both, known as basilisks, are pet trade species. The northern brown basilisk, *Basiliscus vittatus*, of Mexico and northern Central America is the established form. Males have a prominent crest on the back of the head, but lack well-defined vertebral and caudal crests. The status of the very beautiful green basilisk, *B. plumifrons* is uncertain, but it is not thought to be breeding in Florida. The green basilisk, which has cranial, vertebral, and caudal crests, is native to central and southern Central America.

Male basilisks are much larger than the females. The tail of both sexes may be twice to thrice as long as the lizard's head and body length.

Basilisks have fringed rear toes. Buoyed by surface tension and the great surface area of their toes, basilisks are able to run quickly across the surface of quiet water. If they slow down or stop they sink and swim rapidly away.

### Basilisks, Genus *Basiliscus*

The genus contains four species, all of moderate size and all native to the Neotropics. In all cases, the males are the larger sex and variously adorned with head, body, or tail crests, or sometimes with all of these. Two of the four species are common components of the American pet trade, and the other two are occasionally seen. One species, the northern brown basilisk, is now firmly established along many South Florida canals. It is an alert lizard that climbs well and runs rapidly. It flees quickly if approached. Males are especially wary.

This is an oviparous genus.

## 116. Northern Brown Basilisk

*Basiliscus vittatus* (introduced species)

**Abundance:** This lizard is now abundant along many of the canals in several counties of South Florida. It is native from Central Mexico southward to northern Colombia.

**Habitat:** The northern brown basilisk is associated with water. It is most common along canal edges and pond edges.

116a. Northern brown basilisk (photo by Joe Burgess)

116b. Northern brown basilisk, juvenile

**Size:** Adult males are about 2 feet in total length; females are considerably smaller and (except when gravid) more slender. Hatchlings are about 6 inches in total length. Whether adult or juvenile, most of this length is the slender tail.

**Identifying features:** Adult males of the northern brown basilisk are unmistakable. They have long legs. The rear toes are very long and have a foldable flange of scales. Adult males have an olive-brown back and sides, faded flash markings, and a somewhat lighter belly. They have a large crest on the back of the head and a low serrate vertebral crest extends onto the tail. Females, young males, and juveniles tend to be reddish brown and have a light belly and chin. A white dorsolateral stripe begins behind the eye and terminates on the tail base. The head crest and vertebral crests are much reduced. Both sexes may have dark dorsal bars.

**Similar species:** No other lizard now found in the wilds of Florida has the cresting and light dorsolateral lines of the northern brown basilisk.

**Comments:** This alert lizard reacts with speed and agility to any disturbance. Adult males are particularly difficult to approach. This lizard can climb, run, and swim, all with equal facility. When running, either on land or across the surface of water, a bipedal stance is assumed.

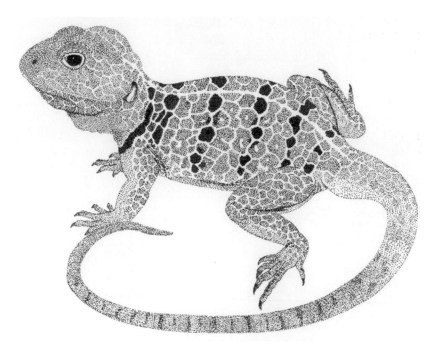

Collared lizard. Illustration by K. P. Wray III.

## Collared and Leopard Lizards, subfamily Crotaphytinae

In their predatory behavior, these beautiful, active lizards are modern-day, dwarfed *Tyrannosaurus rex*. Collared lizards occur in well-drained semiarid to aridland habitats. Leopard lizards are aridland species. Collared lizards typically bask on boulders and leopard lizards on the desert sand. Lizards of both genera are alert and, if startled, able to go from quietly basking to full speed ahead in a fraction of a second. They assume a bipedal position when running. The collared lizards have a broad, enlarged head, a small neck, and a stocky build. During the breeding season adult male collared lizards can be very brightly colored. Females are duller, but develop orange patches on their sides when they are gravid. These fade shortly after egg deposition. The common collared lizard has two black collars on the neck. The collars of the males are more prominent than those of the females. The collars of both sexes of the reticulated collared lizard are comparatively poorly defined.

The leopard lizards are somewhat more slender and have proportionately narrow heads. They are clad in colors of the sand and lack dark collars. They do not assume bright breeding colors. Like the collared lizards, gravid female leopard lizards develop patches of orange on the sides.

Collared and leopard lizards eat both invertebrate and vertebrate prey but both seem to prefer large insects and smaller lizards.

All members of this family are oviparous.

## Collared Lizards, genus *Crotaphytus*

The collared lizards are aptly named. The slender neck is ringed with one or two black collars. Two species occur in our area of coverage. One ranges widely, the other is restricted to southern Texas. The males are the larger sex, although sometimes only marginally so. Additional species and subspecies are found in the American West and in Mexico.

### 117. Eastern Collared Lizard

*Crotaphytus collaris*

**Abundance/Range:** The eastern collared lizard is relatively common in suitable habitats from eastern Missouri to central Texas and southeastern Colorado.

**Habitat:** Look for this lizard conspicuously basking on boulders in rocky hillsides and amid desert boulder fields. It is also found along rock-strewn road cuts, along dry washes, and in other similar habitats.

**Size:** Occasional adult males may exceed 12 inches in total length (the record length is 14 inches), but most are smaller. Adult females are normally smaller than the males. Both sexes are of robust build. Hatchlings are about 3 inches long.

**Identifying features:** Dominant adult males have a dorsal ground color that varies from bluish green (westernmost examples) to grayish green or tan in the east. The dorsum is liberally spangled with tiny light dots. The head, especially near the lips, is usually lighter than the body. The throat is buff to orange. Male collared lizards are brightest during the breeding season. Nondominant males, nonbreeding males, and females are tan to brownish. Gravid females bear vertical, bright orange bars on the sides. Immature specimens of both sexes may also have orange barring on the flanks. Hatchlings are yellowish with crossbars formed of dark spots. The double black collars, present on both sexes, may be interrupted vertebrally. The throat may be orange, white, tan, or green.

**Comments:** Besides eating other lizards (and even tiny snakes), collared lizards opportunistically eat large insects. These lizards bask for long periods of time

117a. Eastern collared lizard, male

117b. Eastern collared lizard, female

on exposed vantage points. When their maximum safe body temperature is attained, collared lizards retire to the shadows or their burrow to cool, then resume basking.

**Similar species:** Some of the larger species of spiny lizards have a *single* collar. They also have keeled, pointed body scales.

## 118. Reticulated Collared Lizard

*Crotaphytus reticulatus*

**Abundance/Range:** This spectacular lizard occurs only in a small area of southern Texas, where it is a protected species, and adjacent Mexico.

**Habitat:** Rocks, dirt clods, road berms, cacti, and desert shrubs are used as vantage and basking sites.

**Size:** The largest measured and authenticated example of this, the largest of the collared lizards, measured 16¾ inches in total length. Hatchlings are about 3¼ inches long.

**Identifying features:** Both sexes of the reticulated collared lizard are quite similarly colored, but adult males are the more boldly patterned.

The ground color is olive brown to olive buff. The color is brightest when the lizard is well warmed. A prominent reticulate pattern of light lines is present when the lizard is warm. Six rows (discounting the collar) of discrete, light-out-

118. Reticulated collared lizard

lined, black spots are incorporated into the reticulum. Adult males often have a brownish orange throat and yellowish on the chest and groin. The collar may be almost entire or it may be broken into spots. Females have only vague indications of the collar. Gravid females often have orange bars between the rows of black dorsal spots and a pinkish orange throat. The orange fades rather quickly after egg deposition. Hatchlings are vividly patterned with orangish cross bands and black dorsal spots against a ground color of olive yellow.

**Similar species:** The eastern collared lizard lacks the prominent black dorsal and lateral spots and has a prominent double black collar. Crevice and blue spiny lizards have a single well-developed collar and spiny scales.

**Comments:** This predatory lizard is wary, fast and difficult to approach. It will bite if carelessly handled.

## Leopard Lizards, genus *Gambelia*

This is a small genus of predominantly southwestern distribution.

A single form occurs sparingly in West Texas. This lizard is associated with shrubby desert habitats where it can see both prey and predators for long distances. Its brownish hues blend well with the sandy habitats in which it is found.

## 119. Long-nosed Leopard Lizard

*Gambelia wislizenii wislizenii*

**Abundance/Range:** In the eastern and central states this lizard occurs only in two disjunct regions of West Texas, where it is not a commonly seen species. Its western range encompasses a vast area of aridlands from northern Nevada and Utah to California and northern Mexico.

**Habitat:** Unlike the related collared lizards, the leopard lizard shuns rocky areas. Rather, it is a lizard of sparsely vegetated, sandy, or gravelly plains. Leopard lizards thermoregulate extensively, retreating when too hot to the shade of creosote bushes or mesquite.

**Size:** This lizard is adult at a total length of 9–12 inches. The record length is 15⅛ inches. It is proportionately more slender of body and narrow of head than the collared lizards. Hatchlings have a total length of about 3½ inches.

**Identifying features:** The leopard lizard's colors blend remarkably with the desert sands of its habitat. The light ground color of the leopard lizard is a sandy tan that may be tinged with olive or gray. The markings are in the form of variably sized rounded spots that are largest dorsally. At cool temperatures the colors

119. Long-nosed leopard lizard

are darkest. Females, somewhat the smaller sex, are similar to the male in color except when gravid. At that time they develop bright orange spots and bars on the sides.

**Similar species:** There are no other lizards in the East with which the leopard lizard could be easily confused.

## Iguanas, subfamily Iguaninae

The true iguanas are found primarily from Mexico southward in the Americas, on Fiji, and in the West Indies. Only the small desert iguana extends its range northward into our southwestern states. However, two species of spiny-tailed iguanas and the green iguana (all important in the pet trade) are now established in southern Florida and the Lower Rio Grande Valley of Texas. All are very cold sensitive and unable to colonize more northerly latitudes.

All are oviparous, producing clutches of 10–50 eggs.

Because the western spiny-tail and the black spiny-tail are of very similar appearance, positive identification can be confusing.

These three iguanas exceed a yard in length, and males of the green iguana may double that size. They are, therefore, the largest lizards now known to occur in the East. Because they can bite, scratch, and slap strongly with their tail, all must be handled carefully.

### Spiny-tailed Iguanas, genus *Ctenosaura*

This is a Neotropical genus of small to large lizards often associated with rocky habitats, but also quite at home in trees. Babies are more arboreal than the adults. Many of the larger species, including the two now found in the eastern and central United States and a third in Tucson, Arizona, are very difficult to differentiate in the field. The spiny-tailed iguanas are now well established in southern Florida, both on the mainland and on some barrier islands, and at least one of the species also occurs in the Brownsville region of southern Texas.

## 120. Western Spiny-tailed Iguana

*Ctenosaura pectinata* (introduced species)

**Abundance/Range:** This lizard is uncommon in the Lower Rio Grande Valley region of Texas, but locally common in Miami-Dade County, Florida. It is native to the Pacific drainages and slopes of southern Mexico.

**Habitat:** In the United States this lizard occurs in disturbed areas that vary from backyards, shopping center parking lots, and public parks in South Miami to the ports and oil refineries of South Texas.

**Size:** Adult males may near or slightly exceed 4 feet; females are about a foot shorter. Hatchlings are about 7 inches long.

**Identifying features:** Hatchlings are grayish but assume a pale green coloration within just a few days. Nonbreeding adults are gray with black saddles. When in breeding color, adult males develop extensive areas of yellow orange on the sides and rump but are tan across the back. The orange may be so bright on

120. Western spiny-tailed iguana

some that they are dubbed "banana iguanas" by observers. After the breeding season is over, the orange fades. Both sexes have a dorsal crest that is more prominent on the males. Banding is evident but best defined dorsally; it fades on the sides. There are *more than* 2 rows of small scales between the whorls of enlarged spiny scales on the anterior of the tail.

**Similar species:** The babies of the black spiny-tailed iguana are bright green and liberally banded with darker pigment. Adults of the black spiny-tailed iguana are heavily banded with black and may become almost entirely black when the breeding season is over. The green iguana never has whorls of spines on its tail.

## 121. Black Spiny-tailed Iguana

*Ctenosaura similis* (introduced species)

**Abundance/Range:** This is the more common of the two spiny-tailed iguanas in Florida. It occurs in Miami-Dade, Charlotte, Lee, and Collier counties, Florida. It is native to southern Mexico and much of Central America.

**Habitat:** This iguana may be found in parks and golf courses on Key Biscayne and Virginia Key, in much of Greater Miami, as well as on barrier islands along Florida's southwestern coast.

**Size:** These are large, robust lizards. At a total length of 4 feet, the males are the larger sex. Adult females are about 3 feet long. Hatchlings are about 7 inches long.

121a. Black spiny-tailed iguana (photo by Joe Burgess)

121b. Black spiny-tailed iguana, hatchling

**Identifying features:** Newly emerged hatchlings are grayish but become bright green within a few days. Soon after they turn green, black barring develops. Adult males in breeding colors have a fair amount of bright orange but retain heavy black barring. After the breeding season is over, the orange fades to gray or charcoal. Females are less intensely colored than males. Both sexes have dorsal crests; that of the male is more prominent. There are usually only 2 rows of small scales between the whorls of large spiny scales on the anterior part of the tail.

**Similar species:** The babies of the western spiny-tailed iguana are pale green and lack most or all of the black barring. Adults of the western spiny-tailed iguana tend to have weak lateral bands and to be predominantly light gray or orange. The great green iguana does not have whorls of spines on its tail.

## Green Iguana, genus *Iguana*

This introduced species is one of the most common of the pet trade lizards. Escapees and released pets have colonized southernmost Florida and the Lower Rio Grande Valley of Texas where they are now seen with regularity. Although often seen on the ground (even on curbs in Greater Miami), green iguanas are agile climbers and spend much time in the trees. The genus has only one additional species, the protected and increasingly rare Antillean green iguana.

## 122. Green Iguana

*Iguana iguana* (introduced species)

**Abundance/Range:** The cold-sensitive green iguana is now established in southern Florida (including the Keys) and in the southern Rio Grande Valley of Texas. Specimens seen elsewhere are merely releasees or escapees that will be killed by the first freeze.

**Habitat:** The green iguana utilizes tree canopy, hides beneath canalside debris, thermoregulates on downtown sidewalks or in urban backyards, swims well, climbs agilely, and runs swiftly. Where present it is a ubiquitous lizard.

**Size:** Adult females may attain 4 feet; adult males are occasionally more than 6 feet in total length, with a strong, whiplike tail making up two-thirds of the length. Hatchlings are slender, long tailed, and 7 inches long.

**Identifying features:** Healthy baby green iguanas are just that—a bright green, either with or without dark bars across the back and sides. Adult coloration is variable and may range from gray green to a rather bright green, again with or without darker barring. Some individuals become suffused with orange during

122a. Green iguana, male

122b. Green iguana, juvenile

the breeding season. A huge dewlap and vertebral crest are present and greatly developed on males. A large rounded scale is present on the jowls. There are no enlarged, spiny scales on the tail.

**Similar species:** The enlarged, circular, jowl scale is diagnostic. Both species of spiny-tailed iguanas have whorls (rows) of spines encircling the tail.

**Comments:** A carelessly held wild iguana will scratch, bite, and tail-slap its captor. Bites and scratches can be severe. Use extreme care when handling an adult green iguana. These lizards often bask high in trees and, if startled, may drop considerable distances, hit the ground or water with a resounding thud, and either run or swim quickly away.

## Horned Lizards, Spiny Lizards, and relatives, subfamily Phrynosomatinae

Representatives of this large family of diverse lizards may be found throughout most of the United States, and from there southward into Central America. The family is particularly well represented in the American West and Mexico. The phrynosomatine lizards differ as much in appearance as they do in habits. Some, like the squat, spiny, horned lizards, are persistently terrestrial, while others, like the slender, agile, tree lizards, are quite arboreal. Many of the spiny lizards (also known as swifts, prairie lizards, and fence lizards) are adapted to either tree bole or rock face habitats. No matter their appearance or microhabitat, many members of this family prey heavily on various ant species.

The lizards of this family have stylized breeding and territorial displays that include head bobs and pushups. None have expanded digital pads, and none are adept at changing color (although most assume a darker color when cold than when hot). The two genera of earless lizards lack external ear openings.

The males of many species have blue, green, or rose ventrolateral and/or throat patches. If these flash-colors are borne by the females, they are smaller and much less brilliant. The horned lizards lack brilliant ventral colors.

Although the females of most phrynosomatines produce one or more clutches of eggs each year, those of some produce instead a single clutch of live young.

### Earless Lizards, genera *Cophosaurus* and *Holbrookia*

These central and western lizards are sand-dwelling speedsters. Both genera lack external tympani (eardrums). All are oviparous, producing one to several clutches of 2–8 eggs annually.

They bask on even the hottest days (if they emerge at all on cloudy days, the lizards are relatively lethargic). Basking lizards often sit, head raised, forelimbs extended, atop sun-heated rocks that are too hot for a human to touch comfortably. When startled they may run only a few feet before coming to rest atop another rock, or they may run a considerable distance. When they are frightened, their colors dull noticeably.

## 123. Texas Greater Earless Lizard

*Cophosaurus texanus texanus*

Texas
Chihuahuan

**Abundance/Range:** This aridland lizard can be quite common in suitable habitats, but may be very wary. However, at some times they may be approached quite closely before darting to another rock. These are one of the many lizards that are best viewed with binoculars. This, the easternmost subspecies of the genus, occurs in a north–south swath several hundred miles wide through central Texas, from mid-panhandle to well into Mexico.

**Habitat:** Look for this earless lizard in boulder fields, rocky flats, rocky washes, jumbled scree at the foot of escarpments, road cuts, and other such rock-strewn habitats.

**Size:** Adult males may attain a full 7 inches in total length. Females are smaller. These are flattened but stocky lizards with a tail slightly longer than the snout–vent length (SVL). Hatchlings are about 2 inches in total length.

**Identifying features:** The scales of this large earless lizard are smoothly granular. There are two skin-folds across the throat. This lizard has a sand tan to pale gray dorsum and sides. Faint darker cross bands or spots may be visible on the back and lighter dots are often present on the anterior sides and dorsum. Males have two prominent vertical black slash marks on each side just posterior to

123. Texas greater earless lizard

midbody. On each side, the coloring between the slash marks may be orange, peach, or yellow. Dorsally the tail bears about 8 darker brown crossbars. The dorsum of the Texas greater earless lizard *does not change in color* posterior to the lateral black slash marks. The belly of this lizard is white (occasionally with an orange or peach blush) anteriorly and along the midline to the tail. Gravid females become suffused with orange or yellow on the sides. Posteriorly males have a field of bright blue on each side containing the bases of the black slash-marks. The undersurface of the original tail is white with 6–8 well-separated jet-black crossbars. The black crossbars are not present on regenerated tails. When the lizard is running the tail may be curved upward, displaying the bars. This lizard stops abruptly after each dash and, were it not for the easily seen black bars on the underside of the upcurved, waving tail, the lizard would be easily lost to sight.

**Similar species:** The smaller and rarer spotted-tailed earless lizard has sub-caudal markings that are spots, not bars, and inhabits areas largely devoid of rocks.

### Additional Subspecies

124. The Chihuahuan Greater Earless Lizard, *Cophosaurus texanus scitulus*, is very similar to, but somewhat more brightly colored than its eastern cousin. It, too, blends remarkably with the color of the boulders over which it scampers.

124. Chihuahuan greater earless lizard

The dorsal coloration can be tan, brown, or gray, even reddish, and *changes rather abruptly* from a darker to a lighter (greenish or yellowish) color at the position of the dark lateral bars. Lighter lateral spots are present, and there may be indications of darker dorsal barring. The venter is white centrally. Gravid females have an orange, peach, yellow, or greenish wash on their sides. Males have a field of bright blue on the sides of the belly. This is crossed by two black bars. Legs and toes are proportionately long. The underside of the tail is prominently barred with black. Vague darker bars are usually present on the dorsal surface of the tail and limbs.

This subspecies ranges westward from West Texas to central Arizona and southward to north central Mexico.

## 125. Northern Spotted-tailed Earless Lizard

*Holbrookia lacerata lacerata*

**Abundance/Range:** This seems to be a locally distributed, seasonally active, and relatively uncommon lizard.
**Habitat:** This earless lizard is restricted to the Edwards Plateau in Texas. Look for it in grasslands, along roadsides, at

northern
southern

the edges of agricultural areas, and on arid flats. Mesquite, prickly pear cacti, and aridland grasses seem to complete the criteria for preferred habitats of this earless lizard.

125a. Northern spotted-tailed earless lizard, male

125b. Northern spotted-tailed earless lizard, female

**Size:** This lizard is adult at 4½–5½ inches, but occasionally attains a total length of 6 inches. It is rather slender and somewhat flattened. The tail is only slightly longer than the SVL. Hatchlings are about 1½ inches in total length.

**Coloration/pattern:** This lizard is darkest when cool or inactive. It is inactive on cloudy days. The dorsal color is tan to brown and about 9 pairs (occasionally broken into 2 rows on each side) of light-rimmed dark dorsolateral blotches run from the back of the head to above the vent. These are separated vertebrally by a light middorsal line. This earless lizard lacks the dark ventrolateral bars and the encircling blue fields that characterize other earless lizards. However, 0–7

126. Southern spotted-tailed earless lizard (photo by Paul Freed)

vague dark bars occur on the sides of the trunk. This species has about 7 small black spots on the underside of the comparatively short tail. When not breeding the sexes are similarly colored. Gravid females assume a yellowish to peach suffusion on the sides. There are usually 13 femoral pores.

### Additional Subspecies

126. The Southern Spotted-tailed Earless Lizard, *Holbrookia lacerata subcaudalis,* is quite similar in appearance to the northern race. The seemingly uncommon lizard ranges south of the Balcones Escarpment throughout most of southern Texas and adjacent northern Mexico. There are usually 4 rows of dorsal markings (2 on each side of the prominent light vertebral line) and 16 femoral pores.

## 127. Great Plains Earless Lizard

*Holbrookia maculata maculata*

**Abundance/Range:** The populations of all three eastern races of this little aridland lizard seem to be diminishing. At present, while it remains common in some areas, it has been extirpated from others. The Great Plains earless lizard ranges northward from the latitude of Winkler County, Texas, to southern South Dakota.

Great Plains
speckled
prairie

127. Great Plains earless lizard

**Habitat:** This lizard inhabits sandy grasslands, dunes, and the verges surrounding agricultural areas.

**Size:** The Great Plains earless lizard is adult at 3¾–5 inches. It is of moderate girth and alert demeanor. The hatchlings measure about 1½ inches in overall length.

**Identifying features:** The ground color of this lizard varies from tan to dark brown. Light dorsolateral stripes and a vertebral stripe are usually very visible. A more poorly defined lateral stripe is usually also present. Dorsolateral and lateral stripes may be orange when a female is gravid. Two rows of dark blotches on each side of the vertebral stripe may be barely or easily visible. A varying amount of faint white speckling is usually present on the back and sides.

Each dorsolateral stripe separates the two rows of dark blotches on each side, and the lateral stripe defines the lowest limit of the dorsal coloration. Two black bars are visible just posterior to the armpit. These may be narrowly edged with blue (male) or tiny and not edged by blue (female). Nonbreeding females are apt to be somewhat paler dorsally than the males. Gravid females become suffused with yellowish, pink, or peach on the sides. The tail is short, being no longer than the SVL.

**Similar species:** Use range for an identification tool. The spotted-tailed earless lizard lacks the well-defined black spots posterior to the forelimb. The black lateral bars of the much larger southwestern earless lizard are nearer the rear legs than the front, and extend far upward onto the sides.

128. Speckled earless lizard

**Additional Subspecies**

128. The Speckled Earless Lizard, *Holbrookia maculata approximans*, a predominantly western subspecies, occurs in our area of coverage only in the Trans-Pecos area of West Texas. From there it ranges northwestward to southeastern Utah, central Arizona, and central Mexico. Males are slightly the larger sex and are often lighter in color and more obscurely patterned than the females. A vertebral stripe is present but the dorsolateral and lateral stripes are vague to absent. Between the nape and the tail base there are 7 (or more) paired dorsal blotches. These are often edged posteriorly with light pigment, but are sometimes quite obscure. There may be obscure lateral blotches alternating with the dorsal blotches. The dorsum is usually peppered with small light spots. Two short black bars, encircled with blue, are present on each side posterior to each forelimb. Although the black bars are present on the female, they are smaller and lack the encircling blue. Although darker and with a stronger pattern, the female becomes suffused with orange or peach color when gravid.

129. The Prairie Earless Lizard, *Holbrookia maculata perspicua*, is rather similar to the northern earless lizard in appearance, but usually lacks any light dorsal or lateral flecking. The dorsal blotches may be well defined or rather obscure. On this race the 2 rows of dark blotches may join, forming a single irregular bar on

129. Prairie earless lizard (photo by R. Wayne Van Devender)

each side of the vertebral stripe. Historically this lizard ranged from south of the Dallas-Fort Worth region of Texas to central Kansas, but it is now considered a declining race over much of its range.

## 130. Northern Keeled Earless Lizard

*Holbrookia propinqua propinqua*

**Abundance/Range:** Although this lizard is seldom seen, in suitable habitat it can be common. It ranges from southern Texas southward into northern coastal Mexico.

**Habitat:** Although it is found well inland, this earless lizard seems most common along the coastline in regions of drifting sands and semistabilized dunes. It forages amid low vegetation.

**Size:** This is a small and rather slender earless lizard. It is adult at 3¾–4¾ inches. The tail length is somewhat greater than the SVL. Hatchlings are about 1½ in total length.

**Identifying features:** The ground color can vary geographically as well as with the body temperature and activity level of the lizard. Cold, inactive lizards, and lizards from inland habitats, are the darkest. The tiny scales are keeled, but it may take a magnifying glass to determine this. There are 2 skin-folds across the throat. An often obscure light vertebral stripe is present. Dorsolateral stripes are better defined and usually visible, at least on males. Rather than a dorsolateral line, the female keeled earless lizard may have a row of porthole-like light spots on her tan sides. Below these she is lighter tan or white. Males usually have

130. Northern keeled earless lizard

variably distinct darker dorsal markings as well as profuse light speckling. A distinct white stripe is usually present on the rear of the thigh. There are no spots beneath the tail. Two black bars are present and not contained in a field of blue on the side of the male, but these are lacking on the female. Prior to the breeding season, females are colored quite like the males. Reproductively active females pale in color and assume a greenish, yellowish, or pale pinkish wash on their sides when gravid.

**Similar species:** The spotted-tailed earless lizards have spots beneath the tail. No subspecies of the lesser earless lizard (the speckled, the northern or the eastern) overlaps ranges with the keeled.

## Horned Lizards, genus *Phrynosoma*

The aridland lizards of the genus *Phrynosoma* are not only very different from the lizards of all other subfamilies, they differ markedly from others in this subfamily as well. Often likened to animated pincushions, even this description is too simplistic. Some are very spiny, others are only moderately so. They are flattened and scurry rather than dash, and some have the disconcerting ability to squirt a few drops of blood from the corner of the eye when frightened. All

Horned lizards

eat at least some ants, and some species are actually ant specialists, feeding on little else. There are three species in the eastern and central United States and an additional eight or so species in our West and in Mexico. In the United States, those species associated with the so-called short-horned group give birth to live babies. The others produce eggs. The horned lizards are terrestrial.

## 131. Texas Horned Lizard

*Phrynosoma cornutum*

**Abundance/Range:** Although it may be uncommon in some areas, in other areas populations of this lizard seem to be increasing. The Texas horned lizard ranges southward from central Kansas to far down Mexico's east coast and westward from north central Louisiana (and adjacent Missouri) to southeastern Arizona. It has also been introduced into two areas of Florida and on some of the islands off the coast of Georgia and South Carolina.

**Habitat:** Look for this lizard in grassland and prairie habitats. It persists in many small cities (such as Alpine, Texas) and may even be increasing in these habitats. It often basks on the edges of paved roads during the early morning or late afternoon. In Florida it is found in urban settings on Eglin Air Force Base and on the innermost dunes along the Atlantic coast in Jacksonville.

131. Texas horned lizard

**Size:** This lizard is 3½–6 inches in length, including the short tail. The record size is 7¼ inches. Hatchlings are about 1¼ inches long.

**Identifying features:** The color of this lizard usually closely matches the substrate on which it is found. The dorsal color may be reddish, tan, or buff, sometimes with olive overtones. The belly is white. A series of 4 pairs of light-edged dark spots run from nape to above the vent. Normally this is a flattened lizard but when frightened it may inflate itself prodigiously. When moving rapidly it folds its ribs backward and then is almost as slender as a spiny lizard. The 2 center horns are noticeably elongated. This species has 2 rows of fringing spine-like scales on each side.

**Similar species:** The round-tailed horned lizard is smaller and less spinose overall, lacks fringe scales, and has all 4 major horns of about equal length. The mountain short-horned lizard has very short horns and only one row of fringe-scales on each side.

**Comments:** Texas horned lizards are often found in the vicinity of the nests of native harvester ants and depend largely on these ants as a food source. This lizard buries itself head first beneath loose sand by employing a side-to-side shuffling motion of its body. It may sit quietly with only its eyes, horns, and nostrils visible, or go entirely beneath the sand.

## 132. Mountain Short-horned Lizard

*Phrynosoma hernandesi hernandesi*

**Abundance/Range:** This little horned lizard often sits quietly when approached, depending on its re-markable camouflage to protect it. It occurs in our area only in West Texas (where it occurs in the Davis and Guadalupe Mountains). From there it ranges westward to south central Colorado and northwestern Arizona.

**Habitat:** In the southernmost portion of its range, the mountain short-horned lizard is associated with open montane grasslands and woodlands.

mountain
eastern

**Size:** This lizard is of moderate adult size. Most examples are 3½–5 inches long. The record length is 6 ⁵/₁₆ inches. Neonates are about 1¼ inches in total length at birth.

**Identifying features:** Like other horned lizards, this pretty lizard is capable of some degree of color change. It is darkest when cold and brightest when at optimum body temperature. The dorsal coloration of this lizard usually closely matches the color of the soil and rocks where it dwells. The dorsal color may be

132. Mountain short-horned lizard

132a. Eastern short-horned lizard

tan to reddish or reddish brown, often with highlights of orange or yellow. It is darkest along a poorly defined vertebral line and just above the orange(ish) area that borders the single fringe of white scales dorsally. Four pairs of dark blotches adorn the dorsum, including blotches on the nape. The tail is banded. The belly is yellow or reddish, often with considerable dark pigment. There is a single row of lateral fringe scales. The horns are very short.

**Similar species:** The round-tailed horned lizard lacks pointed and enlarged lateral fringe scales and has 4 moderately large horns on the back of its head.

These are all of similar size. The Texas horned lizard has the 2 central horns greatly elongated and has 2 rows of lateral fringe scales.

**Comments:** Currently, this species is undergoing extensive taxonomic reassessment. At the moment the subspecies formerly known as the eastern short-horned lizard, *Phrynosoma hernandesi brevirostre* (photo 132a) is in taxonomic limbo. We make mention of it here as it is a very different appearing lizard. This little horned lizard is adult at 2½–3½ inches and not known to exceed 4½ inches in total length. It is brown, buff, tan, or gray dorsally and bears 4 pairs of darker blotches (including the nape blotches). It does not have highlights of brighter colors, has only a single lateral fringe, and has horns so tiny that they are hardly worthy of the name. This lizard enters our coverage area in the western Dakotas and western Nebraska. Its actual range encompasses a vast area from Montana, adjacent western Saskatchewan, and extreme southeastern Alberta southward to northeastern Utah and southeastern Colorado. It is a lizard of shortgrass prairies and sparsely vegetated semiarid habitats.

## 133. Round-tailed Horned Lizard

*Phrynosoma modestum*

**Abundance/Range:** This common horned lizard is often overlooked. We recently saw more than twenty in less than fifteen minutes as they basked in the waning rays of a setting sun on the edges of a paved roadway in the western Big Bend region of Texas. This lizard occurs in suitable habitats over the western half of Texas; from there it ranges westward to southeastern Arizona and far southward into Mexico. An isolated population occurs at the westernmost tip of Oklahoma's panhandle.

**Habitat:** Arid plains and grasslands and open shrubby desert are home to this interesting small horned lizard. It is also commonly seen along the edges of desert roads.

**Size:** This is the smallest of the horned lizards in the United States, being adult at 3–3¾ inches in total length. The record size is a mere 4⅛ inches. The hatchlings are only about an inch in total length.

**Identifying features:** The round-tailed horned lizard occurs in several color phases, and some individuals are capable of considerable color change. The lizards are usually quite dark when cool, lighter when hot. Normal colors are red, dust gray, or almost white. The lizard may or may not bear dark blotches on its back. The 4 largest posterior horns are moderately prominent and are of about the same length. The body lacks a fringe of enlarged lateral scales. The round tail narrows abruptly posterior to the vent.

133. Round-tailed horned lizard

**Similar species:** The Texas horned lizard has the two central horns much longer than all flanking horns and also has a prominent fringe of enlarged scales along each side. The mountain short-horned lizard has very short horns and also has fringing lateral scales.

**Comments:** This strange little lizard has the disconcerting habit of lying tightly against the substrate, body flattened and throwing no shadow. It usually skitters off at the last possible moment. On a desert flat this can be startling to the observer. Because the lizards also use this ploy on dusty desert roads they are frequently run over. Once routed, the lizard makes a short dash, then abruptly stops, again blending perfectly with the dusty substrate.

This horned lizard, may, if prodded, arch its back (like a frightened cat) press its head tightly against the substrate, close its eyes, and assume a rigid catatonic mode. The round-tailed horned lizard preys extensively on the arboreal honey pot ants, apparently catching the ants when they descend from the trees to forage.

### Spiny Lizards, Fence Lizards, and Swifts, genus *Sceloporus*

This is a strongly speciated (and subspeciated) genus of lizards. Unlike the related horned lizards, the spiny lizards are streamlined and very fast. Some are primarily terrestrial, some divide their time between the ground and shrubs,

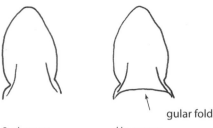

gular fold

*Sceloparus*                *Urosaurus*

some are arboreal, and others are saxicolous (rock dwellers). They range over most of the United States, southward into Central America. Although most species reproduce by eggs, a few give birth to living young. The males of many species have gaudy patches of bright blue (more rarely rose red) along the sides of the belly.

The colors are most intense when the lizards are indulging in territorial or breeding displays. Besides color enhancements, the displays involve head bobbing, flexing and extending the forelimbs in a series of pushups, and other body language understood immediately by other spiny lizards.

The taxonomy of the southern fence lizard group has become problematic. This species contains many subspecies, including six found in the eastern and/or central United States. Among these are forms known as fence lizards (or swifts), prairie lizards, and plateau lizards. Some are quite arboreal, others are more terrestrial. Preferred habitats are here noted for each individual subspecies. It has recently been suggested that many of these entities are full species, not subspecies. We continue to use the subspecies concept here.

## 134. Dunes Sagebrush Lizard

*Sceloporus arenicolous*

**Abundance/Range:** This lizard is fairly common, but of very restricted distribution. It occurs only in the vicinity of the Monahans Sandhills, Texas, and the Mescalero sands in Chavez County, New Mexico. Because of its restricted distribution the dunes sagebrush lizard is protected by state law; it is currently a candidate for federal protection as well.

**Habitat:** This is a specialized lizard that occupies only active and semistabilized dunes. Thick growths of dwarf shin oaks, sagebrush, and grasses are prevalent in these habitats.

**Size:** This 5–6-inch lizard is of moderate girth. The tail is about 125% of the snout–vent length. Hatchlings are about 1¾ inches in total length.

**Identifying features:** Varying from pale tan to pale buff, the dorsal coloration

134. Dunes sagebrush lizard

of this lizard blends remarkably with the sands of its habitat. A broad dorsolateral stripe that is lighter in color than the lizard's back is usually visible on each side. The lower sides are also very light. Males have a blue ventrolateral patch on each side. Each patch is bordered along its inner length by deeper blue or black. The remaining part of the male's belly and the belly of the female is nearly white (sometimes with a yellowish blush). The outer areas of the throat and the lower sides of an ovulating or gravid female are flushed with orange. The scales on the posterior of each thigh are granular and nonspinous. There may be a dark spot anterior to each forelimb.

**Similar species:** Other species of spiny lizard have spiny scales on the thighs. Side-blotched lizards have a dark spot posterior to each forelimb.

## 135. Blue Spiny Lizard

*Sceloporus cyanogenys*

**Abundance/Range:** This lizard may be present in quite considerable numbers but unless it is moving it is easily overlooked. It ranges southward along the Rio Grande from the vicinity of Val Verde and Uvalde counties, Texas, southward to northeastern Mexico.

135. Blue spiny lizard

**Habitat:** The blue spiny lizard is associated with boulder fields, outcrops, and escarpments, but also may be seen on buildings, bridge abutments, and other manmade habitats.

**Size:** This is one of two large rock-dwelling spiny lizards found in the south central states. Average adult size is 6–10 inches. Females tend to be the smaller sex. The record size is 14¼ inches. This is a rather slender-bodied, narrow-headed spiny lizard. The tail is about 150% of the SVL, but is often stubbed. The neonates are about 2¾ inches in total length.

**Identifying features:** The moderately flattened body of this lizard permits access to rather narrow fissures and crevices in the rock faces that it calls home. In color, these lizards are individually variable. At all stages of life, a single, broad, white-edged, black collar is present. The dorsal coloration may be dark gray (assumed when the lizard is cold or has been inactive for some time) or it may be grayish with overtones of blue. It is the adult males, especially during the breeding season and when active, that give credence to both the common and subspecific names. Then the dorsum is overlain with a metallic blue sheen that almost shimmers when the animal is basking in the bright sunlight. Variably distinct, short, dark middorsal bars may be present. Males have large, bright blue ventrolateral patches bordered midventrally with darker pigment, and a blue throat.

**Similar species:** Use range and habitat as identification tools. The lizard that most resembles the blue spiny lizard is the crevice spiny lizard, also a rock dweller. Except at the northwesternmost corner of the blue spiny lizard's range, the two do not come in contact. The crevice spiny lizard is brownish and its tail strongly barred all the way to the tip. The twin-spotted spiny lizard has a black wedge on each shoulder rather than a complete collar. The Texas spiny lizard has neither collar nor wedges and generally is found in trees. None of the smaller species of spiny lizards have a black collar.

**Comments:** We have watched adults of this agile lizard leap and catch grasshoppers in midflight. We have not noticed this behavior with any other spiny lizard.

## 136. Northern Sagebrush Lizard

*Sceloporus graciosus graciosus*

**Abundance/Range:** This is a common lizard. Although it is found over much of the western half of the United States, it enters our region of coverage only in western Nebraska and western North Dakota.

**Habitat:** The northern sagebrush lizard may be seen on fallen trees, rock faces, canyonlands, and road cuts. It prefers sparsely wooded areas where the sun reaches the lizard's chosen micro-habitats throughout most of the day.

**Size:** This small spiny lizard is adult at about 5 inches in length. It is of moderate girth. The tail makes up about half of the lizard's total length. Hatchlings are about 2 inches in total length.

**Identifying features:** Although the dorsal color is variable, this lizard is often quite dark, especially when cool. The ground color is brown to blackish brown.

136. Northern sagebrush lizard

There are 5 buff-colored stripes. The vertebral stripe is broad and usually a little grayer than the dorsolateral and lateral stripes on each side. The lower sides are dark. Males have a blue ventrolateral patch on each side. Each patch is bordered along its inner edge by deeper blue or black. The remaining part of the male's belly and the belly of the female is grayish white. The face, neck, and occasionally the shoulders of a gravid female are orange. The scales on the posterior of each thigh are granular and nonspinous. There may be a dark spot anterior to each forelimb.

**Similar species:** Other species of spiny lizard have spiny scales on the thighs. Side-blotched lizards have a dark spot posterior to each forelimb.

## 137. Mesquite Lizard

*Sceloporus grammicus microlepidotus*

**Abundance/Range:** The range of this lizard parallels the Rio Grande and the Gulf Coast in southern Texas. From there it ranges far southward into Mexico. In its limited range in the United States it is local, wary, and seldom seen.

**Habitat:** This lizard could not be more appropriately named. It is largely restricted to larger mesquite trees, but may occasionally be seen on oaks and other trees as well.

137. Mesquite lizard

**Size:** This spiny lizard is of moderate size. Most are adult at 4½–6 inches in total length. The record size is 6⅞ inches. The tail is about 125% of the SVL. Neonate size is about 1¾ inches.

**Identifying features:** Like most others in the genus, this spiny lizard is dark when cold or inactive but quite light in color when warm and foraging. The body scales are strongly keeled but not particularly spinose. If held the lizard feels more sandpapery than spiny. There is a patch of small scales on each side of the neck. The scales of the tail are larger and more spinose than those of the body. The dorsum is gray to olive gray with 5–7 darker, often obscure, wavy bars across the back. These are better defined on females than on males. The sides are colored similarly to the back and may bear a vague lighter pattern. A thin vertical dark line is usually apparent on each shoulder. The ventrolateral markings of the male are blue outlined with black on the inner edges. The female lacks the blue ventral patches.

**Similar species:** The rose-bellied lizard and the southern prairie lizard are far less arboreal and both have prominent dorsolateral stripes. The arboreal Texas spiny lizard is much larger, brown rather than gray, and very spinose.

**Comments:** The mesquite lizard is the gray ghost of the mesquites. Unlike most arboreal swifts that make skittering sounds as they move about in the trees, the mesquite lizard is virtually silent as it moves. Additionally, the lizards are so wary in most areas of their range that they move to the far side of a branch, or ascend high into their tree nearly as soon as they discern a person coming. They are adept at keeping a branch between themselves and a hopeful observer.

## 138. Twin-spotted Spiny Lizard

*Sceloporus magister bimaculosus*

**Abundance/Range:** This is a common spiny lizard. It ranges northward along the Rio Grande from the Big Bend region of Texas to southeastern Arizona and central New Mexico. It is also found in northern Mexico.

**Habitat:** This is a lizard of the Chihuahuan and Sonoran Deserts. It is common near abandoned homesteads, in mesquite scrublands, on boulder-strewn hillsides grown to scrub and cactus, and in other similar habitats.

**Size:** This is a large and heavy-bodied spiny lizard. The usual size is 8–10 inches, but large males may be 12 or 13 inches in length. Females seldom exceed 10 inches. The tail is about 130% (or more) of the SVL. Hatchlings are about 3 inches in total length.

**Identifying features:** The ground color of this lizard varies from gray through buff to olive brown. The most prominent markings are a pair of large black

138a. Twin-spotted spiny lizard

138b. Twin-spotted spiny lizard, adult male, belly

shoulder wedges. Juvenile lizards have the wedges edged in creamy yellow. There are 4 rows of poorly defined darker spots on the dorsum. All markings are most visible on females and young lizards. Except at breeding time when gravid females become suffused on the lower sides with pale orange or peach, this lizard is of bland coloration with no vivid highlights. Arizona males take on a bluish dorsal blush at breeding time.

**Similar species:** Blue and crevice spiny lizards have prominent full collars. The Texas spiny lizard lacks both the collar or black wedges.

## 139. Merriam's Canyon Lizard

*Sceloporus merriami merriami*

Merriam's
Big Bend
Presidio

**Abundance/Range:** The three subspecies of this small spiny lizard remain common throughout their ranges in the United States. Merriam's canyon lizard is the northernmost of the three races, ranging from Edwards to Jeff Davis counties in the Big Bend region of Texas.

**Habitat:** Seek this lizard at rock-strewn roadcuts, on vertical canyon faces, on abandoned adobe buildings, or in boulder fields. The lizards may occasionally climb into shrubs growing against the rocks the lizards favor. Where boulders and crevices are numerous, the lizards may be abundant.

**Size:** Canyon lizards are among the smallest members of the genus. Merriam's canyon lizard is adult at 4–5¼ inches in length. Occasional examples may reach a total length of 6 inches. The tail is about 150% of the SVL in length. Hatchlings measure about 2 inches in total length.

**Identifying features:** Merriam's canyon lizard is the palest of the three very similar subspecies discussed here. The dorsal spotting and tail banding of this subspecies are often obscure, and in keeping with the rocks of this area of Texas, the body coloration is usually of some shade of gray. The black-edged blue ventrolateral patches of the male do not touch midventrally. There are converging

139. Merriam's canyon lizard

dark stripes on the throat, but these are poorly defined and do not reach the midline of the throat on this race. A vertical shoulder stripe is strongly evident. Although keeled, the dorsal scales are very small and nonspinose. The lateral scales are granular and smooth. The scales on the sides of the neck are noticeably smaller than those at midnape. A *partial* gular fold and black shoulder spots are present. Females and young are paler and lack most ventral markings.

**Similar species:** The range of the rose-bellied lizard does not come in contact with that of the canyon lizard. The rose-bellied lizard has rosy, not blue, belly patches and prominent dorsolateral striping. The various tree and side-blotched lizards have a *full* gular fold.

## Additional Subspecies

140. The Big Bend Canyon Lizard, *Sceloporus merriami annulatus*, usually blends well with the color of rocks over which it animatedly scampers. Gray, olive, tan, and reddish brown are common (but not the only) colors. Four rows of variably distinct dark spots are present on the back. The dorsolateral rows are the most prominent. The male's black-edged blue ventrolateral patches are very brilliant and so large that they may touch medially. On their anterior outermost edges, these blue patches may be weakly suffused with tan or pale pink. Both throat and tail are heavily banded. The throat bands usually (but not always) meet at midline. This subspecies occurs only in the southernmost Big Bend region, western Brewster County, Texas.

140. Big Bend canyon lizard

141. Presidio canyon lizard

141. The Presidio Canyon Lizard, *Sceloporus merriami longipunctatus,* is restricted to rocky habitats in Presidio County and adjacent Mexico. Disjunct populations occur in Chihuahua and Coahuila, Mexico. The dark dorsal markings of this race are usually in the shape of small arches and very evident. Neither throat bands nor ventrolateral patches meet at the midline.

## 142. Texas Spiny Lizard

*Sceloporus olivaceus*

**Abundance/Range:** This common lizard ranges southward from the Red River drainage of northeastern Texas, far into Mexico.
**Habitat:** Seek this big, agile lizard in roadside trees. It also basks on wooden fence poles and occasionally on boulders or building rubble.
**Size:** Most adults of this species measure 8–10 inches in total length. The record size is 11 inches. The tail is fairly long, about 150% of the snout–vent length. Hatchlings are nearly 2½ inches long.
**Identifying features:** This is a long-tailed, large-scaled, very spiny lizard. It is often more easily identified by field marks that are *lacking* than by those it has. Unlike the other three large spiny lizards in the area, the Texas spiny lizard has neither a light-edged black collar nor black shoulder wedges.

Overall, the Texas spiny lizard is brownish with rusty overtones dorsally. It has 6–9 wavy dark bars across the back from between the back of the head to a point above the vent. Broad but poorly defined light dorsolateral lines are present. The sides are nearly the same color as the dorsal ground color, and largely unmarked. The limbs are vaguely barred. Males have narrow blue ventrolateral patches on each side of the belly. These are not bordered on the inside by a

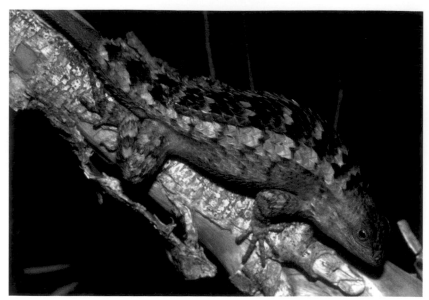

142. Texas spiny lizard

darker color. Females are usually paler than the males. By ruling out the species that have bold identifying marks, you can ease the task of identifying the Texas spiny lizard.

**Similar species:** Both the blue spiny lizard and the crevice spiny lizard have a complete black collar bordered by cream or white. The twin-spotted spiny lizard has black shoulder wedges and lacks a strong dorsal pattern. The northern fence lizard is smaller and has proportionately less strongly keeled scales, the ventrolateral patches of the male are bordered midventrally with black, and the lizard is gray, not brown.

## 143. Crevice Spiny Lizard

*Sceloporus poinsettii poinsettii*

**Abundance/Range:** Although the aptly named crevice spiny lizard is quite common, it is so wary that it usually disappears into a fissure or crevice in the rock long before it is seen by a human observer. This attractive lizard ranges westward to extreme southeastern Arizona from central Texas. It also ranges southward into Mexico.

**Habitat:** Boulder fields, fissured outcroppings, rocky road cuts, and mountain escarpments where exfoliations, fissures, and crevices are plentiful are the preferred habitats of this lizard. Habitats may be nearly devoid of vegetation or

143. Crevice spiny lizard

cloaked with trees and herbs. Crevice spiny lizards occur at altitudes of about 1,000–8,400 feet.

**Size:** Occasional males, the larger sex of this heavy-bodied lizard, may attain 11 inches in length. Most are somewhat smaller. Females seldom exceed 8 inches in length. The original tail is about 135% of the SVL. However, large specimens often have stubbed tails that are proportionately shorter. Neonates of this lizard are about 2¾ inches long.

**Identifying features:** Each dorsal and lateral scale is drawn out into a pronounced spine. The dorsal coloration is olive gray on the sides and a variable brown (often with orange overtones) on the back. The colors usually blend very well with the color of the rock faces that this lizard prefers to colonize. The broad black collar is often bordered both front and back with a poorly defined light (whitish) band. There are several poorly defined but broad dorsal crossbands. The tail is prominently banded along the distal two-thirds. Males have large, bright blue ventrolateral patches bordered on their inner edges with black. The throat is also bright blue. Females have a grayish (sometimes speckled) throat and lack the blue ventral patches (rarely a female may have very pale blue ventrolateral patches but these will lack black borders). Dorsally, neonates are colored like the adults but the banding is more precisely delineated. Some neonates also have a dark vertebral stripe. Neonates lack the blue belly patches.

**Similar species:** Habitat will help identify this lizard. The twin-spotted spiny lizard has a black wedge on each shoulder but no collar. The blue spiny lizard (see account number 134) is variable but often lacks dark dorsal markings and bold banding near the tip of the tail.

## 144. Southern Fence Lizard

*Sceloporus undulatus undulatus*

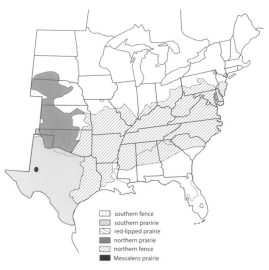

**Abundance/Range:** This is a commonly encountered lizard of moderate size. It ranges northward and westward from central Florida to central South Carolina and eastern Louisiana.

**Habitat:** The southern fence lizard may be found in open pinewoods and pine-oak woodlands and can be particularly common in clearings and on sun-drenched fallen trees. It is often found near dwellings. It also may be found on fences, rails, and uprights and in other similar situations.

southern fence
southern prairie
red-lipped prairie
northern prairie
northern fence
Mescalero prairie

**Size:** Most adult southern fence lizards are in the 5–6½-inch range, but some may actually reach 8 inches. Females are somewhat larger than males. The tail is about 150% of the SVL. Hatchlings are about 1¾ inches in total length.

**Identifying features:** Although spiny, the dorsal and lateral scales are not prominently large. Females are usually of some shade of gray, and adult males

144a. Southern fence lizard, male

144b. Southern fence lizard, female

are brown. The back is patterned with about 7 wavy, rearward-directed chevrons. These are most visible on females and may actually be absent on some older males. The sides are the same color as the back, but largely unpatterned. Males have large bright blue patches on each side of the belly and on the chin. The belly markings are bordered midventrally with black; the chin patch is encircled with black. The light areas of the belly contain black flecks. A dark line is present on the rear of each thigh.

**Comments:** Where it is not accustomed to people, the southern fence lizard is wary and difficult to approach. Those on fences and trees near dwellings become used to human interactions and allow closer approach before fleeing. When frightened this lizard usually ascends a tree, keeping the trunk between it and the frightening object.

**Similar species:** The Florida scrub lizard is smaller and has a prominent, broad, cinnamon to dark brown stripe along each upper side.

### Additional Subspecies

145. The Southern Prairie Lizard, *Sceloporus undulatus consobrinus*, is very different in appearance and habits from its eastern relatives. This is a commonly encountered, primarily terrestrial lizard that ranges westward from Texas to southeastern Arizona and southward well into Mexico. Among other habitats these lizards may be found in open, semidesert scrubland, in grasslands, on rocky hillsides, occasionally on rocky outcrops, or low in aridland shrubs. Typi-

145. Southern prairie lizard

cally, adults measure about 3½–6 inches but may occasionally attain 7 inches. Females are somewhat the larger sex. Although it bears dark dorsal markings the southern prairie lizard is prominently patterned with 5 lengthwise stripes. The vertebral stripe is pale (often light gray) and the dorsolateral and lateral stripes are tan to buff. The dorsal ground color is gray, olive tan to reddish brown. The sides are often somewhat brighter than the back. Males have black-edged blue ventrolateral patches. The remaining part of the venter is grayish. Males may also have a small black-bordered blue patch on each side of the throat (these may be lacking, rarely, or so enlarged that they fuse across the middle of the throat). Females usually lack the blue ventrolateral and throat markings, or if present the blue is very pale and lacks black borders. Gravid females may have orange on the sides of the jaw and develop more brilliant dorsal and lateral colors and an orange wash on the base of the tail. Both sexes have a dark stripe along the rear of the thigh.

146. It is the males of the Red-lipped Prairie Lizard, *Sceloporus undulatus erythrocheilus*, that bear the namesake red lips (which are actually orange or rich rusty brown), but the color is well defined only during the breeding season. The blue belly patches are large and often touch midventrally. At other times the lizards are attractive, but not more colorful than other races of the prairie lizard. This large prairie lizard (to 7½ inches) of boulder fields and cliff faces ranges widely in the West, but occurs in our area of coverage only in extreme western Oklahoma.

147. The Northern Prairie Lizard, *Sceloporus undulatus garmani*, is another of the primarily terrestrial, striped forms. This subspecies may be found from northern Texas to southern South Dakota. At its maximum size it is somewhat smaller than its southern counterpart (topping out at about 5¾ inches).

146. Red-lipped prairie lizard

This is the most strongly marked of the eastern subspecies. Both males and females usually lack the blue throat color. The northern prairie lizard has 5 well-developed lengthwise stripes. The vertebral stripe is pale light gray and the dorsolateral and lateral stripes are tan to buff. The dorsal ground color is gray, olive tan to reddish brown. There are 6–9 dark bars between the vertebral stripe and each dorsolateral stripe. The sides are similar in color to the back. Males have black-edged blue ventrolateral patches. The remaining part of the venter is grayish. Females usually lack the blue ventrolateral markings, or if present the

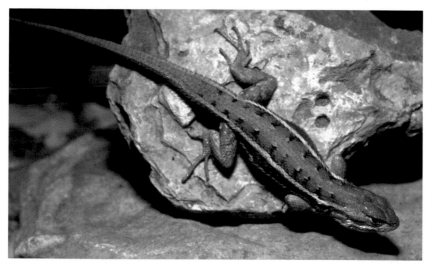

147. Northern prairie lizard

blue is very pale and lacks black borders. Gravid females may have orange on the sides of the jaw and the base of the tail. Both sexes have a dark stripe along the rear of the thigh.

148. The Northern Fence Lizard, *Sceloporus undulatus hyacinthinus*, is found from southern New York to northern South Carolina and westward to eastern Kansas and eastern Texas. It is very much like the southern fence lizard in color but smaller and with less black on the venter. It is primarily an arboreal lizard that is found in pinewoods and open mixed woodlands. These little lizards are commonly seen on both standing and fallen trees in yards and lots, and sunning on wooden fences, rock walls, or derelict buildings. Adults vary from 5 to 6½ inches in total length. Females are slightly the larger sex.

Northern fence lizards are dichromatic—that is, the sexes are colored differently. Females are darker, with a gray to gray-brown dorsum that contains about 8 dark, irregular (but usually chevron-shaped) transverse bars. Females have a dark-flecked white venter that may show indications of blue ventrolateral patches. Males may be grayish, but are usually brown to terra-cotta dorsally and laterally. Males have dark-flecked light chest, pelvic, and midventral areas. The ventrolateral patches are large, bright blue to bluish green, and bordered with black centrally. One or two black-edged blue spots are on the throat. The black edging from the throat spot broadens posteriorly and continues upward onto the shoulder as a black wedge.

Hatchlings are colored like the females.

149. The Mescalero Prairie Lizard, *Sceloporus undulatus tedbrowni*, is a dweller of pale, sparsely vegetated sand dunes and their surroundings. In keeping with its habitat, this lizard is pale tan to the very palest gray. Buffy dorsolateral stripes are usually visible. Males have blue belly patches, but these are paler than the

148. Northern fence lizard

149. Mescalero prairie lizard

patches of other races of this lizard. There is little or no blue on the throat. It ranges in discrete populations southward from Mescalero Dunes, Chavez County, New Mexico, to Monahans Dunes, Ward County, Texas.

## 150. Texas Rose-bellied Lizard

*Sceloporus variabilis marmoratus*

**Abundance/Range:** This species is common but of localized distribution in South Texas. It ranges from Texas southward to northeastern Mexico.

**Habitat:** This pretty lizard is at home amid rocks, building rubble, or low vegetation. It spends much time on the ground but also climbs well. It is not uncommon to see it foraging a foot or two above the ground. Less commonly it may ascend quite high into mesquite trees.

150. Texas rose-bellied lizard

**Size:** Rose-bellied lizards attain 3½–5½ inches in total length. Females are slightly smaller than the males. Hatchlings are 2 inches long.

**Identifying features:** The common name aptly describes the unique belly color of the rose-bellied lizard. The dorsal pattern is complex. The ground color may be pale gray but is more commonly some shade of brown. Light vertebral and dorsolateral stripes are well defined. About 8 dark brown spots run from the nape to above the vent on each side of the back. The sides are often a darker brown than the back. A prominent bluish black spot, an upward extension of the dark edging of the ventrolateral patches, is visible immediately posterior to the axis of each front leg. This reaches onto the shoulder. A smaller dark spot occurs in the groin. Males have extensive pinkish rose ventrolateral patches often edged with blue anteriorly and posteriorly. These almost touch midventrally. A white stripe, edged above and below by black, occurs on the rear of the thigh. The chin, chest, and pelvic areas are white. Females have a white belly. A small, postfemoral skin pocket (situated above the rear of the thigh at the base of the tail) is present.

**Similar species:** The southern prairie lizard, the only other species with prominent dorsolateral stripes in the geographic range of the rose-bellied lizard, lacks the dark shoulder spot.

## 151. Florida Scrub Lizard

*Sceloporus woodi*

**Abundance/Range:** This is a relatively common but very locally distributed small spiny lizard of the central and coastal Florida scrublands. It is probably now found only on Lake Wales Ridge, in Collier County, and along Florida's southeastern coast.

**Habitat:** Oak-palmetto scrublands are the habitat of this aptly named lizard. It climbs well but also spends much time foraging and basking on the ground.

**Size:** This small spiny lizard commonly attains a length of 3½–4½ inches, but may occasionally attain 6¾ inches. Females are somewhat larger than males. Hatchlings are about 1¾ inches long.

**Identifying features:** The dorsal and lateral scales are spiny but quite small. Females and juveniles are gray and males are brown. A broad cinnamon dorsolateral stripe is an excellent field mark. Females and subadults bear about 7 prominent wavy bars on the back. These are often only barely discernable or absent on the brown-backed adult males. Males have a large bright blue patch on each side of the belly and two on the chin. The belly markings are narrowly bordered midventrally with black; the chin patches are encircled with black. Females have some blue on the belly and chin but the blue is not edged with

151. Florida scrub lizard

black. The median chin stripe and the light areas of the chest and belly may be sparsely flecked with black.

**Similar species:** This is the only spiny lizard throughout most of its range. The broad cinnamon dorsolateral stripe is diagnostic of the scrub lizard and lacking on the southern fence lizard.

### Tree Lizards, genus *Urosaurus*

The dorsal scales of the lizards in this genus are rough, but not strongly keeled. A fold of skin is present on the throat. These are small, slender lizards that frequent the trunks of trees and cliff faces. They usually allow rather close approach before scurrying to safety. This is an oviparous genus. Large healthy females often multiclutch, laying 1–3 (rarely to 6) clutches annually, each containing 2–16 eggs. The half-dozen or so species in this genus range from Texas and Utah to southern Mexico.

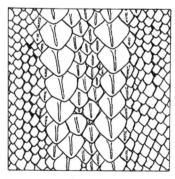

Texas tree lizard

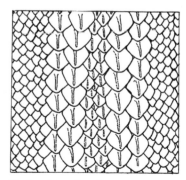

Big Bend tree lizard

Urosaurus skin. Illustration by K. P. Wray III.

## 152. Texas Tree Lizard

*Urosaurus ornatus ornatus*

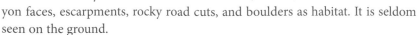

**Abundance/Range:** This is an abundant but easily overlooked lizard. This subspecies is restricted in distribution to central and southern Texas and immediately adjacent Mexico.

Texas
Big Bend

**Habitat:** This tiny flattened lizard utilizes trees, shrubs, canyon faces, escarpments, rocky road cuts, and boulders as habitat. It is seldom seen on the ground.

**Size:** This lizard attains a maximum length of about 5¼ inches. The tail is about 160% of the SVL. Hatchlings are about 1½ inches long.

**Identifying features:** On the dorsal side this alert lizard is clad in the hues of the rocks and bark on which it lives. However, the ventral coloration can be remarkably brilliant.

The dorsal ground color can be gray to brown. The back is marked with 2 rows of about 6 darker spots or bars on each side between the nape and a point above the vent. Highlights of rust or blue may be present. Females have a grayish belly and (usually) a yellow throat. On the gray belly of the male are two large turquoise ventrolateral markings. The throat is yellowish, often with a turquoise central area. A prominent gular fold exists and a fold of loose skin is apparent along each side. The tail is prominently barred, the limbs more obscurely so.

The tree lizards are identified to subspecies by the comparative size of the rows of dorsal scales. On both Texas races, the scales of midback are small and

152. Texas tree lizard

may be keeled or nonkeeled. Lateral to these small scales, on the trunk (and continuing on to the tail) are several rows of large keeled scales. On this subspecies the enlarged scales in the inner row are about twice the size of those in the outermost row.

**Similar species:** The heavier-bodied canyon lizard, a species with which tree lizards share their rocky homes, has only a partial gular fold.

**Comments:** Subspecies are very difficult to differentiate. It will be necessary to have this lizard in hand to determine the comparative sizes of the longitudinal rows of dorsal scales, the differentiating feature.

### Additional Subspecies

153. The Big Bend Tree Lizard, *Urosaurus ornatus schmidti*, may be found in the Big Bend and Trans-Pecos regions of Texas and immediately adjacent New Mexico and Mexico.

The Big Bend tree lizard is very similar to the eastern tree lizard in appearance. However, the scales of the inner row of large scales are less than twice as large as the smaller outermost rows.

153. Big Bend tree lizard

### Side-blotched Lizards, genus *Uta*

Primarily terrestrial, the little side-blotched lizard is one of the most abundant of aridland species. It is often seen sitting atop small rocks, watching alertly for prey or predators. The dark spot behind and not touching the apex of the forelimb is diagnostic. Except for this species, the genus is of Mexican distribution. *Uta* have smooth dorsal scales.

Several clutches of 1–4 (rarely to 6) eggs are produced annually.

## 154. Eastern Side-blotched Lizard

*Uta stansburiana stejnegeri*

**Abundance/Range:** This very common lizard occurs from western Texas, over much of southern New Mexico, to southeastern Arizona, and far southward into Mexico.

**Habitat:** The side-blotched lizard is a terrestrial and rock-dwelling species. It may be seen basking on even the smallest of natural and manmade prominences, including rocks, construction debris, abutments, and clods of dirt.

**Size:** One of the smallest of the spiny lizard relatives, some side-blotched lizards are sexually mature at less than 4 inches in total length. Rarely, a length of 5½ inches is attained. Males are the larger sex. The tail is about 175% of the SVL. Despite the rather small size of the adults, hatchlings may measure 2¼ inches in total length.

**Identifying features:** The dorsal colors of the little side-blotched lizard blend well with the soils and rocks on which it is found. The ground color may be tan, fawn, olive brown, or almost white. Females have prominent thin, light, dorsolateral lines and rather regularly arranged pale dorsal and lateral spots. Males have pale or nonexistent dorsolateral lines and a dorsum heavily flecked with lighter spots interspersed with sky blue dots. The male's tail may be washed with a blue patina. The sides are the same color as the dorsum. Both sexes have a prominent, light-edged dark spot posterior to the apex of each forelimb. Dor-

154. Eastern side-blotched lizard

sal and lateral scales are small and weakly keeled, giving a sandpapery texture to the lizard. A prominent gular fold is present. Hatchlings have very strongly developed dorsolateral stripes. Males may have a bluish venter and dusky chin with a blue center. Females have a light chin and venter.

**Similar species:** Most spiny lizards have heavily keeled, spiny scales and are larger. None have a complete skin fold across the throat. Tree lizards are more slender, are persistently arboreal, and lack the black spot posterior to the arm.

## Anoles, subfamily Polychrotinae

The state of Florida is the anole epicenter of the United States. (Although usually pronounced *ann-nole* the correct pronunciation is *an-ole-ee*.)

There are now nine species of anoles found in the eastern and central United States (none occur in the American West), including seven restricted to the southernmost one-third of Florida.

Of the anoles, one (possibly two, depending on your perspective) is native, and the remainder are West Indian forms that have become established in Florida. Only the green anole is considered a true native. The second possibly native anole is a subspecies of the little bark anole known as the Florida bark anole. If not truly native, it assuredly arrived on our shores long, long ago.

Male anoles of all species are aggressively territorial, especially during the spring and summer breeding season. Territorial and breeding displays are species specific. These displays include dewlap distension, lateral body flattening, pushups, temporary erection of glandular nape and vertebral crests, and sidles that are intimidating to other anoles. Besides interloping anoles, the lizards often display to all other intruders, including humans.

Dewlap coloration is often species diagnostic for human observers. It is, apparently, even more so for the lizards themselves, for they perceive and respond to ultraviolet reflections from the dewlaps.

Anoles are oviparous. Reproduction is stimulated by the increasing day lengths of spring and terminates in late summer when day lengths have again diminished. After an initial annual breeding, sperm retention results in fertile eggs when the female is stimulated solely by courtship displays. Smaller species may lay only a single egg in a clutch, whereas the larger forms may lay several eggs. Eggs may be laid at two-week or somewhat longer intervals. Many anoles prepare no actual nest, instead nudging their eggs into the protection of a grass clump or bromeliad leaf axil or between fallen leaves with their snout. Incubation period may vary, taking 35–65 days.

Although color-changing ability is well developed in many primarily arboreal anoles (many are erroneously referred to as "chameleons"), it is not at all well developed in others and nearly lacking in many primarily terrestrial species. Those that change color do so in response to temperature and attitude rather than as camouflage. Such changes may range from pale to bright green to brown.

Distended, elongate (teardrop-shaped) toepads are characteristic.

## Anoles, genus *Anolis*

Based on comparative toe length and tailbone structure, it has been suggested that this genus be divided into five genera, *Anolis, Ctenonotus, Dactyloa, Norops*, and *Xiphosaurus*. Since these taxonomic entities are not yet in general usage, we have elected to follow the older and better known taxonomy, retaining the generic designation of *Anolis* for all.

There are about 360 species of anoles. The genus is primarily of Neotropical distribution, including the West Indies.

The males (both sexes of some) of these diurnal lizards have distensible dewlaps that are diagnostic in color and pattern.

Small species eat insects and fruit. Larger species may include smaller lizards in their diet.

GREEN ANOLES

### 155. Northern Green Anole

*Anolis carolinensis carolinensis*

**Abundance/Range:** This remains a common lizard over most of its extensive range. It is reduced in numbers in South Florida. This lizard ranges from northeastern North Carolina and eastern Tennessee to Florida (including the Keys) and central Texas.

**Habitat:** This anole is persistently arboreal. It is seen in shade trees and shrubs, on walls and fences, and can be abundant in tall native grasses. It is also common in isolated cypress heads and pine-palmetto scrublands. It often hangs head down on trunks, wooden fence posts, and other such vantage points.

**Size:** Large males may attain a total length of 8 inches. The tail is nearly twice as long as the SVL. Females are noticeably the smaller sex. Hatchlings measure about 2¼ inches in total length.

155. Northern green anole

**Identifying features:** Green anoles have the ability to undergo dramatic and rapid color changes. Green, gray, brown, and combinations of these are the common colors. Resting and content anoles tend to be of some shade of brown. They are darker when cold, and turn a pasty gray when overly warm. Disturbed or frightened anoles may be patchy brown and green. Males involved in aggression, including territorial displays, are often bright green with a nearly black ear patch. Breeding males are often green but lack a significantly darkened ear patch. In some populations, South Florida among them, indications of darker dorsal and dorsolateral streaking may be present. Female green anoles (and some males) have a light vertebral line. Male northern green anoles have a large, decidedly pink dewlap. Females occasionally have a tiny pink dewlap, but more often have none.

**Similar species:** Throughout most of its range, this is the only small color-changing lizard. However, in Dade and Broward counties, Florida, two look-alike species are found. These are the Hispaniolan green and the Cuban green anoles. These can be very difficult to differentiate and both also resemble the northern green anole. The pale-throated green anole can be differentiated by its grayish to white dewlap color.

## Additional Subspecies

156. The Pale-throated Green Anole, *Anolis carolinensis seminolus*, was described in 1991. This subspecies, restricted to southwest Florida, has a gray, white, or greenish dewlap. All else about this form, including appearance and habits, is identical to the northern green anole.

156. Pale-throated green anole

## Green Anole Look-alikes

157. The introduced Hispaniolan Green Anole, *Anolis chlorocyanus*, is now restricted to two small colonies in Broward County, Florida. The species is native to Hispaniola. This very slender anole may attain a total length of 8½ inches but is often smaller. Females are the smaller sex. The tail is a little less than twice as long as the SVL. Hatchlings are about 2¼ inches in total length. This long-nosed anole is very similar to the northern green anole but both sexes have blue dewlaps and whorls of slightly enlarged scales are interspersed between the typical small scales on the tail.

157b. Hispaniolan green anole, female (photo by Joe Burgess)

157a. Hispaniolan green anole, male (photo by Joe Burgess)

158. The introduced Cuban Green Anole, *Anolis porcatus*, is now rather generally distributed in residential neighborhoods in most of Miami-Dade County and possibly northward to southern Broward County. This 8½-inch (females are smaller) anole frequents ornamental trees, fences, yards, and the walls of houses. In southern Florida, where the Cuban and the northern green anoles are sympatric, they can be almost impossible to differentiate. Males, when bright green, usually have some barely visible robin's egg blue striping on the nape between the rows of scales. A dark oval spot is often present on each shoulder. Indefinite darker bars may be visible on the sides. When clad in brown the males often have a series of even darker brown lines laterally and females have a cinnamon vertebral stripe. The dewlap of this species is quite red, its head is

158a. Cuban green anole, male (photo by Joe Burgess)

158b. Cuban green anole, female (photo by Joe Burgess)

bulky, canthal and frontal ridges are prominent, and its nose is proportionately long and very pointed. In some cases, it is necessary to depend on laboratory analysis of DNA to ascertain identification.

GIANT ANOLES

### 159. Western Knight Anole

*Anolis equestris equestris* (introduced species)

**Abundance/Range:** This is a common but not always easily found anole. It is abundant in much of Miami-Dade County, Florida, and being found with increasing frequency in Broward, Collier, Martin, Monroe, Palm Beach, and St. Lucie counties. It may occur in other counties as well. The knight anole is of Cuban origin.

**Habitat:** During the cool nights and short days of late autumn, winter, and early spring, knight anoles are primarily, but not exclusively, canopy denizens. As the weather warms, knight anoles descend more frequently from the canopy and station themselves in a head down position, low on the trunks of palms and other ornamental trees. They are very conspicuous when the very territorial males fan their immense pink dewlaps.

**Size:** This is the largest of all known anoles. Male knight anoles occasionally exceed a total length of 18 inches. The tail is about 150% of the SVL. Females are somewhat smaller. Hatchlings are about 3 inches long.

**Identifying features:** Like many other canopy anoles, the knight anole has the ability to change color dramatically. When warm and unstressed it is usually bright green with yellow flash marks below each eye and on each shoulder. If cold or frightened, the lizards quickly darken their color to chocolate brown or almost black. The flash markings remain visible. Yellow bands may show on the tail, and light (cream to yellow) interstitial (between scales)

159. Western knight anole

skin may be visible. Through muscle contractions, the knight anole can raise a low vertebral crest and a much more prominent nuchal crest. The head is large and bony. Both sexes have dewlaps and indulge in territorial displays.

**Similar species:** No other anole in the United States has as large and bony a head, nor do any attain as great a size as adult knight anoles. The yellow to white flash marks are diagnostic. See also the account for the Jamaican giant anole (account 160).

**Comments:** The knight anole is known in South Florida as "iguana." It will bite painfully if carelessly restrained. When threatened the lizard generally gapes widely, distends its dewlap, and turns its laterally flattened body sideways to the threat. Despite being a cold-sensitive species the knight anole is steadily expanding its range.

## 160. Jamaican Giant Anole

*Anolis garmani* (introduced species)

**Abundance/Range:** This anole now occurs in Fort Myers (Lee County), Naples (Collier County), and Miami (Miami-Dade County), Florida. The Miami-Dade County population seems stable. The long-term status of those in Lee and Collier counties is questionable. Those populations fluctuate noticeably, diminishing tremendously in cold winters.

**Habitat:** During cooler weather the Jamaican giant anole is a canopy species. In summer, it descends to the lower levels and is often seen in a head-down position only 3–5 feet above the ground on the trunks of shade trees.

**Size:** Although males occasionally attain a length of 12½ inches, the females are smaller and less robust. The tail is about twice as long as the snout–vent length. Hatchlings are about 2¾ inches in length.

**Identifying features:** In Florida, this anole is exceeded in size only by the knight anole. Whether unstressed or indulging in territorial displays, Jamaican giant anoles are often bright green. Males may occasionally display vague yellowish banding. When cold they are dark (often chocolate brown) and very wary. A well-defined crest of enlarged scales extends from the back of the head to about a third of the way down the tail. The crest is best defined anteriorly and on males. The dewlap is orange with a yellow border.

160. Jamaican giant anole

**Similar species:** Only the knight anole equals or exceeds the Jamaican giant in size. The knight anole has an angular, bony head and yellow flash markings. Hatchling iguanas have blunter snouts and more prominent cresting.

BROWN ANOLES

## 161. Cuban Brown Anole

*Anolis sagrei sagrei* (introduced species)

**Abundance/Range:** In the last three decades, this lizard has gone from comparative rarity to being one of the best-known lizards in Florida and has now spread to nearby states. It varies from common to abundant over the southern four-fifths of the peninsula but is rarer and more local farther north. It is more common in cities than in rural areas. It is now known from southern Georgia, southern Alabama, the New Orleans region, and the Lower Rio Grande Valley of Texas, as well as some of the larger Texas cities.

**Habitat:** This robust anole is at home in most urban and suburban settings and becoming more common in the surrounding countryside. It prefers tree trunks and terrestrial habitats.

**Size:** Males attain a total length of about 8 inches. Females are adult at about 5 inches and much more slender. Hatchlings are about 2¼ inches long.

**Identifying features:** These anoles are always some shade of brown, never green. Males are usually darker than the females. Males often have bands of light (yellowish) spots and can erect a nuchal, vertebral ridge that extends past the base of the tail. The dewlap is usually bright red orange but occasionally rather pale yellow. The edge of the dewlap is white. When the dewlap is not distended, the white edging is visible as a white stripe on the throat. Female and juvenile brown anoles have a light vertebral stripe edged with dark scallops.

**Similar species:** Of the several brown-colored anoles found in Florida, only this species has a white stripe on the throat when the dewlap is not distended.

**Comments:** These are aggressively territorial anoles that bluff and display throughout spring and summer days. Brown anoles will even distend their dewlaps and indulge in agonistic behavior if a human makes eye contact and bobs his/her head at the lizard. Because of decades of intergradation between the Cuban (*A. s. sagrei*) and the Bahaman subspecies (*A. s. ordinatus*) in Florida, few efforts have been made in recent years to identify this introduced anole to subspecies. However, recent studies align the Florida brown anole more closely with the Cuban race than with the Bahama form.

161. Cuban brown anole

161. Cuban brown anole

## Brown Anole Look-alikes

162. The Puerto Rican Crested Anole, *Anolis cristatellus cristatellus*, has been introduced to Miami-Dade County, Florida, from Puerto Rico. In general appearance it looks like a heavy-bodied, dark brown anole with an olive green to yellow or pale orange dewlap with a darker border. Most males have a wavy crest on the tail. This may be nearly absent or conspicuously high. A vertebral and nape crest can be raised by muscular contraction. Females and juveniles have a dark-bordered light vertebral stripe and lack the tail crest. This species displays from brick walls, brush piles, and cultivated gardens. It climbs well but

162. Puerto Rican crested anole

unless pursued usually remains fairly close to the ground. It often perches, head downward, low on vertical vantage points. Males of this robust anole occasionally attain 7½ inches. The tail is about 150% of the SVL. Females are noticeably smaller. Hatchlings are about 2 inches in length.

163. The introduced Common Large-headed Anole, *Anolis cybotes cybotes*, occurs in Broward and Martin counties, Florida. It has been present in Florida for about 25 years but is not expanding its range quickly. It displays from low on tree trunks, fence posts, building walls, and concrete block fences. When frightened, it is as apt to run downward and seek refuge in ground debris as upward.

The common large-headed anole is noticeably dimorphic. Males may attain 9 inches in length but are often smaller. Females are adult at about 6 inches in length. The tail is more than 200% of SVL. Hatchlings are about 2 inches long. The dorsal color is usually pale gray, gray green, or deep brown, but may occasionally be pale reddish brown. Males have greenish lateral stripes. This anole never assumes a green color. The flanks are lighter. A light (bluish, greenish, or cream) lateral stripe is often present. Adult males have an enlarged head and are proportionately stocky. Females are reddish brown and have a dark-bordered, scalloped, light vertebral stripe, a light lateral stripe, and a light spot on each shoulder. The dewlap is proportionately huge and variably cream to yellow or yellow gray. A pale orange-yellow area may be present in the center of the dewlap. Through muscular contractions, males can erect both a vertebral and a nuchal crest.

163. Common large-headed anole

BARK ANOLE

## 164. Bark Anole

*Anolis distichus* (introduced species)

**Abundance/Range:** This is an abundant anole in Broward, Miami-Dade, and Monroe counties, Florida. It is native to the West Indies.

**Habitat:** Although very arboreal, bark anoles are more often seen on the trunks and low limbs of ornamental trees as well as on vines and herbaceous plantings. They often sleep, with tail tightly coiled, on the upper surface of low, broad-leafed ornamental plants. In south Florida, the bark anole is an urban and suburban lizard.

**Size:** With a total length of only 4½–5 inches, this is the smallest anole now found in Florida. Sexes are about equally sized. Hatchlings are about 1¾ inches in total length.

**Identifying features:** This anole is yellow green to pea green or brown in color. Cold or frightened lizards are

164a. (right) Bark anole

164b. Bark anole (photo by Joe Burgess)

darker than warm or contented ones. Sleeping lizards are lighter than active ones. There are often two small ocelli on the rear of the head, a dark interorbital bar, and a series of dark posteriorly directed chevrons on the back. The limbs and tail are banded, the latter prominently so. The great variation in color is due to interbreeding between two differently colored subspecies (*A. distichus dominicensis*, the green bark anole, and *A. distichus floridanus*, the Florida bark anole) in Florida. The dewlap is yellow to very pale orange.

**Similar species:** No other anole species in Florida has dorsal chevrons and a skittering gait.

**Comments:** Because confusing intergrades between two races of bark anoles are abundant in Florida, most taxonomists no longer attempt to designate subspecies. The Bimini bark anole, *A. d. biminiensis*, was released in Lake Worth in the late 1970s. No information is available on its present status. Bark anoles are often transported across the state in potted plants shipped from South Florida nurseries.

## Curly-tailed Lizards, subfamily Tropidurinae

This is a West Indian and South American lizard family. The three members of this family now in the United States occur only in southern Florida. The northern curly-tailed lizard is firmly established but the others are less frequently seen. In general conformation these lizards look much like robust swifts but they lack femoral pores. Curly-tails may or may not have a fold of skin (a lateral fold) on their sides.

The common name comes from the habit of some species of curling the tip of the tail upward when startled, foraging, or defending territory. When the lizard gets excited (such as when it is stalking an insect), it may wave its tail back and forth.

### Curly-tailed Lizards, genus *Leiocephalus*

This is a large genus of West Indian lizards of moderate size and predominantly terrestrial habits. All species are oviparous. Females are known to double-clutch. A clutch consists of 7–12 eggs. Beside insects, these lizards eat fruits.

### 165. Little Bahama (Northern) Curly-tailed Lizard

*Leiocephalus carinatus armouri* (introduced species)

**Abundance/Range:** This is a common lizard in several counties along Florida's southeast coast. It may be found in Miami-Dade, Broward, Palm Beach, and Martin coun-

165. Little Bahama curly-tailed lizard (photo by Barry Mansell)

ties. A disjunct population occurs near the Brevard County city of Cocoa Beach. This is the most abundant curly-tail in Florida. It is originally from the Bahama Islands.

**Habitat:** This curly-tail can be seen in many kinds of disturbed habitats, including parks, agricultural lands, and canal edges. It is abundant near areas of construction rubble.

**Size:** This lizard ranges 7½–11 inches in total length. Females are usually the smaller sex. Hatchlings are about 3 inches in length.

**Identifying features:** The grays and tans in which this lizard is clad blend well with the sand and limestone boulders among which it lives. Light nape stripes may be present, as may light dorsolateral stripes and a variable amount of light stippling and dark spotting. The tail is rather prominently dark banded; the venter is light. The dorsal scales are strongly keeled, and a low but noticeable vertebral crest is present. Hatchlings are similarly colored but have an orangish throat. This species has no lateral skin fold.

**Similar species:** Swifts (scrub and fence lizards) have prominent femoral pores and lack a vertebral crest.

**Comments:** This curly-tail was introduced into Florida in an attempt to rid sugarcane of insect pests.

## 166. Green-Legged Curly-tailed Lizard

*Leiocephalus personatus scalaris* (introduced species)

**Abundance/Range:** This Hispaniolan species is only tenuously established in Florida. It is known from several areas in Miami-Dade County. It is very cold sensitive and, unless well secluded, perishes during Florida's occasional freezes.

**Habitat:** This very terrestrial lizard may be seen in open land at and near Miami International Airport.

**Size:** This is a moderately robust lizard. Males may attain 8 inches in length, but 6–7 inches is a more normal size. Females are seldom more than 6½ inches in length. Hatchlings are about 2¾ inches long.

**Identifying features:** This is the most brightly colored of the three species of curly-tails in Florida. Males have a brownish back and a greenish venter, green hind limbs, and dark mask. There is a peppering of bright red scales on the otherwise brown upper sides and a red stripe on each lower side. A low dorsal crest is present. Females are less brilliantly colored and tend to retain the juvenile pattern of prominent dorsolateral stripes. Females have a speckled belly. Juveniles are strongly patterned with light (but not red) dorsolateral and lateral stripes. This species has no lateral fold; it does curl its tail but not as readily as the northern curly-tail.

**Similar species:** The red-sided curly-tail is larger, has smoother scales, and has a lateral skin fold.

166. Green-legged curly-tailed lizard

## 167. Red-Sided Curly-tailed Lizard

*Leiocephalus schreibersii schreibersii*

**Abundance/Range:** This robust and pretty lizard is present in small numbers in Charlotte, Broward, and Miami-Dade counties. It is a native of Hispaniola.

**Habitat:** This aridland curly-tail seems to have adapted readily to the climatic conditions of South Florida. It may be found in sandy fields, near the edges of parking lots, and amid construction rubble. It is active even on the hottest of days.

**Size:** Adult males occasionally attain 10 inches in total length. Females top out at about 8½ inches. Hatchlings are about 3 inches long.

**Identifying features:** Males of this curly-tail are more brightly colored than the females. They have a pale brown back and an even paler dorsal keel. Light dorsolateral stripes are also present. Red vertical bars occur on the flanks. Between the bars are patches of pale blue. The belly is white. The dark-banded tail is brown dorsally but often flecked with red ventrally. Females and juveniles are paler and have about 8 dark transverse bars crossing the back. This species curls its tail, but not as frequently or as fully as the northern curly-tail. A prominent lateral fold is present.

**Similar species:** Neither the northern nor the green-legged curly-tails have lateral skin folds.

167. Red-sided curly-tailed lizard

## Typical Old World Lizards, family Lacertidae

This is a large family of Old World lizards of very typical appearance. The largest is the eyed lizard, *Lacerta lepida*, a beautiful species that occasionally exceeds 2 feet in length. The family includes some sand-dwelling species that lack functional eyelids, but there are no cases of truly extreme morphology (such as limblessness) among the many species. The tail can be autotomized and regenerated, but the regrown appendage is quite different in appearance than the original.

In habits and general appearance the lacertids look much like our racerunners and whiptails of the family Teiidae. The lizards of both families are nervous, wary, and quick to react to what they consider adverse stimuli (such as the approach of a human). When foraging, the members of both families move in short spurts of motion, probing with their nose into all manner of nooks and crannies, and scratching insect prey from beneath the sand surface with quick motions of the forelimbs. Fruit and blossoms are also eaten.

The lacertids are sun worshippers, usually not emerging from their lairs until the ground is well warmed. When basking, many species flatten their bodies and angle toward the sun to more quickly warm themselves.

Three species have become established in the eastern United States. Of these, the two wall lizards of the genus *Podarcis* seem firmly established, but the status of the western green lizard (genus *Lacerta*) is more precarious. The populations of these three lizards can be traced to either the deliberate release or the escape of pet specimens.

These three lizards are oviparous. Eggs number 3–20, and more than a single clutch is often produced by a healthy female.

In the city parks and schoolyards of Long Island, New York, in urban neighborhoods and parking lots of Cincinnati, Ohio, and in the sandy fields and open woodlands in Topeka, Kansas, you may find the three established species of this large Old World lizard family. The origin of these lizards in North America was tenuous—an escapee here, a released pet there, but those released somehow found each other, bred, and established viable populations. The two smaller species are attractive. The largest species, the western green lizard, is truly beautiful, and once seen will not soon be forgotten. All three thrive in disturbed areas—in crumbling stonewalls, in construction rubble, and in other such human-generated habitats.

## Old World Whiptails, genus *Lacerta*

This genus of Old World lizards contains the ecological counterparts of the New World racerunners and whiptails. A single species, a European green lizard long identified as *Lacerta viridis* but now found to actually be *L. bilineata*, has been present in the area of Topeka, Kansas, for about forty years. This population is the result of escapees from a reptile dealer once located there. This is a diurnally active lizard. The lizards of this genus have the ventral plates in 6, or rarely 8, rows. They are wary, fast, and agile.

## 168. Western Green Lizard

*Lacerta bilineata* (introduced species)

**Abundance/Range:** Unknown. This beautiful (Mediterranean) European lizard has been known to exist in the vicinity of Topeka, Kansas, for more than thirty years. It appears to undergo population fluctuations, being relatively easy to find some years and almost impossible to find at other times.

**Habitat:** Rubble-filled lots, parking lot edges, fence rows, open woodlands, stone walls, and similar habitats are utilized.

**Size:** Males attain a length of about 15 inches (most are several inches smaller); females are seldom longer than 10–12 inches. Hatchlings are about 3½ inches in length.

168. Western green lizard

**Identifying features:** There is no mistaking the adult males and most of the adult females of this lizard. Although there may be some dark stippling or even vestiges of dark dorsolateral stripes, the overall appearance is of a large lizard of an overall emerald green coloration. Some females, especially young ones, and juvenile males may be brown with dark striping. Breeding males have blue on the sides of the head and neck. The large belly scales are rectangular in shape. The legs are well developed. The juveniles are brownish with a green throat and often a variable amount of green on the sides.

**Similar species:** None. Although the overall shape and behavior of the western green lizard could allow it to be easily mistaken for a racerunner, no other lizard in Kansas is an overall green in color. The prairie racerunner is green anteriorly but always has at least 7 prominent stripes.

### Old World Wall Lizards, genus *Podarcis*

These are small, active, Old World lizards. Two species are established and apparently thriving, one near Topeka, Kansas, and Cincinnati, Ohio, and the other in New York City. The Topeka and New York populations are the result of escapees from reptile dealers; the Cincinnati population is the result of a deliberate release. The lizards of this genus have 6 rows of plates on the belly. These lizards often allow rather close approach before darting to safety, but are adept at evading capture.

### 169. Common Wall Lizard

*Podarcis muralis* (introduced species)

**Abundance/Range:** This is an abundant but localized lizard in certain areas of Cincinnati, Ohio, and more recently from across the Ohio River in Covington, Kentucky. It is a native of much of Europe.

**Habitat:** This little lizard is found in urban areas of both cities, and is particularly abundant in areas where construction rubble has accumulated, near old houses, along stone and brick walls, where sidewalks are broken and slightly tipped, and in gardens.

**Size:** One of the smaller lacertids, the common wall lizard is adult at 6–8 inches. Its long tail comprises a little less than two-thirds of the total length. Hatchlings are about 2½ inches long.

**Identifying features:** This is a small, slender lizard that flattens itself noticeably when basking. Both color and pattern are variable, but the back is usually pre-

169. Common wall lizard

dominantly tan to fawn with or without darker markings. The sides are nearly black and bear round to oval gray-blue spots. The sides of the lower jaw and jowls may be grayish blue. Females are usually the more colorful sex. The 6 rows of rectangular belly scales may be white to orange red.

**Similar species:** None. Although this little lizard looks much like a small race-runner, no racerunners occur in Ohio. Also, the rounded lateral spots will identify this species.

## 170. Italian Wall Lizard

*Podarcis sicula* (introduced species)

**Abundance/Range:** This is an abundant but localized lizard in certain areas of Hempstead, Long Island, and Bronx, New York, and Topeka, Kansas. It was once also known from the vicinity of Philadelphia, but if it still occurs in this latter region it is very rare. It is native to Italy and surrounding countries.

**Habitat:** This little lizard is found in somewhat unkempt grassy urban areas, and can be particularly common where construction rubble or other debris has accumulated, near old houses, and along stone and brick walls. At least one population exists on the grounds of the Bronx Zoo. It is also present in schoolyards and churchyards.

**Size:** Although topping out at only about 9½ inches in length, this is actually one of the larger species in the genus. The tail is about 150% of the SVL in length. Hatchlings are about 2½ inches long.

**Identifying features:** In Europe, up to forty subspecies have been described for this species. Those in the United States are often assigned to two subspecies, but since the supposedly differentiating characteristics overlap widely we have de-

170. Italian wall lizard

clined to mention races. This small slender lizard flattens itself noticeably when basking. Both color and pattern are variable, but the back is usually predominantly green, often with darker markings. A series of dark vertebral dashes are usually visible. The sides, limbs, and tail are brown. The upper sides may bear a variable pattern of black and white. A light dorsolateral line is usually present on each side. The sides of the face are brown. Females are usually more strongly patterned than males. The 6 rows of rectangular belly scales are white.

**Similar species:** None in New York or Pennsylvania. In Kansas, this lizard could be mistaken for a small European green lizard or prairie racerunner. However, the Italian wall lizard lacks the well-defined light stripes of the racerunner, and the green back but brown sides differentiate it from the larger green lizard.

## Skinks, family Scincidae

The skinks (twelve species, twenty subspecies) of the eastern and central United States are contained in three genera. Most (nine species) are in the cosmopolitan genus *Eumeces* (for which the generic name of *Plestiodon* has recently been proposed). The remaining three species are each in separate genera, *Neoseps* for the sand skink, *Scincella* for the ground skink, and *Mabuya* for the introduced brown mabuya.

The skinks of eastern North America are, for the most part, quite small. Only two species attain a foot in length and the rest are adult at a length of 3–8 inches.

Some are fairly large, some are truly tiny, but all are clad in scales so polished and shiny that the lizards actually glisten in the sunshine. Most of the skinks are terrestrial. Indeed, several are actually fossorial, burrowing through yielding sand substrates with ease and agility.

We don't have to leave our own yard to see two of the skink species—the big broad-headed and the tiny ground skink. The former basks on sunny days on the back deck and often skitters through open doors and into the house. The latter is present in incalculable numbers darting through the grass in the yard. Although the ground skink does become infused with a golden sheen during the breeding season, it is the broad-heads that provide the best seasonal displays. The babies, slender and black, have brilliant orange stripes and an electric blue tail. The adults, an overall plain brown in color when they first emerge from hibernation, soon show signs of sexual dimorphism. If the male is sexually mature, his head soon begins to broaden and becomes fire orange in color. Few of our native lizards are prettier or more interesting.

But we do have to travel southward for a hundred miles or so to see the nation's most divergent skink. In the few remaining unkempt sandhills of the Lake Wales Ridge, the sand skink dwells just below the surface of the yielding sugar sand. Tiny and silvery, this minuscule skink has such reduced limbs that when it moves quickly the legs are folded against the body. These creatures are masters of their element and literally swim through the yielding sands, their only habitat.

In general, skinks are short legged, shiny, elongate lizards with long tails. Most have some degree of striping (especially when young) on the back and sides. Many species undergo extensive age-related color and pattern changes. The males of many species develop brilliant orange heads or cheeks during the breeding season. All eastern skinks, save one species, are oviparous (egg layers). Female skinks of the genus *Eumeces* usually remain with the egg clutches for the two-month incubation period. All skinks are wary and secretive. Two of our eastern skinks are persistent burrowers in sandy scrubby areas, one is rather arboreal, one is associated with stream edge habitats and is a capable swimmer. Most, however, are habitat generalists.

Skinks often make a very audible rustling when darting away from danger.

The smooth scales make these lizards difficult to grasp. Most will bite if carelessly restrained; the bite of the larger species can be painful. The tail of all species autotomizes readily, providing a ready escape mechanism.

Except for the live-bearing brown mabuya, all skinks of the eastern and central states are oviparous.

## Typical Skinks, genus *Eumeces*

This large genus comprises species of variable appearance found in Asia, North America, the Near East, and North Africa. There is a remarkable convergence of appearance between some Asiatic and North American forms. These are small to large diurnal skinks with shiny scales. The males of many species develop enhanced head colors (often orange) during the breeding season. Because the females remain with their eggs for lengthy periods, many skinks lay only a single clutch each year.

Most species are secretive and terrestrial, but some have arboreal tendencies. A few swim readily.

### 171. Northern Coal Skink

*Eumeces anthracinus anthracinus*

**Abundance/Range:** Although not uncommon, this is a secretive skink that is seldom seen unless a concerted effort is made. Its main range is northeastward from central Kentucky to central New York. Disjunct populations are found in western Kentucky, western North Carolina and adjacent Virginia, and southern Ohio.

northern
southern

**Habitat:** The coal skink favors cool, moist, humid habitats with ample readily available hiding spots. Look for it near springs and at streamside, in the mud chimneys cast by burrowing crayfish, as well as on rocky hillsides or where fallen trees are strewn and moldering. This skink swims readily and well and may seek refuge beneath submerged rocks or in vegetation.

**Size:** Males, marginally the larger sex, may attain 6½–7½ inches in total length. The tail is 180–200% of the SVL. Hatchlings are about 2 inches long.

**Identifying features:** This skink can have either 4 or 5 light lines. The back is tan to olive tan. The dark brown sides are bordered above and below by a well-defined but narrow off-white to yellow(ish) line. The light lines extend from the head to well onto the tail. Counting toward the side from the middle of the back the light dorsolateral stripe is on scale rows 3 and 4. The vertebral stripe, if present, is best defined anteriorly. Light spots may be present on the supralabial scales from beneath the eye to the rear of the mouth. There are no stripes on the top of the head. The head and face of breeding males become suffused with pale orange. The mental scale (the anteriormost chin scale) is not divided.

171. Northern coal skink

Hatchlings of this subspecies are very similar to the adults in color and pattern, differing primarily in having blue on the tail.

**Similar species:** The mole skink (*E. egregius* ssp.) is tiny and proportionately slender, with a pink to red tail. The three species of five-lined skinks (*E. fasciatus, E. inexpectatus,* and *E. laticeps*) have 5 (to 7) lines when young, but the lines dull with age. These three species have divided mental scales.

### Additional Subspecies

172. The southern coal skink, *Eumeces anthracinus pluvialis,* is associated with damp pine woodlands, streamsides, and cool, moist drainages.

This pretty skink can be very difficult to differentiate from the northern subspecies. Use range as an identification tool. The males are most brightly colored when in breeding condition. This subspecies *may* be paler and *may* have poorly defined light stripes, especially when young. The supralabial (upper lip) spotting is usually very distinct. Hatchlings of the southern coal skink are black with light anterior supralabials and prominent white spots on the posterior supral-

172. Southern coal skink

abials. The white spots often continue onto the sides of the neck. The tail is black with a dark blue patina.

The southern coal skink is found in many disjunct areas of the eastern United States. Intergrades with the northern race occur in the southern Appalachians and Blue Ridge. Consult the range map for specifics.

### 173. Florida Keys Mole Skink

*Eumeces egregius egregius*

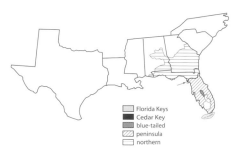

Florida Keys
Cedar Key
blue-tailed
peninsula
northern

**Abundance/Range:** Because of reduced habitats within its limited range, this is an uncommon (and state protected) subspecies of mole skink. It is found only on the Florida Keys, including the Dry Tortugas.

**Habitat:** This, like all races of the mole skink, is found in areas of yielding sands where it can burrow easily and quickly. It often secretes itself beneath surface debris (papers, boards, discarded appliances, fallen leaves, and lichens) and may be most plentiful on the beach side of tidal wrack, near the base of shrubs. These lizards may dig more deeply when the weather is cold, but they thermoregulate very effectively. On cool but clear winter days, when the sand surface is sun warmed, mole skinks may be very near the surface and very agile.

173. Florida Keys mole skink

**Size:** Although this mole skink may attain a length of up to 6 inches, its slender build makes it appear smaller. Males may be slightly larger than females. The tail is about 180% of the SVL. At hatching mole skinks are about 2 inches in total length.

**Identifying features:** Because of color variances and overlapping morphological characteristics, use range as an identification tool. This subspecies usually has 7 supralabial (upper lip) scales. The back and sides are warm brown. The sides may be darker than the back. The tail is dull to bright red. Eight variably discernible light lines are present on the body but often most visible on the tail. When visible the light stripes are of uniform width. A light line is present above each eye and the labial (lip) scales are often of a light color. The tail is heavy and particularly so when moisture and food are abundant. Hind limbs *may* be quite red. Sexually active males usually develop an orange blush ventrally. This may carry over to the sides of the face but fades after the breeding season. The legs are tiny but fully developed and entirely functional. Five toes are present on each foot. The hatchlings are similar to, but usually somewhat paler than, the adults.

**Similar species:** The only other slender skinks found in the range of the mole skinks are the ground skink and the sand skink. The ground skink has a long and slender *brown* tail and a broad, dark dorsolateral stripe on each side. It prefers more heavily wooded and damper habitats than those preferred by the mole skinks. The sand skink is very pale, has a sloping shovel-like snout and degenerate legs, with only one toe on each front foot and two on the hind feet. Hatchlings of the coal skink and all three of the five-lined skinks, *E. inexpectatus, E. fasciatus,* and *E. laticeps,* have a blue tail like that of the blue-tailed mole skink, but have a black body and 4–7 prominent yellow stripes on the dorsum.

**Comments:** These little lizards are both fast and agile. Even where common the mole skinks are so secretive that their presence may go unsuspected. When unearthed these lizards dive back beneath the sand so quickly that one is often left wondering whether one has truly seen a lizard.

Although both tail color and striping may differ somewhat by subspecies, these characteristics can be confusingly variable. Counting the scales around the trunk at midbody and on the upper lip is difficult but may help to confirm a subspecies identification.

Usually 22 or more scale rows at midbody: Keys mole skink, *E. e. egregius*
Usually fewer than 22 scale rows at midbody: All races except the above.
Usually 6 supralabial scales: Northern mole skink, *E. e. similis*
Usually 7 supralabials: All races but the above.

174. Cedar Key mole skinks (photo by Barry Mansell)

## Additional Subspecies

174. The Cedar Key Mole Skink, *Eumeces egregius insularis*, is restricted in distribution to Cedar Key and surrounding keys (including, among others, Seahorse, North, and Atsena Otie Keys) in Florida's Gulf Hammock area. The body stripes are inconspicuous or absent; the tail is orange to orange red, brightest on moderately large adults. Hatchlings of this uncommon race are black.

175. The Blue-tailed Mole Skink, *Eumeces egregius lividus*, is protected by both state and federal regulations. Although most young examples do have the namesake blue tail, the amount of blue is variable. The tail may be almost entirely blue or blue only on the distal half. As they age, the tail color of this skink darkens.

175a. Blue-tailed mole skink

175b. Blue-tailed mole skink

Some old adults may have a reddish or purple tail. The body stripes, when present, are short. The range of this race follows the yielding white sand habitat of Florida's Lake Wales Ridge northward from southern Highlands County to northern Polk County. A single blue-tailed example was found in the Ocala National Forest. This is the largest of the mole skinks, and an occasional large adult may reach 6½ inches in total length.

176. The Peninsula Mole Skink, *Eumeces egregius onocrepis*, is found over most of peninsular Florida. This is an uncommon lizard. The tail of this race may vary from whitish to nearly red, rarely to purplish blue or purplish red. The tail color becomes less brilliantly contrasting with age. The stripes, if present, usually terminate anterior to midbody. This race of mole skink is occasionally found in the sandy mounds of the pocket gopher or in other exposed patches of sand.

176. Peninsula mole skink

177. Northern mole skink

177. The Northern Mole Skink, *Eumeces egregius similis*, occurs in North Florida, including the panhandle, southern and eastern Alabama, and southern Georgia. The body coloration may vary from pale to rich brown; the stripes are variable both in intensity and length. This red-tailed race has only 6 supralabial scales.

### FIVE-LINED SKINKS

Although it may be sufficient for some to know that a particular lizard is one of the three species of five-lined skinks, others will wish to know exactly which one of the three it is.

There are actually some reasonably easy to see identifying marks—if the skink is in hand.

At hatching, all three of these lizards have black bodies with usually 5, but sometimes 7, bright yellow lines. All have electric blue tails. And, as they grow, all three species undergo very similar color changes (see individual accounts).

The males of these species are larger than the females.

The common five-lined skink has the broadest stripes, the southeastern five-lined skink the narrowest.

Here are some other differences:

Subcaudal scale size: The median row of scales beneath the tail (the subcaudals) of the southeastern five-lined skink are not noticeably wider than the other rows of tail scales while those of broad-headed and the five-lined skinks are noticeably wider than the other scale rows.

Ear opening: If only two small scales touch the anterior edge of the ear open-

*Broad-headed*

*Broad-headed*
*and five-lined*

*Southeastern*
*five-lined*

Skink heads and subcaudal scales.
Illustration by Dale Johnson.

*Common five-lined*

ing the skink is a common five-line; if four small scales touch the anterior edge of the ear opening the skink is a broad-head.

Supralabial (upper lip scale) count: Variable, but the common five-lined skink *usually* has 4 supralabials whereas the broad-headed skink *usually* has 5.

## 178. Common Five-lined Skink

*Eumeces fasciatus*

**Abundance/Range:** This abundant skink occurs southward from Michigan and Vermont to eastern Texas and northern Florida.

**Habitat:** The common five-lined skink is essentially terrestrial, but climbs well. It is also very capable of swimming and burrowing. This skink can be quite common at the edges of damp woodlands, in logged areas where decomposing stumps and fallen trunks remain, and amid debris near rural dwellings.

**Size:** Males attain 8½ inches in length but are usually an inch or so shorter. Females are a bit smaller. The tail is about 150% of the SVL. Hatchlings are about 2¼ inches long.

**Identifying features:** Juveniles are black with five broad white to yellow(ish) lines and an electric blue tail. The dorsolateral stripes are usually the brightest. Females fade to brown or olive brown (darkest on the sides) but usually retain well-developed stripes. The vertebral stripe is broad but less brilliant than the lateral stripes. Adult males are like the females but their stripes fade almost to invisibility and they have a somewhat broader head. During the breeding season adult males develop an orangish blush on the jaws.

178a. Common five-lined skink, adult male

178b. Common five-lined skink, juvenile

**Similar species:** Compare the accounts of the southeastern five-lined skink and the broad-headed skink. Coal skinks and southern prairie skinks often have only four light lines. Northern prairie skinks have an overall busier pattern.

## 179. Southeastern Five-lined Skink

*Eumeces inexpectatus*

**Abundance/Range:** This common skink ranges southward in the Atlantic seaboard states from Virginia and southern Maryland through Florida, westward in the Gulf states to eastern Louisiana. It also may be found west of the Appalachians in southern and central Tennessee.

**Habitat:** Expect to see this species in pinewoods, humid hammocks, and at the edges of pastures and fields. This primarily terrestrial lizard basks on the trunks of inclined and fallen trees, cement walls, or piles of rubble. It is commonly seen in dumps and trash piles but may also be encountered in backyards.

**Size:** Males attain a length of 5½–8½ inches. Females are somewhat smaller. The tail is somewhat more than 150% of the SVL. Hatchlings are about 2¼ inches long.

**Identifying features:** The blue-tailed, black hatchlings are vividly patterned with 5 narrow yellow to orange lines. Females fade to olive brown and develop a dark brown lateral stripe that is bordered above and below by a light stripe. The vertebral stripe of adult females is very pale. Adult males are like the females but the 4 side stripes fade almost to invis-

179a. Southeastern five-lined skink, male

179b. Southeastern five-lined skink, juvenile

ibility and vertebral stripe is usually entirely lacking. Males have a somewhat broadened head, often with an orangish blush that is most prominent during the breeding season.

**Similar species:** Compare the accounts of the common five-lined skink and the broad-headed skink. Coal skinks often have only four light lines.

## 180. Broad-headed Skink

*Eumeces laticeps*

**Abundance/Range:** Like the two smaller look-alike species, this large skink is common to abundant in suitable habitat. It is found from eastern Kansas and southern Maryland to eastern Texas and northern Florida.

**Habitat:** This skink is a common resident of yards, city and state parks, as well as of moist deciduous and mixed hammocks and woodlands. It is the most arboreal of our eastern skinks, often scampering up a tree to safety if approached. It is often seen sunning or foraging on high limbs amid the resurrection ferns and poison ivy vines but is also found in terrestrial situations.

**Size:** This is the second largest of our skinks. An occasional male may reach 12½ inches in total length. Females are smaller. Hatchlings of the broad-headed

180. Broad-headed skink, adult male

skink are about 3 inches long and have proportionately longer tails than the adults. The tail of an adult is about 120% of the SVL.

**Identifying features:** The yellow to orange lines of the blue-tailed, black juveniles of this large skink are usually intermediate in width between those of the southeastern five-lined skink and the common five-lined skink. There may be 5 or 7 lines. The striping of both sexes pales with growth, usually disappearing entirely on adult males. Females have a light brown back and may have darker sides. The uniform warm brown coloration of the male is relieved only by some amount of orange on his head. During the spring breeding season the head of the reproductively active male widens toward the rear and becomes an intense fire orange.

**Similar species:** Size alone will identify the adults of this skink. There is no other species in the range of the broad-head that even approaches it in size. Compare the accounts of the common five-lined skink and the southeastern five-lined skink. Coal skinks and southern prairie skinks often have only four light lines. Northern prairie skinks have an overall busier pattern. The Great Plains skink has a light spot in each scale.

OTHER SKINKS

## 181. Northern Many-lined Skink

*Eumeces multivirgatus multivirgatus*

northern many-lined
variable skink

**Abundance/Range:** This skink is not uncommon, but is very secretive and seldom seen. It ranges southward from southwestern Kansas to central Colorado.

**Habitat:** This skink is usually associated with irrigated, riparian, or pond bank habitats in semiarid to arid terrain. Look for it in scrubby deserts with ample rocky cover. It also may be found amid talus, in canyons, and in pine and oak woodland habitats.

**Size:** This is a slender skink of moderate length. When adult it measures 5½–7½ inches in total length. The tail is about 135% of the snout–vent length. Hatchlings are about 2½ inches long.

**Identifying features:** Ontogenetic changes are apparent. The hatchlings have a ground color of dark olive buff with poorly defined stripes. The tail is bright blue. Adults are variably marked with dark stripes and lineate rows of tiny dark spots against a ground color of tan or buff. There are usually 4 well-defined dark stripes. The light vertebral stripe is paralleled by a solid dark stripe on each side.

181. Northern many-lined skink

A light stripe then occurs on the third rows of scales counting outward to each side from the light vertebral stripe. This and the related variable skink (next account) are the only eastern skinks to have a light stripe on the 3rd rows of scales. Rarely, unicolored examples are seen.

Breeding males develop some orange on the lips. All phases have a gray(ish) belly.

**Similar species:** Both the short-lined and the four-lined skinks lack stripes on the tail. The two races of prairie skinks lack lineate rows of dots. Hatchling Great Plains skinks are jet black on the trunk, have a very deep blue-black tail, white or orange labial markings, and lateral scale rows diagonal to the dorsal rows. Adult Great Plains skinks lack solid dark lines and have diagonal lateral scale rows.

### Additional Subspecies

182. The Variable Skink, *Eumeces multivirgatus epipleurotis*, is the southern representative of this species. Both lineate and unicolored examples may occur in the same clutch. As with the many-lined skink, the pattern of the striped form is complex and variable. Whether striped or plain in color, hatchlings are darker than the adults and have bright blue tails.

When striping is present, a light stripe occurs on the third scale row outward from the vertebral stripe. Breeding males develop some orange on the lips. All phases have a gray(ish) belly.

The primary range of the variable skink is west of our area of coverage but it also occurs in several disjunct areas of western Texas. Look for it beneath cover in mountain meadows, lowland, mesquite creosote bush, deserts, and, of course, intermediate areas. It is associated with surface rocks and at least a small amount of moisture.

The lined morphs are more common in moist, high-altitude habitats, while the nonstriped phase dominates dry, low-altitude areas. Currently, the population in the western panhandle of Texas is considered of intergrade status.

182. Variable skink

## 183. Great Plains Skink

*Eumeces obsoletus*

**Abundance/Range:** This, arguably the largest of our skinks, remains common, but is so secretive that it is seldom seen. It occurs in the western two-thirds of Texas, then ranges westward and northward to central Arizona, southern Nebraska, and extreme southwestern Iowa.

**Habitat:** Despite its large size, this skink is adept at hiding. Surface debris, both natural and human generated, is utilized. The Great Plains skink is a common resident of rock-strewn grasslands, scrublands, trash piles, and dumps.

**Size:** With a record size of 13¾ inches, the Great Plains skink is a full 1 inch longer than the next eastern runner-up, the broad-headed skink. The tail of an adult is about 150% of the SVL. Hatchlings are 2¼–2¾ inches in length.

**Identifying features:** Juveniles of this skink are black with a tail of deep blue. The black head is variably marked (most strongly on the labial scales) with orange or white. Adults are tan, yellowish, buff, or olive gray to pale brown with variably wide dark edging on the free edges of each scale. The upper labials are barred with black. The venter is yellow(ish). Breeding males develop a slight widening of the head and a vague suffusion of orange at the angle of the jaws. The dorsal and ventral coloration is usually separated by an irregular stripe of

183a. Great Plains skink, adult

183b. Great Plains skink, juvenile

orange. The lateral scale rows are diagonal. This latter is a characteristic unique to this species.

**Similar species:** None. Size, and the lack of light striping, will identify the adults of this skink. Juveniles of the variable skink are gray rather than black and lack the white to orange facial markings of juvenile Great Plains skinks.

## 184. Northern Prairie Skink

*Eumeces septentrionalis septentrionalis*

**Abundance/Range:** Like most skinks this species can be rather common, but its secretive habits assure that its presence goes all but unknown. It is distributed from northwestern Wisconsin to southeastern Kansas. A disjunct population occurs in southwestern Manitoba.

**Habitat:** The northern prairie skink prefers areas of soft substrate in which it can construct its burrows. If either natural or human-generated surface debris (flat rocks, boards, building rubble, piles of vegetation, etc.) is present, so much the better. Rocky hillsides, sandy stream and pond banks, alluvial fans, or other easily burrowed substrates are especially favored. Fully capable of making its own burrows, this skink may occasionally use the deserted burrows of small mammals.

**Size:** This is a skink of moderate size and build. Males may attain 8½ inches in total length; females are a little shorter. The tail is about 150% of the SVL. Hatchlings are about 2 inches long.

**Identifying features:** This is a busily patterned, striped skink of dry areas. The light dorsolateral stripe may be on either scale row 4 or rows 4 and 5. A dark side stripe two scale rows wide is bordered both above and beneath by a narrow

184. Northern prairie skink

but prominent light stripe. Both dark and light stripes extend far onto the tail. The dorsal area between the uppermost two light dorsolateral lines is a warm brown to an olive brown and contains two narrow dark lines and a narrow light vertebral line. The lower sides are olive gray, the belly is lighter. Juvenile northern prairie skinks look much like the adult but have a darker ground color, more vivid striping, and a bright blue tail. Breeding males develop an orange blush on the sides of the face and on the chin. The postmental scale is divided.

**Similar species:** Both subspecies of the four-lined skink lack stripes on the tail. The southern coal skink has a nondivided postmental scale and the dark field between its dorsolateral and lateral lines is more than 2 scale rows wide. The Great Plains skink appears speckled rather than striped. The many-lined skink has the light dorsolateral stripe restricted to scale row 3. Common five-lined and broad-headed skinks, *E. fasciatus* and *E. laticeps*, are less busily, but more precisely patterned dorsally.

### Additional Subspecies

185. The Southern Prairie Skink, *Eumeces septentrionalis obtusirostris*, is much less busily patterned than its northern counterpart. The olive gray to olive tan back is only weakly striped if patterned at all. The darker lateral stripe, 2 scale rows wide, is delineated above and below by pale yellow lines, the uppermost of which extends from the back of the head to far onto the tail. Occasionally both the dark field *and* the light lines may be largely obscured. The lower sides are gray. The belly is light gray to white. Juvenile southern prairie skinks are patterned much like the adult but have a blue tail and darker ground color. Breeding males develop an orange blush along the lips, chin, and sides of the face. The postmental scale is divided in two.

This subspecies ranges northward from the Gulf Coast of eastern Texas to eastern Oklahoma and extreme south central Kansas. Look for it beneath sur-

185. Southern prairie skink

face objects on grassy prairies, amid mesquite scrub, and in open woodlands. It is most abundant in habitats where moisture is available. It seems to have become uncommon in some areas where it was once plentiful, such as in the vicinity of the sprawling Dallas–Fort Worth metroplex.

## 186. Four-lined Skink

*Eumeces tetragrammus tetragrammus*

**Abundance:** Because it is very secretive, this abundant skink is seldom seen. It occurs in the Lower Rio Grande Valley of Texas as well as northern Mexico.

four-lined
short-lined

**Habitat:** The four-lined skink burrows extensively (and sometimes deeply) during the hottest weather and is adept at remaining beneath surface cover even when surface active. It is often common in piles of trash or building rubble.

**Size:** While most specimens are 5–6 inches in total length, the record size is 7⅞ inches. The tail of an adult is about 120% of the SVL. Hatchlings are close to 2 inches long.

**Identifying features:** The ground color of the adults is a warm but rich brown or more rarely an olive brown. The dorsolateral and lateral stripes, and the dark field between them, reach almost to the groin. A pale Y with irregular arms is present on the top of the head. Males have pale orange jowls during the breeding season. Hatchlings are black with orange stripes and an electric blue tail.

186. Four-lined skink

**Similar species:** The striped phase of the variable skink has the dorsolateral stripe restricted to the third scale row from the midline of the back. The stripes of the southern prairie skink extend well onto the tail. The stripes of the short-lined skink terminate anterior to midbody.

## Additional Subspecies

187. The Short-lined Skink, *Eumeces tetragrammus brevilineatus*, is a paler rendition of the four-lined skink with much shorter stripes. The back and sides of adults are essentially a warm fawn to olive brown or olive gray. The belly is somewhat paler. Four stripes—2 dorsolateral and 2 lateral—begin anterior to the eye and fade out posterior to the shoulder. Contained between these two stripes on each side is a field of brown that is usually darker than the dorsal color. Juveniles are darker dorsally and have orange lines and a bright blue tail.

This subspecies ranges from central northern Texas southward to northern Mexico. Look for it on well-drained rocky hillsides, near and in trash piles, and in dumps. Brushlands, thorn scrub, the edges of open, pine-oak woodlands, and other such habitats as well as pond edges and riparian corridors are also ideal habitat. This is one of the most secretive of lizards.

187. Short-lined skink

## Mabuyas, genus *Mabuya*

*Mabuya* is a large African, Asian, and Neotropical genus with only a single species found in the United States. This is the Asian *M. multifasciata*, a common pet trade species. Since no reptile dealers are known to have been located near this skink's Miami range, it must be assumed that its presence there is the result of a deliberate release. A secretive skink, the live-bearing brown mabuya is present in its restricted Miami habitat in considerable numbers but very easily overlooked. Evidence of its presence is often nothing more than the sound of rustling leaves as it scuttles to safety when approached.

## 188. Brown Mabuya

*Mabuya multifasciata* (introduced species)

**Abundance/Range:** This lizard is found only in Miami-Dade County, Florida, where it has apparently been established for well over a decade. It is native to much of southeast Asia and Malaysia.

**Habitat:** In Florida, this is a species of mulch piles, ground litter, irrigated plant beds, and other such habitats where seclusion can be readily accessed. It can climb but is primarily terrestrial. This is an often-imported pet trade lizard.

**Size:** This skink commonly attains an overall length of 9–10 inches. An occasional example may attain a foot in length. The tail is about 150% of the SVL. The neonates are about 3½ inches long.

**Identifying features:** This skink has sturdy, well-developed legs and is very active. It is a warm to olive brown dorsally and darker brown on the upper sides. The lower sides and belly are gray. Females are often lighter dorsally than the males and may have olive-gold spangles on the sides of the neck and sides. They may lack the darker sides and have the dorsal coloration wrapping around to the middle of the sides. During the breeding season the dark brown upper sides

188. Brown mabuya

of the male turn a bright orange and his chin and throat become suffused with light orange.

**Similar species:** None in Miami-Dade County, Florida. This is the only large skink that is overall brown above, does not have an orange head during the spring and early summer breeding season, and has broad dark brown stripes on the sides.

## Florida Sand Skink, genus *Neoseps*

It has recently been suggested that this skink is merely a divergent *Eumeces*. This small skink is the North American ecological equivalent of the Old World sandfish. The genus *Neoseps* comprises a single species restricted in distribution to Central Florida. It is a persistent burrower in sandy soils and not often seen unless deliberately sought. Its legs are much reduced in size, and held against the body as the lizard bulldozes its way through the sand. Despite the tiny limbs, this is a fast and agile species that is adept at evading capture. It is a protected species.

## 189. Florida Sand Skink

*Neoseps reynoldsi*

**Abundance/Range:** Although both a federally and state threat-ened species, the sand skink can be locally common in suitable habitat. It is essentially restricted in distribution to the Lake Wales Ridge and the Winter Haven Ridge in central peninsular Florida but is occasionally found on the Mount Dora Ridge as well.

**Habitat:** This very specialized sand swimmer is endemic to white sugar-sand habitats in the low, rolling, sparsely vegetated scrublands. Associated plants consist of lichens, rosemary, turkey oak, saw palmetto, and sand pine. Sand skinks may be found by raking through the surface sand and are most common near the base of plants and beneath leaves, fronds, and trash.

**Size:** This skink is adult at 3½–5 inches in total length. The tail is 90–100% of the SVL. Hatchlings are about 2¼ inches in length.

**Identifying features:** The silvery to buff coloring of this species is shared by no other skink in the United States. Tiny darker dots are present on most scales, imparting a vague lineate pattern that is often most visible laterally. A dark bar (mask) is present. All legs are greatly reduced, but the forelegs are especially so. Each hind foot bears two toes; the forefeet have only one toe each. The eyes are small but functional. The lower eyelid has a transparent window. The snout is wedge shaped and the lower jaw countersunk to prevent the entrance of sand.

189. Florida sand skink

**Similar species:** There is no other skink species in the United States with such reduced limbs or a dark mask.

### Ground Skink, genus *Scincella*

The genus *Scincella* is monotypic, encompassing but a single species that is a tiny and secretive skink of the southeastern United States. The lower eyelid bears a transparent scale (a window) through which the lizard may see even when the eye is closed. This is an amazingly abundant species that occurs not only in remote woodlands and scrublands but in suburban backyards as well. It is alert and darts hurriedly for cover when approached.

## 190. Ground Skink

*Scincella lateralis*

**Abundance/Range:** This is an abundant lizard throughout most of its extensive range. It may be found from the Pine Barrens of New Jersey and eastern Kansas southward to southern Texas and throughout Florida and its Keys (except for the Everglades). It occurs in urban, suburban, and open woodland habitats.

**Habitat:** This secretive little skink may be seen skittering away from approaching lawnmowers in urban yards, darting from the cover of one fallen leaf to another. It occurs in dry upland woodlands as well as along stream and pond

190. Ground skink

edges. The ground skink can swim if necessary. These tiny lizards often hide beneath logs, boards, and other ground litter.

**Size:** This slender lizard may attain 5½ inches in total length. The tail is about 125% of the SVL. Hatchlings are about 1¾ inches in total length.

**Identifying features:** This active little lizard is of an overall dark coloration. The broad, dark brown dorsolateral stripes, which extend from the snout to well on to the tail, separate the light brown dorsum from the grayish tan sides. There is no light striping. The top of the head may be coppery colored, especially on juveniles and breeding males. The tail is not contrastingly colored. The legs are tiny. Each foot bears five toes.

**Similar species:** The four-lined and short-lined skinks have at least vestiges of light lines and, if young, blue tails. The many-lined skink and the patterned phase of the variable skink have many dark dorsal and lateral lines. The nonpatterned phase of the variable skink lacks a brown back. The sand skink is light colored with a reduced number of toes. The various races of the mole skink have a contrasting tail color and (often) light lines.

## Racerunners and Whiptails, family Teiidae

There are currently fourteen described species of racerunners-whiptails in our eastern and central states. None occur in Canada. Three species, the giant whiptail, the rainbow whiptail, and the giant ameiva, are Neotropical species that have become established in South Florida.

All are fast, nervous, smooth-scaled lizards that routinely move in short bursts of speed. Most either construct home burrows, utilize burrows made by other animals, or zip into human-generated surface debris when frightened. To find insect prey the teiids scratch through ground litter and loose sand. Many species also consume some vegetation. The teiids are most active on hot, sunny days from about nine o'clock in the morning to noontime but may forage well into the afternoon. All species in eastern and central North America are essentially terrestrial.

The dorsal and lateral scales of all racerunners and whiptails are small and evenly granular. The ventral scales are large and platelike and arranged in either 8 or 12 parallel rows.

Several species of whiptails are of hybrid origin and are parthenogenetic. Ovulation is stimulated by a pseudocourtship; the unfertilized eggs then develop into clones of their mother.

Whiptails of a given species may vary somewhat in appearance. Males of the bisexual species are usually larger and more brilliant than the females. Many whiptails are *very* difficult to identify to species.

Three terms, not normally seen elsewhere, are used to help identify whiptails. *Field(s)* pertains to the lines or stripes (fields) of dark pigment borne by most. The *postantebrachial scales* are those on the rear of the forearm; their relative size may help with species identification. *Supraorbital semicircles* are small scales in a pattern of semicircles between the large scales (the supraoculars) above the eye and the large head scales.

For some inexplicable reason, the bisexual species of whiptails are usually more wary and difficult to approach than the unisexual types.

The whiptail currently identified as the Laredo whiptail, *Aspidoscelis laredoensis*, a Texas species, is actually a complex of two very similar appearing species of different lineages.

Based on several morphological criteria, all native racerunners and whiptails and the Central American giant whiptail have been moved from the genus *Cnemidophorus* to the genus *Aspidoscelis*. This leaves only the rainbow whiptail in the former genus.

Although the hot, dry aridlands of the central and western states are the stronghold of the whiptails, one species, the six-lined racerunner, occurs in the humid, rainy Southeast. There this pretty lizard inhabits old fields and parking lot edges, and persists even in suburban areas. The racerunner's habitat and speed have earned it the vernacular name of "fieldstreak"—an entirely appropriate appellation.

When we embarked on the mission of photographing the whiptails of the United States (none occur in Canada) we knew we had a daunting task ahead. The lizards are not only fast, but also so wary and nervous that it takes a stroke of luck to succeed with each one. We soon learned that whiptails are more easily approached in national and state parks and on zoo grounds and college campuses where the lizards have become accustomed to the milling throngs of people. Whiptails have also readily accepted roadsides, sidewalks, and curbstones as suitable—indeed, preferred—basking areas. Although such backgrounds were not those we preferred, we were unable to convince the whiptails otherwise.

## Ameivas, genus *Ameiva*

These are Neotropical whip-tailed lizards of moderate to large size. A few species are popular in the pet trade. A single species with two distinctly different color morphs now occurs in South Florida. The Ameivas are terrestrial lizards able to colonize the disturbed habitats that are so abundant in South Florida. The species is often seen around office and warehouse complexes as well as at the grassy perimeters of parking lots, near canal edges, along beachfronts, and in botanical gardens.

This large lizard lays one or two clutches of about 4 eggs each in the early summer. The eggs hatch in somewhat more than two months.

## 191. Giant Ameiva

*Ameiva ameiva* (introduced species)

**Abundance/Range:** This variable Neotropical species is restricted in distribution to Miami-Dade County, Florida, where it is locally common.

**Habitat:** In Florida this lizard prefers disturbed open areas such as fields, parklands, and weedy canal banks. It is also found among the low shrubs at the edges of lawns of suburban office complexes.

**Size:** Adult males of the dark-colored population on Key Biscayne may attain 2 feet in overall length. The populations of green-rumped lizards present on

190a. Giant ameiva, green morph

191b. Giant ameiva, dark morph

mainland Florida seldom exceed 18 inches in total length. Hatchlings of both forms are nearly 5 inches long.

**Identifying features:** The two color phases of this lizard now found in Florida were once considered subspecies.

The dusky phase undergoes extensive age-related color changes. Males are the larger and more colorful sex. Adult females are dusky olive gray anteriorly but usually retain some evidence of striping posteriorly. Adult males are charcoal to bluish gray with rather regular cross rows of pale yellowish or whitish spots that shade to blue on the lower sides and outermost belly plates. Blue to bluish white spots also appear on the limbs.

The dorsal color of the green-rumped phase varies. Some are warm tan anteriorly shading to brilliant green posteriorly whereas others may have almost entirely green backs. In both cases, the sides are darker and liberally peppered with prominent dark-edged white spots. There are brilliant blue spots on edges of the belly.

The hatchlings of both phases are prominently striped with green against a body color of light gray, tan, or brown.

There are 12 rows of large belly scales.

**Similar species:** Only the giant whiptail (account 198) approaches these lizards in size and form. It has a blue or bluish spangled, brownish dorsum.

## Racerunners and Whiptails, genera *Aspidoscelis* and *Cnemidophorus*

These are small to moderate-sized lizards that can be abundant in suitable habitats. They abound in disturbed areas and are most reliably found along the edges of parking lots, dumps, sidewalks, roadways, and road cuts. They are particularly diverse and abundant in our southwest and Mexico and range well southward into South America. In this genus hybridization is well documented, and it has been demonstrated that some forms currently recognized as species have been derived from the long ago interbreeding of two, or even three, parent species. Many of these hybrid species are parthenogenetic. The parthenogenetic species indulge in a pseudocourtship to induce ovulation. All racerunners and whiptails are oviparous. All of these lizards are diurnal, largely inactive during cloudy weather, and able to tolerate comparatively great heat. They are alert, shy, agile, and very fast.

## 192. Gray-checkered Whiptail

*Aspidoscelis dixoni*

**Abundance/Range:** Although not an uncommon species, this whiptail is restricted in distribution to Presidio County in western Texas, and a small area of southwestern New Mexico. It has been suggested that the Texas population is specifically distinct from the New Mexico one.

**Habitat:** This is a whiptail of rocky plains, dry washes, canyon bottoms, and desert scrub (ocotillo, creosote bush, opuntia). It can be quite common where human-generated surface debris creates labyrinths of passageways and readily accessed hiding spots.

**Size:** This is one of the larger whiptails. Large adults may attain 10 inches to 12½ inches in total length. The tail comprises about two-thirds of this length. Hatchlings are about 4¼ inches long.

192. Gray-checkered whiptail

**Identifying features:** The ground color of this lizard blends well with the gray soils of its habitat. The adults have a ground color of gray or grayish tan anteriorly. This may shade to grayish fawn near the hips. The dark lateral markings are vertically oriented. Dark dorsolateral markings are in two (or more) rows on each side of the irregular vertebral line. There are from 6 to 14 poorly defined (but strongest anteriorly) light lines on the back and sides. Both the crown of the head and the tail are largely devoid of markings. The underside of the tail is light. The posterior scales of the gular fold are noticeably enlarged. The supraorbital semicircles extend far forward. The limbs are mottled. There are no significantly enlarged scales on the posterior of the forearm. The light (white to pale blue) belly is sparingly marked with flecks of dark pigment. The chin is usually light in color and unmarked.

The hatchlings bear 6–14 broken light stripes (formed of dots) against a ground color of black or dark brown. These markings often obscure quickly with age.

**Similar species:** The various "spotted" whiptails can be very difficult to differentiate, even when in hand. The marbled whiptail has a dark-spotted peach colored chin; the scales anterior to the gular fold are only moderately enlarged and are narrowly separated from fold by a row or two of tiny scales. The Chihuahuan spotted whiptail has a patch of enlarged scales on the rear of each forelimb and the underside of the tail is dark. The checkered whiptail is virtually identical in appearance to the gray-checkered whiptail, but may have a darker ground color and more contrasting pattern. Depend on range when trying to identify these confusingly similar lizards.

**Comments:** This species was derived from hybridization between the marbled whiptail, *C. marmoratus*, and the plateau spotted whiptail, *C. septemvittatus*. This is a unisexual, all-female (parthenogenetic) whiptail.

## 193. Chihuahuan Spotted Whiptail

*Aspidoscelis exsanguis*

**Abundance/Range:** This whiptail is a habitat generalist of West Texas, southern New Mexico, extreme southeastern Arizona and northern Mexico. It is a common species.

**Habitat:** Expect to see this lizard in sparsely wooded hillsides, rocky plains, grasslands, dry washes, canyon bottoms, and desert scrub. It is a difficult lizard to approach.

**Size:** Large adults range 10–12¼ inches in total length. The tail is greater than 200% of the SVL. Hatchlings are about 4 inches long.

**Identifying features:** This is a dark whiptail with a busy pattern of (usually) 6 lighter stripes overlain with even lighter spots in both the dark fields and the light stripes. The ground color is dark brown to brownish gray. The stripes are pale cream to pale yellow. The paravertebral stripes (those on each side of the midline of the back) are separated by 5–8 scale rows and, because of the placement of the lighter spots, often appear wavy. The lower sides are (often vaguely)

193. Chihuahuan spotted whiptail

patterned with vertical bars. Younger lizards have a darker ground and more contrasting yellows than old adults. The posterior scales of the gular fold and the antebrachial scales are significantly enlarged. The light belly is usually devoid of dark pigment but may have a faint blush of blue. The chin is usually light in color and unmarked. The tail is gray, brown, or greenish.

**Similar species:** The Texas spotted whiptail is confusingly similar, but often has 8 stripes, a reddish (rather than gray or brown) tail, some pink or orange on the throat, and light spots largely restricted to dark fields. The New Mexican whiptail has a more vividly contrasting pattern and 7 rather than 6 light stripes.

**Comments:** This is another of the all female (parthenogenetic) whiptail species. Of hybrid derivation, this whiptail has a complex lineage involving three species. The parental species are the little striped whiptail, *C. inornatus*, probably the giant whiptail, *C. burti*, and the plateau spotted whiptail, *C. septemvittatus*.

## 194. Texas Spotted Whiptail

*Aspidoscelis gularis gularis*

**Abundance/Range:** This is a common to abundant whiptail species that is found through most of Texas, adjacent southern Oklahoma, southeastern New Mexico, and northern Mexico.

**Habitat:** The Texas spotted whiptail is found in gravelly, sandy areas. They are most common where there is a sparse cover of low herbs and shrubs. They are often commonly seen near nature centers, park buildings, and other such habitations. Rocky hillsides, grasslands, rocky washes, and road cuts are also favored habitats.

**Size:** This is a moderately large and fairly robust whiptail. Large males may attain 10½ inches in total length. Females are fully grown at 7½ to 8 ½ inches. The tail is nearly twice as long as the SVL. Hatchlings are about 4 inches in total length.

**Identifying features:** This is a very colorful lizard. It may have either 7 or, if the vertebral stripe is narrowly divided, 8 stripes. The ground color can vary from warm brown to rather dark brown. The stripes may vary from nearly white to yellow to pale green. The 2 lowermost dark side stripes are liberally marked with light spots. During the breeding season males develop a pink to pinkish orange throat. The venter may have a black area surrounded by blue or be entirely blue. There are large scales on the rear of the forearm and along the posterior edge of the gular fold. The tail may be orange brown to reddish. Females are smaller, and have light venters (including chin). Hatchlings have yellow stripes on a black ground, poorly defined lateral spots, and rather bright reddish tails.

194. Texas spotted whiptail

**Similar species:** This is one of the most easily identified of the whiptails. No related lizard, from Texas east, bears the same suite of colors borne by the male Texas spotted whiptail.

**Comments:** This is a bisexual whiptail.

## 195. Trans-Pecos Striped Whiptail

*Aspidoscelis inornatus heptagrammus*

**Abundance/Range:** In the range covered by this guide, this whiptail occurs only in western Texas, where it is a commonly encountered species. It is also found in immediately adjacent New Mexico and south into northern Mexico.

**Habitat:** This little whiptail is common in rocky or gravelly areas. Look for it in desert grasslands, on rocky hillsides, amid low vegetation along dry washes, and in other such areas.

**Size:** This is a small, very long-tailed whiptail. Typically, the body, including head, measures only about 2¼ inches, while the tail is about 6½ inches long. Occasional adult males may attain 9½ inches in total length. At hatching these lizards are about 3½ inches long.

**Identifying features:** The only easily seen splash of bright color on this prominently striped, nonspotted whiptail is its bright blue tail. It normally has 7 cream to yellow stripes against a very dark ground color. Males have a rather bright blue belly and chin and a brighter tail than the females. Females have a pale

195. Trans-Pecos striped whiptail

blue belly and chin. Hatchlings have bright yellow stripes and a pale blue tail. The posterior scales of the gular fold and a patch of scales on the rear of each forelimb are only slightly enlarged.

**Similar species:** The desert grasslands whiptail has a pale bluish green tail. The New Mexico whiptail lacks a bright blue tail; it has spots on the dark stripes and a wavy vertebral stripe. The body of the prairie racerunner is suffused with green.

**Comments:** This is a bisexual species. This whiptail has been shown to be a parent species in at least thirteen of the parthenogenetic hybrid species of whiptails!

## 196. Laredo Striped Whiptail

*Aspidoscelis laredoensis*

**Abundance/Range:** Initially thought to be restricted to the vicinity of Laredo, this species, in its two pattern morphs, actually occurs from near Brownsville, Texas, to the vicinity of Del Rio in the Rio Grande Valley.

**Habitat:** Although for the most part this whiptail prefers open sandy spaces and sparse vegetation, it can adapt to pathside life amid rather dense vegetation. In some portions of the range, both pattern morphs occur.

**Size:** This all female species is adult at 9½–11¼ inches in total length. The tail is about 240% of the SVL. Hatchlings are about 4¾ inches in length.

**Identifying features:** The Laredo whiptail (field identified as LAR-A) is appar-

196a. Laredo striped whiptail, type A

196b. Laredo striped whiptail, type B

ently derived from the breeding of a female Texas spotted whiptail and a male prairie whiptail. The second form (LAR-B) is apparently of a similar parentage (interbreeding sexes unknown, but perhaps reversed) but a separate origin.

The Laredo whiptail has 7 stripes. The vertebral stripe is noticeably narrower than the others. The stripe color is from cream to yellow, often with a greenish tinge. The ground color is a very dark greenish brown. Some poorly defined light spotting is usually visible in the lowermost dark fields. The belly is white until two years of age, when the outermost belly plates may become suffused with sky blue. The chin is white. The upper surface of the hindlimbs is variably (often prominently) reticulated. The tail is brown to brownish gray, often suffused with pale green, and bears stripes. Hatchlings are similar to the adults but more precisely patterned. The posterior scales of the gular fold as well as the antebrachial scales are *moderately* enlarged.

**Similar species:** The Trans-Pecos striped whiptail has a decidedly blue tail. The more westerly New Mexico whiptail has a wavy vertebral stripe. The range of the six-lined racerunner does not abut that of the Laredo striped whiptail. The prairie racerunner is green. The Texas spotted whiptail has a broad vertebral stripe. The body stripes of the plateau spotted whiptail terminate near the hips.

**Behavior:** These lizards are active throughout the morning hours, but seek seclusion during the hottest part of the afternoon. They may become active again in the late afternoon. These alert lizards move nervously between patches of cover. They either dig burrows or utilize the unused burrows of small mammals for their afternoon siesta and at night. When frightened they usually dart from one clump of vegetation to another. It has been found that this whiptail is very fast growing and essentially an annual species; most die before their second winter hibernation. The outer belly scales of the small percentage that do survive the second hibernation often become suffused with blue.

**Comments:** This is a unisexual, all-female (parthenogenetic) whiptail species.

## 197. Western Marbled Whiptail

*Aspidoscelis marmoratus marmoratus*

western
eastern

**Abundance:** This is a common species through the western Trans-Pecos, central New Mexico, and northern Mexico.

**Habitat:** This whiptail is found in sandy desert regions that bear a cover of sparse vegetation such as ocotillo, creosote bush, and opuntia. It can be particularly common along river flood plains and near dry washes.

**Size:** Large adults may measure up to 12 inches in total length. The tail is about 200% of the SVL. Hatchlings are about 5 inches long.

**Identifying features:** This wary and attractive whiptail is often seen as a pale brown blur as it streaks across the desert sands. Typically the adults have a ground color of brownish tan to brownish gray. Up to 8 complete or broken light lines *may* be visible, but often are not. It is most often perceived as a large-spotted lizard. Although the markings, when present, are only a few shades lighter than the ground color and of variable shape, they are precisely delineated. The light lateral markings are vertically oriented. Light dorsal markings may have squared corners, but are more often rounded and arranged in more or less lineate fashion between the light lines (or where the light lines would be if extant). The limbs are reticulated on the upper surface and the tail is of the ground color and unmarked. The venter is light posteriorly, light with darker markings anteriorly, and chin and throat are white to peach to salmon colored, often with a variable amount of dark speckling. The posterior scales of the gular

197. Western marbled whiptail

fold are only moderately enlarged and separated from the fold by at least one row of small granular scales. The supraorbital semicircles extend far forward. There are no significantly enlarged scales on the posterior of the forearm.

The hatchlings have many light spots arranged in a lineate pattern against a dark ground color.

**Similar species:** You can immediately rule out all prominently lined whiptails. The other spotted whiptails of the eastern United States have a patch of enlarged scales on the rear of each forelimb and/or along the rear of the gular fold. Despite these differences, determining an exact identification can be most exasperating and will require having the lizard in hand.

**Comments:** This is a bisexual whiptail. It is one of the wariest species in the genus. Many researchers continue to consider this species a race of *C. tigris*, the more westerly tiger whiptail.

### Additional Subspecies

198. *Aspidoscelis marmoratus reticuloriens*, the Eastern Marbled Whiptail, is the easternmost race of this species. Though its range is east of that of the nominate race, it involves only the western half of Texas, southeastern New Mexico, and northern Mexico. This race is very similar to the western form but usually more precisely marked, having fewer reticulations. The lateral bars are well defined

198. Eastern marbled whiptail

and there are often 4–8 variably defined light stripes. Occasional specimens lack all pattern, being a uniform sandy gray both dorsally and laterally.

### 199. Giant Whiptail

*Aspidoscelis motaguae* (introduced species)

**Abundance/Range:** These lizards occur only in South Miami, Miami-Dade County, Florida. They are indigenous to northern Central America.

**Habitat:** Open fields, canal banks, grassy parking lot edges, and road shoulders are all favored habitats.

**Size:** Males grow to slightly more than 13 inches in total length. Females are smaller. Hatchlings are 4¼ inches long.

**Identifying features:** This whiptail has a golden brown back, and darker brown sides that bear golden spangles. The lower sides are the darkest and spangled with white spots. The venter is gray with bright blue spangles at the edges. Females are somewhat paler than the males. The tail is brown anteriorly, shading to reddish brown terminally.

**Similar species:** Of the whiptails, only the giant ameiva equals this species in size. However, giant ameivas are either darker (blue black) or have a variable amount of green on the dorsum.

**Comments:** This appears to be a bisexual whiptail species.

199. Giant whiptail

## 200. New Mexican Whiptail

*Aspidoscelis neomexicanus*

**Abundance:** This is a fairly common lizard along the Rio Grande Valley from Presidio County, Texas, to El Paso (where it is also present on the Mexican side), then northward in a narrow spur to central northern New Mexico. It can actually be abundant in old fields, public gardens, parks, and zoo grounds.

**Habitat:** Like many other whiptails, the New Mexican whiptail is a lizard of open sands and urban lots. Look for it in and along sandy dry washes, at the edges of parking lots, and wherever else sandy soils predominate.

**Size:** Adults are most often 8–10 inches in length (including a tail that may be slightly longer than 200% of the SVL). The record length is 11⅞ inches. Hatchlings are about 4 inches long.

**Identifying features:** This long-tailed whiptail has a brownish ground color that blends well with the sands of its habitat. All seven of the cream to yellow stripes are well defined, but usually do not contrast sharply with the ground color. The vertebral stripes (and occasionally the paravertebral stripes) are wavy.

200. New Mexican whiptail

Pale spots in the dark fields on the side are readily visible. The venter is often an immaculate white, but may have a blue wash. The chin may be a pale bluish white to a definite blue. The brownish tail is a pale greenish blue distally. Hatchlings have a tail of rather bright blue. This fades to the adult color quickly with growth. Neither the gular fold scales nor the antebrachial scales are noticeably enlarged. The limbs are mottled.

**Similar species:** Range will help identify this whiptail. The Trans-Pecos striped whiptail retains a decidedly blue tail throughout its life and has no spotting in the dark fields. The Chihuahuan spotted whiptail has prominent spots in all dark fields. The desert grassland whiptail has no spots in the dark field. The Texas spotted whiptail has strongly defined spots laterally and males have a pink throat.

**Comments:** This is a unisexual, all female (parthenogenetic) species. This species was derived from hybridization of the Trans-Pecos striped whiptail, *C. inornatus heptagrammus*, and the western marbled whiptail, *C. marmoratus marmoratus*.

## 201. Big Bend Spotted Whiptail

*Aspidoscelis septemvittatus septemvittatus*

**Abundance/Range:** This whiptail is fairly common in suitable habitat. It ranges southward from the Big Bend of Texas to northern Mexico.

**Habitat:** The Big Bend spotted whiptail is associated with sparsely vegetated gravelly or rocky hillsides and canyon habitats. It is common in Big Bend National Park and other such heavily trafficked sites.

**Size:** Adult at 11 inches in total length, large males may occasionally attain 12¼

201. Big Bend spotted whiptail

inches. The tail can be 225% of the SVL in length. Females are smaller. Hatchlings are nearly 5 inches long.

**Identifying features:** This is a quietly colored but pretty whiptail. The 6 or 7 pale stripes separate rows of lineate spots anteriorly. The striping is especially well defined on juvenile specimens. The stripes and spots terminate anterior to the hips and fade somewhat with age. The hips and rear legs may be fawn or russet. The venter and often the front of the forelimbs are tinged with the palest blue (brighter on the male). Males have a white chin while females, especially adults in breeding readiness, have an orange chin. Black flecks may be present. Females are somewhat paler than the males. The tail is grayish to fawn anteriorly, shading to greenish blue distally and brightest on juveniles.

**Similar species:** None. This is the only Texas whiptail on which the pattern, including the striping, fades anterior to the hips.

**Comments:** This is a bisexual whiptail species. Although the scientific name used here seems now to be stabilized, this whiptail may occasionally be referred to as a subspecies of *C. gularis*, *C. scalaris*, or *C. semifasciatus*.

## 202. Six-lined Racerunner

*Aspidoscelis sexlineatus sexlineatus*

**Abundance:** This is a common lizard of sandy soils throughout most of the southeastern United States. It has a greater range than that of any other whiptail of the east and is the only whiptail to occur in the Atlantic states (except in Dade County, Florida, where two introduced species are found). It ranges from Maryland and Illinois southward through Florida and eastern Texas.

**Habitat:** Look for this eastern speedster in well-drained sandy fields, openings in scrubby woodlands, sandy parking lot and sidewalk edges, and myriad other such habitats.

**Size:** Adult males attain 7–9½ inches in total length; females are an inch or so smaller. The tails is 225% of the SVL or longer. Hatchlings are about 3 inches in total length.

**Identifying features:** Range alone will identify this racerunner through-out most of the eastern United States. Males, females, and juveniles have 6 (rarely 7) yellow lines against a ground

□□ six-lined
■ Texas yellow headed
□ prairie

color of variable brown. If a light vertebral line (the 7th) is present, it is paler than the other 6 lines. The ground color is lightest middorsally and darkest low on the sides. This race has no suffusion of yellow or green on the neck or sides. However, adult males do have a suffusion of light blue over their entire bellies. Females have almost white bellies. Juveniles have light bellies and bluish tails.

**Similar species:** Female rainbow whiptails (Dade County, Florida) have 7 prominent lines and may have a pale greenish tinge on the throat. Small ex-amples of the giant whiptail (also Dade County, Florida) have light spangles on the side. Immature skinks have shiny mirrorlike scales.

**Comments:** This is a bisexual species.

202. Six-lined racerunner

203. Texas yellow-headed racerunner

## Additional Subspecies

203. The Texas Yellow-headed Racerunner, *Aspidoscelis sexlineatus stephensae*, differs from the wide-ranging six-lined racerunner and the prairie racerunner by being smaller (to about 8½ inches), lacking a vertebral stripe, having more poorly developed lateral stripes, having yellow coloration on the face and sides of the neck, and lacking green on the body. In truth, specimens that we photographed on South Padre Island had more extensive bright areas laterally than expected, and were more green than yellow. This racerunner occurs in eastern Texas, from about the latitude of Kingsville (including the barrier islands) southward to the latitude of Harlingen (it is absent from the immediate environs of the Rio Grande). There it is common in sparsely developed and undeveloped areas where the vegetation is low and often sparse, and soils are sandy and sharply drained.

204. The Prairie Racerunner, *Aspidoscelis sexlineatus viridis*, is the largest, most brightly colored, and most westerly distributed of the three races. It occurs over much of central Texas northward in the central states to southern South Dakota. Breeding males are suffused over nearly their entire body with a flush of green, brightest laterally and especially so on the sides of the neck. There are 7 or 8 distinct light lines. The darkest field of color on each side is between the paravertebral and the dorsolateral stripe. Adult males may attain 10½ inches in total length. The tail length is at least 225% of the SVL.

204. Prairie racerunner

## 205. Common Checkered Whiptail

*Aspidoscelis tesselatus* complex

**Abundance/Range:** This primarily western species ranges eastward to west Texas and north Texas. Lizards of this species occur in many discontinuous and localized populations rather than generally throughout the range.

**Habitat:** This is a whiptail of rocky plains, roadside dumps, dry washes, canyon bottoms, floodplains, and rocky areas of desert scrub.

**Size:** This is one of our larger whiptails. The total length of a large adult is often slightly more than 12 inches, rarely to 15½ inches. The tail is very long, often nearing 300% of the SVL. Hatchlings are 4½–5 inches in total length.

**Identifying features:** This confusing species has at least six pattern classes.

Dorsally and laterally the lizards of this complex are clad in a ground color of tan, yellowish, cream, or gray. They may be strikingly patterned with vertically oriented lateral bars and paired or entire heavy dorsal crossbars, or may be finely peppered with longitudinal rows of black or dark brown spots. The body bears 6–14 light stripes. The belly is light and immaculate or may bear some dark spotting. The tail is spotted, most prominently on the sides. The supraorbital semicircles extend far forward. The posterior scales of the gular fold are noticeably enlarged. The limbs are mottled. There are no significantly

205. Common checkered whiptail

enlarged scales on the posterior of the forearm. The chin is usually light in color and unmarked.

The hatchlings are marked with broken lines or spots, straw yellow on a black or dark brown ground.

**Similar species:** The marbled whiptail usually has a dark-spotted peach-colored chin; the scales anterior to the gular fold are only moderately enlarged. The Chihuahuan spotted whiptail has a patch of enlarged scales on the rear of each forelimb and the underside of the tail is dark. The gray-checkered whiptail, present in Presidio County, Texas, and southwestern New Mexico, is virtually identical in appearance to the checkered whiptail, but may have a lighter ground color and a more contrasting pattern. Use range extensively when trying to identify these confusingly similar lizards.

**Comments:** This is a diploid, unisexual, all female (parthenogenetic) species that was derived from the hybridization of *C. marmoratus*, the marbled whiptail, and *C. septemvittatus*, the plateau spotted whiptail. Hybridization between diploid checkered whiptails and *C. sexlineatus viridis*, the prairie racerunner, has produced populations of all female triploid lizards (Colorado checkered whiptails, *C. neotesselatus*) with an appearance very similar to the common checkered whiptail but all of these appear to occur just to the west of our coverage area.

# 206. Desert Grassland Whiptail

*Aspidoscelis uniparens*

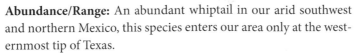

**Abundance/Range:** An abundant whiptail in our arid southwest and northern Mexico, this species enters our area only at the westernmost tip of Texas.

**Habitat:** As its common name indicates, this is a whiptail of the desert grasslands and adjacent areas of desert scrub.

**Size:** With an adult length of only 9½ inches, this very long-tailed lizard is one of the smaller species of whiptails. The tail is about 240% of the SVL. Hatchlings are about 4¼ inches long.

**Identifying features:** This is a prominently striped, nonspotted whiptail. It has 6 (rarely 7) yellow stripes against a very dark ground color. Hatchlings have a bright blue tail. The blue of the tail fades with age, eventually becoming little more than a pale greenish tinge toward the tip. Adults (especially the males) may have a pale blue wash on the throat and sides of the neck. The posterior scales of the gular fold and the antebrachial scales are noticeably enlarged. The forelimbs are mottled with light spots and the thighs have light stripes on the dorsal surface. The belly is white and unmarked. Except for the brighter blue of their tail, the hatchlings are very much like the adults in appearance.

**Similar species:** The Trans-Pecos striped whiptail retains a decidedly blue tail throughout its life. The New Mexican whiptail has a wavy vertebral stripe and

206. Desert grassland whiptail

vestiges of light spots in the dark stripes. The range of the prairie racerunner, a lizard usually having an overwash of green on its body, does not near that of the desert grasslands whiptail in Texas.

## 207. Rainbow Whiptail

*Cnemidophorus lemniscatus* complex (introduced species)

**Abundance/Range:** In the United States, this species is found only in Dade County, Florida, in the vicinity of several urban warehouses. The rainbow whiptail occurs widely in the Neotropics.

**Habitat:** In Florida, the habitat of this lizard is a mixture of pebbles and sand with a sparse cover of low weeds.

**Size:** Males may occasionally attain a 12-inch total length. Females are usually 6–8 inches long. The tail is at least 200% of the snout–vent length. Hatchlings are about 3½ inches long.

**Identifying features:** Males of this beautiful lizard have an intricate coloration. Middorsally they are warm brown. This color is bordered with a thin yellow stripe below which is a lime green stripe. Another thin yellow stripe separates the green stripe from a broad, yellow spangled, golden lateral area. The face, throat, and anterior surface of all limbs are turquoise or robin's egg blue. The tail is green. A white-spangled purplish shoulder spot is often present. The belly is

207a. Rainbow whiptail, male

207b. Rainbow whiptail, female

grayish. Females have 7–9 yellow stripes on a field of greenish brown. The head is orange(ish) and the hindlimbs and tail are greenish. The venter is white.

**Similar species:** Adult males of this species can be confused with no other lizard in Florida. Six-lined racerunners have only 6 yellow lines.

**Comments:** The rainbow whiptails in Florida are bisexual.

**Comments:** This unisexual, all female (parthenogenetic) species was derived from hybridization of the little striped whiptail, *C. inornatus*, and possibly the giant whiptail, *C. burti*.

## Monitors, family Varanidae

These lizards are all of Old World distribution, but a few species are popular in the American pet trade. In size the monitors range from the tiny 8-inch short-tailed monitor of Australia to the huge, 9-foot or more Komodo monitor of the Sunda Islands. They are primarily insectivorous or carnivorous; one described and one as yet undescribed Philippine species are the exception, being fruit eaters. Many of the smaller monitors are arboreal, semiarboreal, or saxicolous. Most are found in aridland habitats. Others, especially the larger ones, are firmly associated with watercourses, arboreal when young but terrestrial when adult. Interestingly, the young of many large monitors have sharp grasping teeth while the adults have heavy crushing teeth.

At present, only the large and voracious Nile monitor, a sub-Saharan species, is established in the United States. It is restricted to South Florida. Little about its population densities or lifestyle statistics is known. Its reproductive biology in Florida is also unknown.

Nothing is known about its nesting habits in Florida. In Africa, incubation may vary between 6½ months to more than a year. A clutch may contain 15–60 eggs.

## Monitors, genus *Varanus*

The African Nile monitor is a comparative newcomer to the state of Florida. Because it is large and predatory the presence of this lizard is of considerable concern to conservationists. This is a pet trade species, but its normal temperament and adult size render it unsuitable as a pet. We speculate that its presence in the state is the result of the release of no longer wanted "pets" that had outgrown their facilities or become intractable.

When a biologist with our state wildlife commission told us that Nile monitors were now present in Florida, we both thought we were being kidded. It turns out that the joke was on us. Not only were the big, aggressive lizards present, they had by then become rather firmly established in Cape Coral, a bustling city on Florida's southwestern coast. Even more unsettling was the fact that the lizards had become established quite near a colony of Florida burrowing owls, engaging and protected birds.

I initially thought that since these lizards are large, hence conspicuous, they would be rapidly eradicated from their newly found range. But it appears that the Nile monitors are not only large and conspicuous, but wary and unapproachable as well, and that it will take more than a casual program to rid Florida of these efficient predators. Are the monitors, then, in Florida to stay? Only time will tell.

## 208. Nile Monitor

*Varanus niloticus* (introduced species)

**Abundance/Range:** This lizard is known to breed only in Cape Coral, Lee County, Florida. However, feral specimens are often observed in numerous other Florida counties from the vicinity of Orlando southward.

**Habitat:** This huge lizard is found in many areas of Cape Coral, Lee County, Florida. It has now been found amid mangroves, along canals as well as some distance from the water. It seems probable that, among other areas of seclusion, the lizards are utilizing the burrows of birds and mammals as shelter.

208a. Nile monitor, juvenile

208b. Nile monitor, adult

**Size:** Hatchlings and juveniles of this impressive predator are slender and big headed. The adults, which might occasionally attain a length of 6 feet, are heavy bodied but quite agile. Hatchlings are about 9½ inches in length.

**Identifying features:** The slender juveniles are predominantly black on their back and upper sides and predominantly yellow on their lower sides and belly. The neck, back, and tail bear well-defined crossbars (actually rows of spots) of yellow. The lower sides are banded with black. The preciseness of the pattern becomes obscured with growth and the colors dull. Adults are usually grayish black on the upper sides and back and predominantly grayish white on the lower sides and belly. Traces of banding may remain visible on the neck and trunk but are best defined on the lower sides and tail. The neck is long and sinuous and an immensely long forked tongue is frequently extended. The legs are well developed and powerful; if carelessly restrained, the lizard will scratch its captor painfully.

**Similar species:** None. Iguanas may be nearly as long but have large dewlaps and noticeable nape and vertebral crests.

**Comments:** The Nile monitor can be difficult to handle. It will bite, scratch, and whip with its powerful tail. Large examples can produce severe wounds and should be handled with extreme care. This lizard is a powerful swimmer and can also run rapidly. Babies climb with agility. If cornered the Nile monitor will inflate its body, loll the tongue out with tips drooping, and huff and hiss. Use care in approaching large examples.

# Glossary

**Aestivation**—A period of warm weather inactivity, often triggered by excessive heat or drought.

**Alveolar ridge** (or **plate**)—A broad crushing plate posterior to the mandibles.

**Ambient temperature**—The temperature of the surrounding environment.

**Anterior**—Toward the front.

**Annulated**—Bearing rings around the body.

**Annuli**— Rings or ringlike structures; the growth rings on the carapace of some turtle species; rings around the body of worm lizards and earthworms.

**Anus**—The external opening of the cloaca; the vent.

**Arboreal**—Tree dwelling.

**Bridge**—The "bridge of shell" between fore and rear limbs that connects a turtle's carapace and plastron.

**Brille**—The clear spectacle that protects the eyes of lidless-eyed geckos.

**Carapace**—The upper shell of a chelonian.

**Caudal**—Pertaining to the tail.

**Chelonian**—A turtle or tortoise.

**Cloaca**—The common chamber into which digestive, urinary, and reproductive systems empty and that itself opens exteriorly through the vent or anus.

**Congeneric**—Grouped in the same genus.

**Crepuscular**—Active at dusk and/or dawn.

**Deposition**—As used here, the laying of eggs or birthing of young.

**Deposition site**—The nesting or birthing site.

**Dichromatic**—Exhibiting two color phases, often sex linked.

**Dimorphic**—A difference in form, build, or coloration within the same species, often sex linked.

**Diurnal**—Active in the daytime.

**Dorsal**—Pertaining to the back or upper surface.

**Dorsolateral**—Pertaining to the upper side.

**Dorsum**—The upper surface.

**Ectothermic** (also **poikilothermic**)—"Cold-blooded," pertaining to an organism that absorbs heat from the environment. All groups included in this book are ectothermic.

**Endemic**—Confined to a specific region.

**Endothermic**—"Warm-blooded," pertaining to an organism that produces its own body heat.

**Femoral pores**: Openings in the scales on the underside of the hind legs of some lizards.

**Femur**—The part of the leg between the hip and the knee.

**Form**—An identifiable species or subspecies.

**Fossorial**—Burrowing.

**Fracture plane**—A naturally weakened area in the tail vertebrae of some lizards, a natural breaking point.

**Genus** (pl. **Genera**)—A taxonomic classification of a group of species having similar characteristics. The genus falls between the next higher designation of Family and the next lower designation of Species. The first letter of the generic name is always capitalized and the name is always written in italics.

**Gravid**—The reptilian equivalent of mammalian pregnancy; carrying unborn young or eggs.

**Gular**—Pertaining to the throat.

**Herpetology**—The study (often scientifically oriented) of reptiles and amphibians.

**Hybrid**—Offspring resulting from the breeding of two species or noncontiguous subspecies.

**Intergrade**—Offspring resulting from the breeding of two adjacent subspecies.

**Interorbital**—Between the eyes.

**Interstitial**—Between the scales.

**Juvenile**—A young or immature specimen.

**Keel**—A carapacial or plastral ridge (or ridges) or a longitudinal ridge on the scales or shell of reptiles.

**Lamellae**—The transverse divisions that extend across the bottom surfaces of the toes of anoles and geckos.

**Lateral**—Pertaining to the side.

**Lateral fold**—A longitudinal expandable fold that is found on the lower sides of anguid lizards.

**Lateral ridge**—A longitudinal ridge of skin that runs along the sides of some curly-tailed lizards.

**Mandibles**—Jaws.

**Mandibular**—Pertaining to the jaws.

**Melanism**—A profusion of black pigment.

**Mental**—Scale on the tip of the lower jaw.

**Middorsal**—Pertaining to the middle of the back.

**Midventral**—Pertaining to the center of the belly.

**Monotypic**—Containing but one type.

**Nocturnal**—Active at night.

**Nominate**—The first named form in a group of subspecies.

**Ocelli**—Dark- or light-edged circular spots.

**Ontogenetic**—Age related (color) changes.

**Oviparous**—Reproducing by means of eggs that hatch after laying.

**Parthenogenesis**—Reproduction without fertilization.

**Phalanges**—The bones of the toes.

**Photoperiod**—The daily/seasonally variable length of the hours of daylight.

**Plastron**—Turtle's bottom shell.

**Postocular/Postorbital**—To the rear of the eye.

**Race**—A subspecies.

**Rugose**—Wrinkled, warty, or rough.

**Scute**—Scale; especially the large scales on a turtle's shell.

**Setae**—The hairlike bristles in the lamellae on the toes of anoles and geckos.

**Sibling species**—Two or more similar appearing species supposedly descended from the same ancestral parental stock. Sibling species are often not separable in the field.

**Species** (abbr. **sp.**)—A group of similar creatures that produce viable young when breeding. The taxonomic designation that falls beneath Genus and above Subspecies.

**Subcaudal**—The underside of the tail.

**Subdigital**—The underside of the toes.

**Subocular**—Below the eye.

**Subspecies** (abbr. **ssp.**)—The subdivision of a species. A race that may differ slightly in color, size, scalation, or other criteria.

**Subsurface**—Beneath the surface.

**Supraocular/Supraorbital**—Above the eye.

**Supratympanal**—Above the tympanum.

**SVL**—Snout–vent length.

**Sympatric**—Occurring together.

**Taxonomy**—The science of classification of plants and animals.

**Terrestrial**—Land-dwelling.

**Thermoregulate**—To regulate (body) temperature by choosing a warmer or cooler environment.

**Vent**—The external opening of the cloaca; the anus.

**Venter**—The underside of a creature; the belly.

**Ventral**—Pertaining to the undersurface or belly.

**Ventrolateral**—Pertaining to the sides of the belly.

# Additional Reading

*The following list includes just a few of the publications that pertain to herpetology of eastern North America.*

Ashton, R. E., Jr., S. R. Edwards, and G. R. Pisani. 1976. Endangered and Threatened Amphibians and Reptiles of the United States. Herpetology Circular no. 5. Lawrence, Kans.: Society for the Study of Amphibians and Reptiles,

Ashton, R. E., Jr., and P. S. Ashton. 1985. Handbook of Reptiles and Amphibians of Florida. Part II, Lizards, Turtles and Crocodilians. Miami: Windward Publishing.

Bartlett, R. D. 1988. In Search of Reptiles and Amphibians. New York: E. J. Brill.

Bartlett, R. D., and Patricia P. Bartlett. 1999. A Field Guide to Texas Reptiles and Amphibians. Houston: Gulf Publishing.

———. 1999. A Field Guide to Florida Reptiles and Amphibians. Houston: Gulf Publishing.

Behler, John L., and F. Wayne King. 1979. The Audubon Society Field Guide to North American Reptiles and Amphibians. New York: Alfred Knopf.

Carr, Archie. 1952. Handbook of Turtles. Ithaca, N.Y.: Cornell University Press.

Collins, Joseph T. 1982. Amphibians and Reptiles in Kansas, 2nd ed. Lawrence: University of Kansas.

Conant, Roger, and Joseph T. Collins. 1991. A Field Guide to the Reptiles and Amphibians of Eastern and Central North America, 3rd ed. Boston: Houghton Mifflin.

Crother, Brian I. (Chair). 2000. Scientific and Standard English Names of Amphibians and Reptiles of North America North of Mexico, with Comments Regarding Confidence in our Understanding. Herpetology Circular no. 29. Lawrence, Kans.: Society for the Study of Amphibians and Reptiles.

Degenhardt, William G., Charles W. Painter, and Andrew H. Price. 1996. Amphibians and Reptiles of New Mexico. Albuquerque: University of New Mexico Press.

DeGraaf, Richard M., and Deborah D. Rudis. 1983. Amphibians and Reptiles of New England. Amherst: University of Massachusetts Press.

Dixon, James R. 1987. Amphibians and Reptiles of Texas. College Station: Texas A & M University Press.

Duellman, William E., and Albert Schwartz. 1958. Amphibians and Reptiles of Southern Florida. Gainesville: Bulletin of the Florida State Museum 3.

Dundee, Harold A., and Douglas A. Rossman. 1989. The Amphibians and Reptiles of Louisiana. Baton Rouge: Louisiana State University Press.

Ernst, Carl H. 1992. Venomous Reptiles of North America. Washington, D.C.: Smithsonian.

Ernst, Carl H., Jeffrey E. Lovich, and Roger W. Barbour. 1994. Turtles of the United States and Canada. Washington, D.C.: Smithsonian.

Green, N. Bayard, and Thomas K. Pauley. 1987. Amphibians and Reptiles in West Virginia. Pittsburgh: University of Pittsburgh Press.

Halliday, Tim, and Kraig Adler (Eds.). 1986. The Encyclopedia of Reptiles and Amphibians. New York: Facts on File.

Harding, James H. 1997. Amphibians and Reptiles of the Great Lakes Region. Ann Arbor: University of Michigan Press.

Hunter, Malcolm L., Aram J. K. Calhoun, and Mark McCollough (Eds.). 1999. Maine Amphibians and Reptiles. Orono: University of Maine Press.

Johnson, Tom R. 1987. The Amphibians and Reptiles of Missouri. Jefferson City: Missouri Department of Conservation.

Lazell, James D., Jr. 1976. This Broken Archipelago, Cape Cod and the Islands, Amphibians and Reptiles. New York: Quadrangle/The New York Times Book Co.

Lazell, James D., Jr., and J. A. Musick. 1973. The Kingsnake, *Lampropeltisgetulus sticticeps*, and the ecology of the Outer Banks of North Carolina. Copeia 1973(3): 497–503.

Martof, Bernard S., William M. Palmer, Joseph R. Bailey, and Julian R. Harrison III. 1980. Amphibians and Reptiles of the Carolinas and Virginia. Chapel Hill: University of North Carolina Press.

Miller, D. J. 1979. A Life History Study of the Gray-banded Kingsnake, *Lampropeltis mexicana alterna*, in Texas. Alpine, Tex.: Chihuahuan Desert Research Institute.

Minton, Sherman A., Jr. 2001. Amphibians and Reptiles of Indiana. Indianapolis: Indiana Academy of Science.

Mitchell, Joseph C. 1994. The Reptiles of Virginia. Washington, D.C.: Smithsonian Institution Press.

Moler, Paul E. 1990. A Checklist of Florida's Amphibians and Reptiles (Revised). Tallahassee: Florida Game and Fresh Water Fish Commission.

Moler, Paul E. (Ed.). 1992. Rare and Endangered Biota of Florida. Vol. 3, Amphibians and Reptiles. Gainesville: University Press of Florida.

Mount, Robert H. 1975. The Reptiles and Amphibians of Alabama. Auburn, Ala.: Auburn University Agricultural Experiment Station.

Neill, Wilfred T. 1971. The Last of the Ruling Reptiles. New York: Columbia University Press.

Oldfield, Barney, and John J. Moriarty. 1994. Amphibians and Reptiles Native to Minnesota. Minneapolis: University of Minnesota Press.

Palmer, William M., and Alvin L. Braswell. 1995. Reptiles of North Carolina. Chapel Hill: University of North Carolina Press.

Reeder, Tod W., Charles J. Cole, and Herbert C. Dessauer. 2002. Phylogenetic relationships of whiptail lizards of the genus *Cnemidophorus* (Squamata: Teiidae): a test of monophyly, reevaluation of karyotypic evolution, and review of hybrid origins. American Museum Novitates 3365: 1–61.

Schwartz, Albert, and Robert W. Henderson. Amphibians and Reptiles of the West Indies. 1991. Gainesville: University Press of Florida.

Schwartz, Vicki, and David M. Golden. 2002. Field Guide to Reptiles and Amphibians of New Jersey. Vineland: New Jersey Division of Fish and Wildlife.

Schulte, James A. II, John Pablo Valladares, and Allan Larson. 2003. Phylogenetic relationships within Iguanidae inferred using molecular and morphological data and a phylogenetic taxonomy of iguanian lizards. Herpetologica 59: 399–419.

Smith, Hobart M. 1946. Handbook of Lizards. Ithaca, N.Y.: Comstock.

Tyning, Thomas F. 1990. A Guide to Amphibians and Reptiles. Boston: Little, Brown, and Co.

Vogt, Richard Carl. 1981. Natural History of Amphibians and Reptiles of Wisconsin. Milwaukee: Milwaukee Public Museum.

Webb, Robert G. 1962. North American recent soft-shelled turtles (family Trionychidae). University of Kansas, Publications of the Museum of Natural History 3(10): 429–611.

Wilson, Larry David, and Louis Porras. 1983. The Ecological Impact of Man on the South Florida Herpetofauna. Lawrence: University of Kansas.

# Index

Richard D. and Patricia Bartlett have coauthored numerous books, including *A Field Guide to Florida Reptiles*, *Reptiles and Amphibians of the Amazon*, and *Florida Snakes: A Guide to Their Identification and Habits*. Together they lead interactive tours to many areas of the Amazon Basin. Richard has published more than 500 articles about herpetology in *Tropical Fish Hobbyist*, *Reptiles*, *Reptile and Amphibian*, and others. Patricia is former director of the Fort Myers Historical Museum.

Related-interest titles from University Press of Florida

*30 EcoTrips in Florida: The Best Nature Excursions (and How to Leave Only Your Footprints)*
HOLLY AMBROSE

*A Field Guide and Identification Manual for Florida and Eastern U.S. Tiger Beetles*
PAUL M. CHOATE, JR.

*Florida's Snakes: A Guide to Their Identification and Habitats*
R. D. BARTLETT AND PATRICIA BARTLETT

*Guide and Reference to the Amphibians of Eastern and Central North America, North of Mexico*
R. D. BARTLETT AND PATRICIA BARTLETT

*Guide and Reference to the Snakes of Eastern and Central North America, North of Mexico*
R. D. BARTLETT AND PATRICIA BARTLETT

*A Guide to the Birds of the Southeastern States: Florida, Georgia, Alabama, and Mississippi*
JOHN H. RAPPOLE

*Hiker's Guide to the Sunshine State*
SANDRA FRIEND

*Reptiles and Amphibians of the Amazon: An Ecotourist's Guide*
R. D. BARTLETT AND PATRICIA BARTLETT

*Wild Orchids of the Canadian Maritimes and Northern Great Lakes Region*
PAUL MARTIN BROWN WITH DRAWINGS BY STAN FOLSOM

*Wild Orchids of North America, North of Mexico*
PAUL MARTIN BROWN WITH DRAWINGS BY STAN FOLSOM

*Wild Orchids of the Southeastern United States, North of Peninsular Florida*
PAUL MARTIN BROWN WITH DRAWINGS BY STAN FOLSOM

*The Windward Road: Adventures of a Naturalist on Remote Caribbean Shores*
ARCHIE CARR

For more information on these and other books, visit our website at www.upf.com.